# BUYING
# AND CARING FOR
# YOUR FABULOUS
# FUR

# BUYING
# AND CARING FOR
# YOUR FABULOUS
# FUR

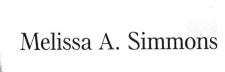

Melissa A. Simmons

FAWCETT COLUMBINE
·
NEW YORK

A Fawcett Columbine Book
Published by Ballantine Books
Copyright © 1986 by Melissa Ann Simmons
Illustrations copyright © 1986 by David Guinn
All rights reserved under International and Pan-American Copyright Conventions. Published in the United
States by Ballantine Books, a division of Random House, Inc., New York, and simultaneously in Canada by
Random House of Canada Limited, Toronto.

Photo credits may be found at the end of this book.

Library of Congress Catalog Card Number: 86-90744

ISBN: 0-449-90172-6
Cover photo by Don Banks
Cover design by James R. Harris
Text design by Michaelis/Carpelis Design Associates
Fur sampler photos by Ben Rosenthal
Manufactured in the United States of America

First Edition: January 1987

10 9 8 7 6 5 4 3 2 1

To my beloved family (Sasha and Ingrid too),
whose encouragement, support, and faith have helped me
weather many a *fur*ious storm.

## ACKNOWLEDGMENTS

When I first began to write this book, I knew as much—or as little—about fur as the average person. While seeking the advice and expertise of a number of professionals in the fur business, I had the opportunity to meet some very interesting people, from animal-rights activists to mink farmers. All of them were helpful, but there are those whose assistance went above and beyond the call of duty, and these individuals deserve special recognition: Adrienne Weinfeld-Berg, Public Relations Director for Kip Kirkendall, Inc., New York; Harold DeHart of the Fur Farm Animal Welfare Coalition, Tomahawk, Wisconsin; and Ernest Graf of Ben Kahn Furs, New York.

I would also like to thank the following people: Angie Berchielli of the New York State Trappers Association; Sandy Blye of the American Fur Industry; Marilyn Blumer; Jerry Brown of Jerry Brown Furs; Laura Brockway Bodor of Revillon, Inc.; Judy Bonds of Neiman-Marcus; George Contaxakis of Amsel & Amsel, Montreal, Canada; E. B. Gold of Fairchild Books and Visuals; Mary Frentz of J. Mendel; Lili Glassman of SAGA Furs of Scandinavia; David Goodman of Gus Goodman; Henry Foner, president, Local 1-FLM; Liz Greenfield of Cosmos Sirochio; Bernard Groger of *Sandy Parker's Fur World Reports*; Richard Harrow; Alan Herscovici; Dean Hilda Jaffe of the Fashion Institute of Technology; Ray Kelly of the Ray Kelly Mink Farm, Medina, Ohio; Kip Kirkendall; Sue Krost of Sue Krost Associates; Adrienne Landau; Gabrielle LaRue of Furrari; Karen Lawer of The Fashion Institute of Technology; Paula Lishman; Harriet Love; Richard Mackie of Matric Computer Ltd., Franklin, Pennsylvania (without him, this book literally would not have been written!); James McQuay and his lovely assistant Dreana; Gilles Mendel; Ben Mendisch of Furs by Antonovich; Dave Monture of Indigenous Survival International; Karen Myerhoff of The Costume Institute at the Metropolitan Museum of Art; Barry Novick of Evans, Inc.; Evelyn Paswall of Martin Paswall, Inc.; Jim Preston of the Jim Preston Mink Farm, Greenville, Pennsylvania; Karen Raaber of Furs by Antonovich; Helmut A. Rothe, vice president, Rosenberg & Lenhart, Inc.; Fred, Andrew, and Suzanne Schwartz of The Fur Vault, Inc.; Lawrence Schulman of Alixandre; Kirk Smith of the Fur Institute of Canada; Arlette Smolarski; Keith Tauber of the Ritz Thrift Shop; Carol Teitelbaum; Carol Ware of the Carol and Irwin Ware Fur Collection at I. Magnin, Chicago.

Last but not least, special thanks go to my agents, Michael Larsen and Elizabeth Pomada, San Francisco, California; my editor at Ballantine, Ann LaFarge; and my parents, Gertrude and Albert Simmons of Erie, Pennsylvania, and Ernest O. Denny.

# CONTENTS

Introduction: The Allure of Fur
• xi •

**CHAPTER ONE**
Fur in Fashion History
• 1 •

**CHAPTER TWO**
Adventures in the Skin Trade
• 21 •

**CHAPTER THREE**
From Catch to Consumer
• 32 •

**CHAPTER FOUR**
Profiles of the Most Important Furs
• 50 •

**CHAPTER FIVE**
How to Select and Buy the Right Fur
• 87 •

**CHAPTER SIX**
Fur and the Working Woman
• 134 •

**CHAPTER SEVEN**
Wear, Repair, and Care: Maintaining Your Fur
• 146 •

**CHAPTER EIGHT**
Previously Owned Furs
• 167 •

**CHAPTER NINE**
The Accessory Story
• 178 •

**CHAPTER TEN**
Fur for Men
• 190 •

**CHAPTER ELEVEN**
Fur and the Environment
• 199 •

Glossary of Fur Terms
• 212 •

Bibliography
• 216 •

Index
• 219 •

# THE ALLURE OF FUR

"Fur." he word conjures up a variety of images, from the cave dwellers who wrapped themselves in the stiff, uncured hides of scrawny prehistoric beasts, to the rough-hewn trappers whose lust for beaver pelts opened up hitherto unexplored sections of North America; to the glamorous movie stars of the thirties and forties, resplendent in their fox tails and mink.

After briefly falling into disfavor, fur is back in vogue with a vengeance. Retail fur sales have been increasing steadily, and in 1985, reached approximately 1.8 billion. Sales are expected to increase by at least 5% annually, and in general, industry analysts are optimistic about the future.

What's behind this unprecedented rise in sales? Part of the fur boom can be traced to the increase in two career couples with high disposable incomes and, more specifically, the enormous purchasing clout of affluent young career women, a group that fur retailers are pursuing with vigor.

Fur has also shed the image of being something that only the older woman wears. According to a recent survey in *The Business of Fur*, a leading trade magazine, four out of ten fur customers are thirty-five years old or younger, and in Canada, this percentage is even higher—sixty-one percent were in this age bracket.

What are some of the reasons behind the perennial appeal of fur?

## WARMTH

Historians conclude that soon after man discovered that the flesh of animals was good to eat, he found that their hides, or pelts, provided much-needed protection from the harsh elements. Indeed, for the first two or three millennia that humankind went without central heating, the primary function of fur was to keep the wearer warm.

In many frigid parts of the U.S. and Canada a fur coat is still more of a necessity than a luxury, and fur coats are far more energy efficient than even the warmest woolens. Chicago furriers Carol and Irwin Ware of I. Magnin have developed a system for ranking furs according to their BEPS (Body Energy Performance Standard) rating. On a scale of 1 to 10, sable has the highest rating of 8.4 (the Wares have yet to find a "perfect ten") while mink gets 7.1. Most cloth coats score only around 4.7. Says Carol Ware: "Our winters are very cold, and you can freeze when the wind starts to blow off the lake . . . in a climate like Chicago's, a fur is a very warm and wise investment."

## DURABILITY

Although some may think of a fur as being anything but practical, a quality coat of a fur such as raccoon, sable, mink, or Persian lamb, with proper care, can last twenty years or more. Although its initial cost is high compared to even the best cloth coat, a fur will outlast the cloth coat and will provide the wearer with years of enjoyment.

## A WIDE RANGE OF PRICE—FROM AFFORDABLE TO OUT-OF-SIGHT

A fur garment, whether a full-length coat, a jacket, or even a scarf or hat, is the fulfillment of a fantasy, and, unlike a trip around the world or the Hope diamond, it is a dream attainable by even the least well-heeled among us. From a hundred dollar rabbit jacket to a coat made of white Russian lynx bellies (which, at $100,000 or more, is currently the costliest fur in the world) fur is an increasingly affordable luxury. There is something to fit every lifestyle, budget, and taste.

There are fur capes, parkas, and shrugs, as well as fur coats for children and even dogs. And adding new meaning to the expression,

"Oh, you beautiful doll!," the Fur Galleria of Cedarhurst, Long Island, hoping to cash in on the mid-eighties craze for Cabbage Patch Kids, introduced a line of 25 miniature coats and jackets made just for them (after first clearing the idea with the manufacturer, Coleco). The furs came in every variety from raccoon to sable, and ranged in price from $200 to $595. During the first three weeks, forty coats were sold, prompting one to wonder what is next—fur dust protectors for plants?

## GLAMOUR

A man or woman wearing fur stands apart from the crowd like a Ferrari in a parking lot full of Volkswagens. While it may offend the egalitarian sensibilities of some, it is part of human nature to want to be admired, emulated, and even envied a bit. A fur garment says that the wearer is a success, that he or she is worthy of such unabashed luxury. Says Edythe Cudlipp in her book, *Furs: An Appreciation of Luxury, A Guide to Value*, "Furs have a status that's within the reach of everyone's pocketbook . . . You may get out of your own Rolls-Royce or you may get out of a battered Checker cab, you may be wearing diamonds or no jewelry at all, but if you're wearing furs—whether it's a sable coat, a fling of fox, or a sheared rabbit warm-up jacket—you're chic, glamorous, and perhaps more than a little fantastic."

## AVAILABILITY

The potential fur owner has never had more options. New and exotic types of furs, such as tanuki and Finnish raccoon, are widely available, in addition to old standbys such as mink and beaver. The style-conscious, or "fashion forward" woman is no longer limited to traditional let-out garments either, as a crop of young designers are producing an array of exciting styles, some of which incorporate such disparate materials as suede, snakeskin, and semiprecious stones, and involve complicated processes in which fur is actually woven like cloth or knitted like yarn.

## BE AN INFORMED BUYER

Besides the dilemma over the type of fur, there are other bewildering aspects of fur selection which might lead the consumer to ask, "What fur can I afford?" "Is the fur I want from an endangered species?" "As a petite, can I wear a long-haired fur?" "What about furs for men?" "When is the best time of year to buy a fur?" and a question important to most big-city dwellers, "Will a fur enhance my image or just cause me to get mugged?"

The purpose of this book is to answer all these questions, and those you may have never thought of, and to educate you completely about fur—its history, its uses, and its changing role in fashion. In the process, you'll learn that fur is not only fabulous, but functional and fun as well. So turn the pages, and step inside the wonderful world of fur!

# BUYING
# AND CARING FOR
# YOUR FABULOUS
# FUR

# FUR IN FASHION HISTORY

## THE ANCIENT WORLD

Since earliest times, people have worn fur garments for a variety of reasons, not all of them practical. Fur was not only a means of keeping warm; it was also one of the first symbols by which early men and women could establish prowess or leadership, setting them apart from others. Neolithic cave paintings, their earth-toned hues still vibrant after the passage of thirty centuries, have been found in Spain and southwestern France. The people in these paintings wear garments of animal hides. Some authorities believe that the rudiments of fur processing may have been known even before this: one surviving stone scraper, which was once used to clean bits of tissue from animal hides, has been estimated to be almost one million years old.

Perhaps the earliest written reference to the wearing of animal pelts can be found in the Bible (King James version) in the Book of Genesis. Here it states that "unto Adam and his wife did the Lord God make coats of skins and clothed them," in response to the sudden sense of modesty felt by the pair after tasting the forbidden fruit of the Tree of Life.

---

1

The ancient Egyptians were also fond of fur, although obviously, in that tropical climate, it was used more for ceremonial reasons than for everyday wear. Leopard skin was particularly popular, and in the fabled Middle Kingdom, its use was restricted to members of the ruling elite. However, like the furriers of modern-day America, who are also forbidden to use leopard skin, the enterprising peasants learned to paint or stencil the big cat's characteristic rosettes on sheepskin or other less costly hides.

Jason's Golden Fleece notwithstanding, the ancient Greeks considered furs smelly and barbaric, and restricted their use to rugs and decorations. The Romans shared this sentiment to some degree, and were probably influenced by the fact that the fierce Teutonic tribes that they enslaved—and who, in an ironic twist of fate, later conquered them—wore the skins of bears, wolves, foxes, and many other animals. Some Greek and Roman gods, however, are depicted wearing furs, and early Roman senators were called *pelliti* because of the animal hides they wore.

The Medes, Persians, and other Middle Eastern peoples wore furs and there is evidence that in China, fur was used as an indication of rank and prestige more than three thousand years ago. Mongol tribes used skins extensively, and Marco Polo, on his visit to China, was astounded by the enormous *yurts*, or tents, which, with their circular shapes, were "symbolic of the cosmos." These tents could hold thousands of people, and were covered with "skins so well joined that they shed rain and snow." Variations of the yurt are still used by nomadic peoples in the desert wastelands of the world.

During the period between the fall of the Roman Empire and the Renaissance, the use of fur reached its height.

## THE MIDDLE AGES

If time travelers from the twentieth century were able to visit the London of the 1300s, they would be quite surprised by what they saw, for

---

**Fur Facts and Fancies:** *Queen Semiramis, the semilegendary ruler and founder of Babylon, brought eight thousand tiger skins back from India in 21 B.C. to decorate the floors and walls of the Hanging Gardens.*

---

the Middle Ages was not a time of armored, gallant knights and splendidly garbed ladies, as Hollywood and the writings of Alfred Lord Tennyson would lead us to believe. Our twentieth century cosmopolites would have to hold their noses because of the overpowering stench of raw sewage that was dumped into the River Thames and the narrow, dark streets. They would have to be careful in even the most prosperous of neighborhoods, for the knights of yore were more often hooligans than heroes. But most of all, they would be astounded by the ragtag assortment of clothing worn by the people of the Middle Ages—the *houppelands* (a voluminous outer robe), *cotehardies* (a tightly fitting men's outergarment); the *surcoats* (a sleeveless vest often worn over armor), and the *succenes* (another kind of long vest). On almost every garment, from the velvet cloaks of the gentry to the drab homespun jerkins of the lowest serf, there was fur in some form or another, ranging from sensuous sable to revolting ratskin.

During this period, fur was more of a necessity than a luxury, for even the wealthiest nobleman lived in a cold, drafty building which the summer heat could barely warm. Fur blankets, bedspreads, and curtains were the norm, as was a fur lining for almost every conceivable piece of clothing, even shoes and dresses. Fur coats as we know them, however, with the texture outside, were almost unheard of until centuries later.

It was also during this time that so-called *sumptuary laws*—rules determining the day-to-day conduct of the people—were passed. Many of these laws affected the wearing of fur garments, specifying what types could or could not be worn by whom. For example, in 1337, Edward III of England made ermine a royal fur. Generally, rich furs such as sable, marten, miniver, and ermine were the exclusive property of the nobility while the average run-of-the-manor peasant had to be content with sheepskin, coney (rabbit), fox, or plain old alley cat. Curiously, in some countries, squirrel was considered a fur fit only for commoners, while in other nations it was limited to the elite.

Even the clergy was not immune to class distinctions. While the lower orders had to be content with sheepskin, the upper levels of the Christian hierarchy could wear ermine and sable. Fur garments were commonly worn by both nuns and monks, and there even existed a special group of friars, called the *fraties pelippari*, who were caretakers of the furs used by the religious community. Even today, the very highest orders of the Catholic clergy, including the Pope himself, don magnificent fur-trimmed robes on special occasions.

**Fur Facts and Fancies:** *Although they are often confused, ermine and miniver—two "royal furs" of the Middle Ages—were not one and the same. Garments made of ermine, the white winter coat of a member of the weasel family, are often embellished with the black tips of the animals' tails. Miniver, the white underbelly of a certain type of squirrel, was often decorated with small pieces of other black fur, usually from a special kind of sheep called budge.*

As widespread as the sumptuary laws were, they appeared to have little effect, and despite the penalties associated with their breakage, including heavy fines and even whippings, they were largely ignored, which must have made the haughty nobility *fur*ious!

The latter part of the Middle Ages was marked by a number of new developments, including the Crusades, which opened up trade routes to the East with its many splendors. The gradual transformation of European cities from closed, feudalistic societies into centers of cultural activity left its mark on every aspect of Western life, including fashion.

## THE RENAISSANCE

The Renaissance was a period marked by many changes. The arts reached their heights in such places as Venice and Paris, and the New World was slowly being opened up to exploration—and exploitation. A general spirit of open-mindedness and a keen sense of discovery were the hallmarks of this era.

The winds of change also affected fashion. Gone were the graceful, flowing lines of medieval costumes, which allowed relative ease of movement; clothing took on a more rigidly defined, stylized appearance. Although this era saw several major changes in fashion, the masculine garment most often associated with this period is the wide-shouldered, puff-sleeved *doublet*, a short gown which was worn with tight hose, as seen in the portraits of the notorious Henry VIII. For women, the most important garment was a dress with a snug, V-shaped bodice widening into a huge skirt that was made to stand away from the body in stiff folds by the use of the farthingale, a coarse linen petticoat stitched over iron, wire, cane, bone, or whalebone into a cone-like shape. In many countries, the width of the farthingale was determined by the wearer's social status. Hence, the gowns worn by Queen Elizabeth I were often four feet wide or more.

Fur was very popular in the Elizabethan period (1558–1603), when "great fur collars, huge fur sleeves, which sometimes flared out to fall nearly to the knees, and at other times were separate, detachable items, and luxurious fur linings were features of the clothes of wealthy men as well as women." Elizabeth herself is often shown wearing garments which illustrate the lavish use of lynx and ermine.

Even though this period was marked by increasing wealth and power in western Europe, the use of fur in clothing was generally on the decline. This was due to three main factors. One was that other means of embellishing garments to show the wealth and status of the wearer were prevalent. Clothing was encrusted with embroidery, often in gold thread, and sometimes even with precious stones. Exquisite laces and beautiful velvets, brocades, and satins, in colors that dazzled the eye, were available. Secondly, houses were warmer, eliminating the need for cumbersome layers of fur. The wealthier classes could afford to have glass windows, and fireplaces were becoming more efficient. Lastly, furs were simply scarcer. By the 1400s much of Europe's animal population had become extinct or was greatly diminished. In the forests of Britain, which once covered most of the island, the beaver and the brown bear had vanished by the tenth century. Sources of fur from other nations, such as Russia and northern Europe, were unreliable, and the New World, with its seemingly endless abundance of wildlife, had yet to be fully explored.

However, fur did play a minor role in Renaissance fashion. Three new fashions stand out: the beaver hat (which would enjoy great popularity well into the nineteenth century); the muff, an accessory worn by both men and women; and the tippet, a long fur scarf that was often worn with the head and claws of the animal still intact, and sometimes encrusted with costly jewels.

An interesting, if rather disgusting variation of this last accessory was the "flea fur," or *countenance*. It must be remembered that although ladies and gentlemen of this period wore costumes so intricately constructed that they sometimes had to be taken apart to be washed, they doused themselves in rare and costly perfumes because they rarely bathed, and thus were host to many species of vermin. To remedy the problem of unwanted bugs appearing at inopportune times, the flea fur—an untanned pelt, often of marten, sable, or squirrel—was draped around the neck, in the hope that fleas and other creatures would be attracted to it instead of to other parts of the wearer's body, or to his dinner plate. The fur would be shaken out later, fleas and all, like a dirty rug. Whether this invention was successful or not is unclear, but the flea fur, like mood rings and other ill-conceived accessories, was short-lived.

Toward the end of the 1500s, explorers began to venture into other parts of the world, bringing back with them tales of untamed lands, brown-skinned peoples who worshipped strange gods, and, most importantly, a limitless store of natural resources.

## THE SEVENTEENTH CENTURY

The clothing of the period from 1600–1700 is a study in contrasts, from the flamboyant dress of the Cavaliers to the somber garments of the Puritans. The 1600s also stands out as "the great age of the hat." The Royalists and Cromwell's men had one thing in common—their costumes would have been incomplete without some type of head covering, which was almost always made out of beaver. A man of substance would sooner go naked than be seen without his beaver in public.

So insatiable was the demand for beaver that new sources for it had to be discovered. North America offered a seemingly inexhaustible supply of the silky pelts, attracting thousands to Canada and America. A new chapter in world history was written as a result of the almost fanatical search for beaver.

During this time, fur was often used as a trimming for cloaks and other garments, and fur accessories were quite popular. A well-dressed woman of the 1600s might carry a fur muff, trimmed perhaps with a big silk bow, and would wear a long, flowing cape, fully lined in fur, which might also include a detachable hood. As a finishing touch, she might wear a black silk mask, à la the Lone Ranger, a fashion that was very much in vogue for a brief period.

Hats were popular with both sexes and all ages. Berets, caps, and hats of fur—sometimes grotesquely tall—were worn by all, from commoner to king. A Germanic woman, for example, might wear a *pelzkappe*, which was a large bonnet, usually made in a long-haired fur.

All things considered though, fur was a minor fashion element in the seventeenth century, which was not the case during the next hundred years.

*Above:* A fashionable woman in a winter costume of the 1600s, with a fur muff and a silk mask. *Right:* A young French dandy of the pre-Revolutionary period (about 1787), with a huge beribboned muff.

# THE EIGHTEENTH CENTURY

The years from 1700 to 1800 were marked by turmoil on both continents. A series of upheavals—social as well as political—left their mark, and as fashion is the mirror of a society's mores, these changes were reflected in the clothing worn by the men and women of the era.

By this time, the rigidity of Elizabethan dress had long given way to less severe styles, but by today's standards, the clothing of this period was cumbersome and uncomfortable. The *pannier* (French for basket), a framework of wire, bone, or cane worn under skirts to extend the hips, was popular in the early part of this century, and as these "baskets" were often very wide, one can imagine that it was no picnic trying to maneuver through doorways. These elaborate dresses were often very expensive. At a time when the average peasant earned pennies a day, it was not unusual for noblewomen to spend the equivalent of $3,000 for a single gown, which was rarely worn twice.

Of course, over such voluminous dresses only loose-fitting garments were practical, and these were lined with fur. Fur accessories continued to be predominant, and tippets, often with muffs to match, were popular. The muffs were trimmed with artificial flowers, ribbons, feathers, or contrasting pieces of fur.

Not to be outdone, the men of the 1700s also decked themselves in fur finery. They continued to carry muffs, although these were usually smaller and not so elaborate as the ones used by women. Dressing gowns lined with fur were very popular for those who could afford them, particularly in the Colonies. Fur-lined cloaks, capes, and coats were also favored by the man-about-town, and the famous philosopher Voltaire possessed a magnificent sable-lined cloak given to him by Catherine the Great.

Inspired by a variety of forces, such as the back to nature philosophy of Rousseau, the French Revolution, and a growing interest in neo-classicism, the women of the late 18th century abandoned the fussy fashions of earlier decades in favor of loose-fitting, flowing gowns in thin, fine fabrics. These simple, columnar dresses were often trimmed with fur, and a fashion plate at the turn of the century might wear a gown edged in fox, squirrel, or ermine, accompanied by a fur-lined cape, and would have wound around her neck a long, thin, fur *snake*, which is nowadays called a *boa*. Completing the ensemble would be, of course, the ubiquitous muff, which by this time had mushroomed to outlandish proportions.

---

> **Fur Facts and Fancies:** *So huge were muffs during the eighteenth century that a small lapdog could fit quite comfortably inside one, and a prominent female member of society would include in her entourage a servant whose sole duty was to walk behind her, carrying the muffled mutt!*

Despite this lavish use of everything from ermine to otter, the next century could truly be called "the great age of fur display." During this period, fur garments "arrived," becoming a part of fashion instead of a footnote to it.

## THE NINETEENTH CENTURY

The years from 1800 to 1900 were a time of tumult all over the globe, from Washington, D.C. to Waterloo. Fashion also went through a number of revolutions, and a comparison of the graceful, neoclassical garments that dominated the opening years of the century and the exaggerated, bustled styles of the late 1800s presents a startling contrast.

Empress Josephine, the wife of Napoleon I, was noted for her extravagant taste in clothing, jewelry, and furs. Always conscious of her small-busted, lean-hipped figure—which was then considered unfashionable—the vain, mixed-blood beauty commissioned the equally difficult designer Hippolyte Roy to fashion a garment that would flatter her childlike figure. Thus was born the "Empire" gown, a high-waisted dress with a seam that ended just below the bust and a square, low-cut neckline. These dresses were often trimmed with deep bands of fur, perhaps inspired by the lavish, ermine-trimmed robe worn by Josephine at her coronation. Even wedding gowns of this period were embellished with fur.

As these dresses were often made of sheer muslins and other light fabrics, a wide variety of capes, cloaks, and other outer garments were employed to keep the ladies of the First Empire from freezing in their flimsy gowns. These cloaks were often lined with fur. One particularly popular style was the *wizcheria*, a full-length fitted coat modeled after the wolfskin outerwear of eastern Europe.

The elegant lines of this period gradually gave way to a wider silhouette, and to skirts that were given their characteristic bell shape by use of a stiffly starched petticoat called a crinoline, which was worn during

A fur shop, c. 1830. Note the fur stoles, capes, and "snakes," or boas.

the 1850s and 1860s. The petticoat was attached to a hoop of whalebone, metal, or even a lightweight, pliable wood, such as willow. Like many popular styles, it was carried to an extreme—it was not unusual for these crinolines to have a circumference of five feet or more.

Full-length, tightly fitted outer garments would have been unwearable over these styles, and the mid-century woman could choose a fur-lined cloak, stole, or mantle, often accompanied with a coordinating muff, to keep her warm. Fox, sable, and squirrel were popular choices.

As the century progressed, the silhouette was once again transformed, mainly by use of the *bustle*, a "pad, cushion, or other arrangement which gave a bulging effect in the rear." At its height, the bustle could be quite unwieldy; some were large enough to hold a tea tray. More important, however, were two developments that were to change the use of fur in fashion permanently: the evolution of fur garments as fashions in themselves, and the introduction of two "new" varieties of fur.

Up to this time, fur had been used mainly in accessories or as trimmings. However, with the rise of the affluent middle classes, fur became a status symbol, particularly for women. Elizabeth Ewing writes in *Fur in Dress:* "The leisured, expensively and conspicuously dressed

Bustled garments of the 1890s with fur lined capes and muffs.

woman was, by a kind of unofficial revival of long past sumptuary laws, a social phenomenon, a status symbol by which not only she herself but her husband and family too were given their place in the stakes in a class-conscious society, which, for the first time in modern history, equated class with money before anything else."

Secondly, the use of astrakhan (known as Persian lamb in the United States) and sealskin increased greatly, introducing new segments of the population to fur. Astrakhan was often seen in men's garments, and sealskin remained in vogue for men, women, and children well into the early 1900s. Sealskin came to symbolize upper-middle-class affluence, much as mink does today, and was in such demand that by 1912 the seal herds of the Pribilof Islands, off the coast of Alaska, had nearly been decimated.

It was around this time that male dress began to be standardized, with the suit jacket, trousers, and some form of neckwear becoming the uniform of the middle and upper classes. With such conservatism holding sway, the ostentatious use of fur in male clothing nearly disappeared, being relegated to coat linings and collars. By the end of the century, beaver hats had largely been replaced by those made of silk.

As the nineteenth century closed, fur garments were more widely worn than ever before, and their popularity continued and even increased in the next century.

## THE TWENTIETH CENTURY AND BEYOND

The year is 1900, the country is France, and the event is the Paris Exposition. In the fashion section of this international affair, Madame Paquin, the first woman to achieve worldwide fame as a fashion designer, displays elegant fur garments, including sumptuous dresses with trimmings of ermine, sable, and chinchilla; elegant wraps with huge collars of fox, and an innovative idea—coats with the fur on the *outside*.

The Paris Exposition was important in that it marked the display of fur garments as fashions in themselves, for the first time, in an international exhibition. Although fur coats as we know them—with the texture outside instead of inside—had already made sporadic appearances (Victor Revillon, for example, featured fur fashions in a show in Paris in 1862), the Paquin collection was a milestone. It was also during this time that fur began to be cut and shaped, as cloth is, on a large scale, a procedure which had also been pioneered by Monsieur

Revillon. (Before the late nineteenth century, fur had just been made into shapeless garments that hung from the body.)

The early 1900s was the heyday of the wasp-waisted, hourglass figure, which was achieved by the use of a rib-crushing corset. This S-shaped silhouette was set off by elegant fur stoles, scarves, and muffs, the latter being a small shadow of its once extravagant self. There was a fur garment for every season—full-length coats for fall and winter and lightweight wraps for spring. Madame Paquin suggested carrying a muff in all but the hottest weather, and in 1911, summer furs were all the rage. The men of this period also enjoyed wearing furs, and a symbol of male Edwardian affluence was the fur-lined coat with a fur collar.

Just before the First World War, Paul Poiret shocked the world with his elegantly draped, Oriental-inspired styles, which freed women from the tyranny of the corset. His clothing was often trimmed with deep bands of fur, creating an elegant soignée effect.

By the turn of the century, fur was seen not only in accessories, but in full-length garments as well.

A fur coat (*above*) and cape (*right*) from the 1920s.

In wartime skirts were shortened, and the corset all but disappeared. The popularity of fur garments remained stable, and even increased a bit. As women began to work outside the home, fur became affordable to even the humblest working girl, who could at least buy herself a fur muff or a pair of fur-lined gloves.

After the war, fur became even more popular, and the fur coat became the chief status symbol of the well-dressed of all classes. Innovations in the garment industry made mass production of furs more feasible, and lower-priced varieties, such as muskrat (known in Europe as *musquash*, an Indian word), coney, and pony were in style. Sable was still popular, as was ermine, another costly fur. Seal gradually became associated with the older, more conservative woman, much as Persian lamb is today. Surprisingly, mink did not come into vogue until much later.

The image many associate with the 1920s is one of freewheeling, flat-chested flappers with dangling pearls, and men in long-haired raccoon coats. However, during those years fur was also used for trimmings on capes, evening wraps, and even lingerie. Fragile, lovely Russian broadtail was often seen in formal attire, and monkey and ocelot were popular as well.

The most coveted fur of the 1920s and 1930s, however, was silver fox. Says fashion historian J.G. Links of this period: "to be bereft of fox was almost to be naked." The fur-farming industry—which had been started in the previous century—grew dramatically during those years, mainly in response to the huge demand for fox fur.

One great influence on the popularity of furs in the 1930s and 1940s was Hollywood. During and after World War II, stars such as Ava Gardner, Rita Hayworth, and Betty Grable appeared on the screen bedecked in mink, fox, and other glamorous pelts, inspiring the furry fantasies of American women.

The war had little effect on the demand for fur; consumers were even encouraged to buy it, as wool was needed for the armed forces. In Britain, and to a lesser extent, the U.S., the utility fur coat, a lower-priced garment which could be bought by carefully accumulating ration coupons, was "one of the few good things to come out of the war." It might have been made of opossum, fur seal, or "beaver lamb"—sheepskin cleverly processed to look almost, but not quite, like beaver.

One important innovation to come about after the war was Christian Dior's New Look, "an ultra-feminine silhouette incorporating yards of material in an almost ankle-length skirt, with tiny waist, snug bodice, rounded, sloping shoulders, and padded hips." Along with this smoothly sculpted shape came the need for "ladylike" furs with dress-maker details. Mink came into its own as the ultimate feminine luxury in status-conscious postwar America, and the mink coats of the fifties, with their roomy sleeves and classic styling, are still in demand by collectors of antique furs. Accessories such as scarves, stoles, and the diehard muff, were also popular.

With the youth movement of the early 1960s, the "fun fur"—a low-er-priced garment or accessory, often with unusual styling—was the rage. Younger women, who had previously regarded fur as something for the older woman, began to wear furs. The search for new and unique furs sent the "youthquakers" of the sixties to the attics of their mothers—and grandmothers—in search of something different. Bar-onduki, fitch, monkey, and other unusual furs were popular, as were the skins of big cats such as leopards and tigers, which had a very detrimental effect on these species.

The ecology movement of the late sixties and early seventies, howev-er, soon dampened the enthusiasm for fur garments. A flurry of legisla-tion was enacted to protect certain dwindling species. "Fake" furs, made of synthetic pile fabrics, were touted as alternatives to wearing fur garments, while wearing the real thing came to be regarded as cru-el, inhumane, and in short, not a very nice thing to do.

In the late seventies, the tide seemed to turn, as burgeoning fur sales indicated. Critics suggest that the men and women of the late twentieth century have retrogressed to the value system of their counterparts of a hundred years ago, who judged an individual's worth by the size of his or her bank account. Others suggest that the increased interest in fur garments is a reaction to the coldness and superficiality of the modern world; fur can be taken to represent the all-enveloping warmth and security of the womb. But whatever the case, fur is "in" again, thanks in part to such fashion trendsetters as Nancy Reagan.

---

**Fur Facts and Fancies:** *In the late 1880s, the general taste for furs and feathers in fashion took a gruesome turn, as women took to wearing tiny (artificial) monkey and cat heads on their cos-tumes, as well as (real) stuffed mice!*

What will the mirror of fashion reflect in its fickle silver eye with regard to fur in the twenty-first century? As new techniques and innovations, such as weaving and knitting fur and combining it with materials such as leather and ribbon, become more sophisticated, and furriers try to appeal to the younger, more affluent, and style-conscious customer, we might see some startling creations that would shock the ladies of Victorian days out of their sealskins. But as fashion, like history, tends to repeat itself, it is also likely that the furs of the near future will not be too unlike those of the recent past. As the French say, "the more things change . . . the more they remain the same."

## CLOSEUP
# SUPERNATURAL FURS

For centuries, man has not only used fur to adorn and protect himself, but he has also considered the skin of certain animals to possess magical, mystical, or malevolent powers. The ancient Romans believed that seal and hyena pelts could protect an individual from lightning, and deerskin offered immunity from snakebites. Roman physicians also prescribed "beaver skins for burns and scalds and beaver skin shoes for gout."

The curative powers of the pelts and other parts of the beaver (in France called a *castor*) were also highly thought of in more recent times. In colonial America, "leave it to beaver" didn't refer to a television show, but to the alleged healing powers of beaver hats, which, when worn religiously, were supposed to be a cure for deafness. The hats were also thought to cure lapses of memory, particularly if the "oil of castor" from the hat was massaged into the scalp.

Early naturalists ascribed near-human characteristics to the beaver. The animals were believed to assemble in communities of two hundred or three hundred to build their lodges and, in a melodramatic "death before dishonor" scenario, the gnawing rodent was thought to castrate itself if its virtue were threatened, thus becoming a symbol of purity and chastity in the early Christian church.

Another animal which came to symbolize virtuous attributes was the ermine. Elizabeth I, the Virgin Queen, was often painted wearing the fur, and is sometimes portrayed with a tiny, live, gold-collared ermine by her side. Some of the early Christian martyrs, such as Saint Ursula, who according to legend was killed with eleven thousand other virgins in Cologne when returning from a pilgrimage to Rome, is often pictured wearing the soft, white fur.

In many societies, wearing the fur of a certain animal was supposed to convey the strength, cunning, and prowess of that beast to the wearer. Says J.G. Cooper in *An Illustrated Encyclopedia of Traditional Symbols*: "wearing animal skins or masks . . . reproduces the paradisal state of understanding and speech between man and animals; it also means access to animal and instinctive wisdom." Thus, a resident of ancient China might have wrapped himself in bearskin to capture the bravery and strength of the animal, while the early Christian would at all costs avoid the shaggy pelt of the bruin, as this animal symbolized evil, greed, and the devil himself.

In most cultures, the fox is regarded as intelligent, resourceful, and somewhat crafty. In an unusual reversal of color symbolism, the Japanese believed that wearing black fox would bring good luck, while white fox would invite calamity. Elsewhere in Japan, the Ainu, a mysterious, pale-skinned tribe whose members live primarily on the island of Hokkaido, would never eat the flesh or wear the skin of the otter, as they believed that to do so would confer the animal's alleged forgetfulness on whomever ate or donned it.

The big cats in particular were thought to possess magical powers, and their skins brought to their wearers bravery, cunning or cruelty, depending on which side of the globe you were on. In ancient Egypt, the leopard, with its many eyelike spots, was called the Great Watcher, and symbolized Osiris, Lord of the Underworld. But in early Christian societies, the leopard and its skin were thought to symbolize aggression, sin, and unbridled carnality. In Rome, the lynx was believed to have the ability to see through walls.

The leopard, lynx, and their kin, with their beautiful markings, bravery, and hunting prowess, fascinated the people of many cultures, and roared their way into myth and legend. In East Indian cultures, the tiger symbolizes bravery and nobility, and in Hindu mythology, the God Siva is shown wearing the skin of a tiger, as did many Indian princes and nobles. In feudal Japan, the *oni*—mischievous, sometimes malicious spirits who were fond of playing tricks on hapless humans— were often portrayed wearing tiger skins, and in China, the big striped cat was one of the Three Thoughtless Creatures of mythology, symbolizing anger (the other members of this hapless trio were the monkey and the deer).

Fighting men on every continent have garbed themselves in the skins of aggressive animals, believing that the animals' ferocity would be imparted to them. The tall, regal Zulu warriors of southeastern Africa often wore leopard skins into battle for this reason. In ancient Scandinavia, *berserkers*—from the Norse words "bear sarks," referring to the hairy garments these soldiers wore, were feared because of their viciousness and insane fury in battle. Believing themselves to be possessed by the spirit of Odin, they bit into their shields and often fought with their bare hands, sometimes literally tearing their opponents to pieces. More likely, however, these individuals were "men to whom tumult and violence and the wild desire to murder were normal."

Even in this century, the Leopard Societies have terrorized the countryside of many West African nations. By attaching leopard claws to their hands, and draping the skins of this beautiful beast over their backs, these men believed that they actually became the creature, and proceeded to kill their many victims, most of them young women, quite horribly. Some even ate parts of the victims' bodies, as leopards do. One of the few clear benefits gained from colonial rule in this part of the world was the eventual eradication of the Leopard Societies, although murders suspiciously reminiscent of these gruesome rites still occur from time to time.

The American Indians also believed that the *mana* or spirit of an animal could be transferred to the human wearer of its skin. The Plains Indians had great reverence for the buffalo, and the finest skins from this awesome creature were reserved for the *shamans* or priests of the tribe. To native Americans, the buffalo represented the all-encompassing power of the whirlwind, which is probably why they were so appalled by the white man's gratuitous slaughter of this animal in the late nineteenth century. The Blackfoot Indians, renowned for their skill and prowess in hunting and trapping, could not be persuaded to kill beaver, because they considered it sacred.

Although few today believe in magic symbolism, certain furs do send out specific messages. Mink International, a trade organization for producers of this fur, recently commissioned the J. Walter Thompson advertising agency to survey women in five American cities about their attitudes toward fur. They discovered that a woman wearing mink is seen as "mature, affluent, and socially active," while the wearer of raccoon seems "young and sporty." The woman who chooses lynx is thought to be "wealthy." Most interesting, however, is the perception of the wearer of fox as being "fashion-oriented and good-looking, a career woman." In fact, this "foxy lady" has many of the attributes ascribed to the crafty reynard of yore, which suggests that we are not too far removed from the beliefs of our ancestors after all.

# ADVENTURES IN THE SKIN TRADE

## TWO

The fur trade is America's oldest continuously operating industry. Its 350-year history, combining intrigue, glamour, and suspense, could provide raw material for several best-selling novels. Starting with the exploration of the New World, the fur industry has played a vital role in the shaping of North America.

## BEGINNINGS

### Fortunes in the Forest

By the advent of the fifteenth century, Europe's once rich supply of natural resources had been depleted. The idea that wildlife should be carefully conserved to ensure its survival for future generations was unheard of, and overexploitation was the name of the game.

In Shakespeare's day, and even until the dawn of the twentieth century, fur was more of a necessity than a luxury. Even the manors and castles of the wealthy were very cold. With Europe's animal population dwindling, and the riches of Russia yet to be explored, it was only natural that the merchants of the Age of Exploration should look to

North America for new sources of fur. Some types, such as marten, very nearly extinct in the Old World, were almost worth their weight in gold.

Much of the early trade in furs centered around the beaver. The rich brown fur of this aquatic animal—a cousin of the porcupine and the rat—was so highly valued that in Europe a man's status was often judged by the height of his beaver—hence the term "high hat." The importance of the beaver to the early North American economy is illustrated by the fact that in many of the original colonies beaver skins were used as currency. (William Penn, founder of Pennsylvania, had to pay an annual token rent of two beaver skins to the British.)

The French were the first to settle in the New World. With the blessings of Henry IV of France, a small band of colonists settled in Newfoundland and Nova Scotia in 1600. However, the harsh Canadian winters took their toll, and many returned to their native land. Those who stayed became *coureurs de bois,* wood or forest runners, who lived a rough-and-ready existence, trading furs with friendly tribes such as the Hurons and Algonquins. The importance of these early French fur traders is illustrated by the many American place names with a Gallic flavor—including Champlain, Duluth, and Joliet.

The English and Dutch soon followed. In the early 1600s, the Dutch established a trading post called Fort Manhattan in what is now Brooklyn, New York. Their presence in what was to become New York City continued until the end of the century, and many of the city's well-known neighborhoods—including Bedford-Stuyvesant, Harlem, and Spuyten Duyvil—attest to The Big Apple's Dutch heritage.

One of the most important and long-lived British contributions to the fur trade—and the development of the New World—was the establishment of The Governor and Company of Merchants of England trading into Hudson's Bay—better known as the Hudson's Bay Company. The company was granted a charter by Charles II of England on May 2, 1670. The primary purpose of this organization was to trade

---

**Fur Facts and Fancies:** *In 1779, Jean Baptiste Point du Sable, a fur trader of African and French heritage, established a permanent settlement at the mouth of the Chicago River, which was to become the city of Chicago.*

---

The Hudson Bay Company Trading Store.

furs with the Indians, with whom relations were deteriorating. The Indians were at first paid with guns, whiskey, or cooking pots. Once again, the most important fur traded was beaver. A system of exchange was set up by which eight to twelve beaver skins equaled one gun, or one beaver skin was traded for a half pound of gunpowder, eleven pounds of tobacco, and a half pound of beads. The colorful Hudson's Bay blankets, which are still coveted today for their warmth and beauty, were also used in trade, with each long black mark or "point" on the blanket signifying how many beavers were traded for it.

Today the Hudson's Bay Company is still in existence. The fur trade is only one aspect of its many diversified operations, but the early importance of beaver to the company is shown by the four castors that still decorate its coat of arms.

## A New Era

By the early 1800s, the eastern U.S. had largely been depleted of its wildlife. The ever-increasing demand for fur, especially beaver, was the driving force that led many westward across the Appalachians.

John Jacob Astor buying furs in Western New York.

However, the independent frontiersmen of the 1600s and 1700s had almost disappeared, and the fur trade was increasingly controlled by a handful of large trading companies.

By this time, the Dutch had lost their power in North America to the British, and the French presence was similarly diminished. After her defeat in the French and Indian War, France ceded to England all of her North American possessions east of the Mississippi, and the Hudson's Bay Company gained control of the Eastern fur trade. Meanwhile the North West Company of Montreal further developed the fur trade in the West, extending its operations to the Arctic in the north, the Rockies to the west, and the Big Bend of the Missouri River to the south.

One man who was instrumental in developing the fur business was John Jacob Astor. In a classic rags-to-riches story, he started out toiling in the fur trade and ended up controlling much of the American fur market. He dreamed of establishing trading posts throughout the west, and his Pacific Fur Company succeeded in building the city of Astoria at the mouth of the Columbia River. Although Astor never succeeded in establishing a nationwide fur empire, he dominated the industry and built a huge fortune. Later his interest turned to real estate, earning him more millions, so that by the time of his death in 1848, he was one of the country's wealthiest men.

By the end of the nineteenth century the fur trade was at its height. The steel trap had been invented, which made the taking of furs much easier, and the Hudson's Bay Company had absorbed the North West Company. Fur was becoming more of a symbol of affluence than a necessity, and the demand for marten, fisher, otter, mink, and of course, beaver, was enormous.

It was around this time that large numbers of Jews from Germany and Austria-Hungary, later followed by those from Russia and Eastern Europe, began arriving in the United States, fleeing centuries of religious persecution. In many European nations, strict laws kept Jews from owning land, and quotas severely limited the number admitted to universities, particularly in Germany.

Faced with such discrimination, many became small shop owners and skilled craftsmen, particularly in the needle trades. They became the seamstresses, tailors, and furriers for all of Europe, establishing such cities as Leipzig and Vienna as centers of fur-garment production. These immigrants brought their highly developed skills to the New World, and by the early twentieth century, they controlled the industry.

The late nineteenth century also saw the first organized labor movements. Although the early struggles of coal miners, auto workers, and garment-industry laborers are well chronicled, little has been said about the first fur unions, whose growing pains were just as dramatic. Early fur workers often faced hazardous working conditions. Twelve-hour days and seven-day workweeks were common, and the pay was pennies an hour. Workers who expressed an interest in union activities were often fired, verbally and physically harassed, or sometimes even killed.

Today, however, the fur industry's dressers, dyers, machine operators, and other workers are represented by several locals, which in turn are affiliated with the United Food and Commercial Workers Union, a division of the AFL-CIO. Fur workers are among the most highly organized and well paid in the garment industry, averaging more than four hundred dollars a week.

## THE FUR INDUSTRY TODAY

Although the fur industry is fairly small in comparison to other garment trades, it spans many countries, and supplies the livelihood of thousands. In America, the nucleus of the fur industry is in New York, while in Canada it is centered in Montreal and, to a lesser extent, Toronto.

In the United States, approximately a quarter of a million men and women earn all or part of their living from the fur industry—including manufacturers, skin dealers, trappers, and many others. In Canada, this figure is about a hundred thousand. It is safe to assume that on a worldwide scale, the fur industry employs more than half a million people.

Most furriers, at both the wholesale and retail level, are small, family-owned businesses that employ fewer than twenty people. One notable exception is Evans, Inc., the largest retail furrier in the world, with locations all over the United States and Japan. The Chicago-based firm operates its own stores, and also leases the fur salons in fourteen major department stores nationwide.

Another company, The Fur Vault, Inc., recently made history when it became only the second fur company to be listed on a stock exchange in America. Under the leadership of Fred Schwartz (better known as "Fred the Furrier" to thousands in the New York–New Jersey metropolitan area), the firm not only includes a wholesale division—Mademoiselle, "America's Furrier"—but also leases the salons of several well-known department stores. The Fur Vault also operates several independent fur shops, including the world's first fur department store.

## A Look at the American Fur Industry

The bulk of the United States's fur manufacturers are located in midtown Manhattan, in the heart of the garment district, which has been described as "a sort of very small, very crowded, and very rich country inside another slightly larger and richer country."

The fur industry encompasses only a few blocks, from West Twenty-sixth to West Thirtieth streets between Sixth and Eighth avenues. It is easy to recognize this fabled area of the city by the sight of the ubiquitous pushboys who aggressively roll huge racks down the street. These racks-on-wheels bear bolts of cloth, dresses of everything from crepe de chine to polyester, sportswear, and formalwear, and of course furs. Along the way they frequently mow down any obstacles in their path, including hapless tourists.

Many of the small family-owned furriers have been in the business for two or even three generations, and a small but significant number of "fur brats"—young people who grew up in these family businesses, hanging around fur machines—are entering the field, bringing with them new blood and fresh ideas. The ethnic makeup of the industry is also changing: Greeks, many of them from the city of Kastoria, a fur manufacturing center for centuries, are rapidly replacing Jews as manufacturers.

A visitor to the fur district, noticing the hustle and bustle, would guess that the fur industry is enjoying the best of times, but in reality, it has its share of problems. Manufacturers, who numbered about twenty-five hundred in the late 1940s, have dwindled to about six hundred, and the number is decreasing yearly. Why is this?

As with other sectors of American manufacturing, imported furs—mainly from the Far East—are edging out American-made garments. Furs imported to the United States climbed from $90 million in 1980 to $307 million in 1984, and this amount is increasing every year. In 1984, imported garments accounted for 45% of all furs sold in the U.S.—up from 16% in 1980. Korea, Canada, Hong Kong, Greece, and West Germany are the five leading exporters of fur garments to this country. In contrast, the number of fur garments exported by the U.S. to other countries has declined from a peak of $83.1 million in 1980 to about $32.9 million in 1985.

Although American-made garments are considered the best in the world, many furs manufactured abroad are much cheaper because wages overseas, particularly in the Orient, are much lower. In many Asian countries fur workers are paid one third or less the weekly wage of their American counterparts. In fact, the average hourly pay of a manufacturing worker in South Korea in 1983 was $1.36, while in the U.S. it was $12.59!

Although the burgeoning percentage of imported garments gives the consumer a wider variety of furs to choose from, the impact of low-priced imported furs has been detrimental to U.S. manufacturers. In the long run it seems that the fur industry will be able to hold its own when it comes to higher-priced garments, while manufacturers who concentrate on producing middling quality, or commercial-grade coats, will gradually disappear.

In addition, as in other sectors of the American economy, relations between labor and management have not always been cordial. In 1982 and 1984, the industry was nearly paralyzed by two lengthy strikes, the latter of which lasted more than two months. At issue was not only the question of wages, but the increasing tendency of many manufacturers to contract work out to nonunion shops. Although the unions gained much of what they demanded, some feel that these strikes did the industry more harm than good. The fur unions are still influential, but their memberships are declining, and some manufacturers are turning to nonunion labor from such places as the Dominican Republic, and even from just across the river in New Jersey.

Many manufacturers also complain about the lack of skilled workers. Few young people are interested in becoming fur craftsmen, and as older, highly trained workers retire, it is difficult to find replacements.

To remedy this problem, New York's famous Fashion Institute of Technology—alma mater of such internationally known designers as Calvin Klein and Norma Kamali—has implemented a Fur Design and Marketing Program, the only one of its kind in this country. The two-year course prepares students to "function at various levels of the design, marketing, and production areas in the fur industry." Students accepted into the program must have an associate-level college background in some area of fashion design or merchandising; they graduate with a Bachelor of Fine Arts degree. Topics include such diverse areas as "Breeding and Wildlife Management," "Selling Furs: The Dynamics of Great Selling," and "Fur-Design Patternmaking." Although the first class graduated only recently, Jill Lawer, consulting chairperson of the program and an F.I.T. alumna, comments that the new graduates have been enthusiastically received by industry professionals. By all indications, the program is a success.

## THE FUR INDUSTRY AND THE FUTURE

Where will the fur industry be in the year 2000? One furrier quips, "in New Jersey." This may be true if more and more manufacturers and other firms involved in the industry decide to relocate, partially because of escalating rents. The New York branch of the Hudson's Bay Company, after years at the same location, recently moved lock, stock, and barrel to New Jersey.

In all likelihood, however, Manhattan will always be the spiritual, if not the physical center of the American fur industry. It is equally probable that American furs will continue to be coveted because of their high degree of workmanship, and that sales will continue to increase even as the number of manufacturers is decreasing. The fur industry will survive, for, in a sense, it represents the American spirit—tough, proud, independent, and remarkably resilient.

# FROM RUSSIA WITH LOVE: THE SOVIET FUR INDUSTRY

In the early 1970s, the Khakas Archaeological Expedition of Moscow University discovered a 2,000-year-old tomb—a small, low, wooden chamber which, having been hermetically sealed in the bitter cold of Siberia, was almost perfectly preserved. Among the items found were cooking utensils and clothing, including what is thought to be the world's oldest fur coat.

The coat, which appeared to be for a child, was made of dog or wolf fur, and is trimmed with sable. The skirts of the garment were cut from sheepskin, and have side gussets that create a flaring, graceful hem. The coat—now on display at the State Hermitage Museum in Leningrad—is no worse for wear and is surprisingly contemporary in appearance, so much so that if worn by a trendsetting youngster enamored of the "ethnic" look it would not be the least out of place today on the streets of any large city in America.

Somehow it is more than fitting that the world's oldest fur should be of Russian origin, for fur has played an important part in Russian history for centuries. Like North America, Siberia was settled largely by men eager to exploit its rich supply of furs, particularly sable, which for centuries has been prized as the fur of kings. In fact, in prerevolutionary Russia, sable was the exclusive fur of the royal family.

Although the U.S.S.R. government does not release any figures, thousands are said to be employed by the fur industry. The world's largest fur processing plant is located in Moscow. As with every other aspect of Soviet life, the fur industry is highly regulated, with fur farms under state control. The government has even cracked down on citizens who were raising fur animals as a hobby, disapproving of the pocket money earned from these homegrown enterprises.

The sole agent for the fur collectives is a fifty-year-old firm called V/O Sojuzpushnina. In 1980, this organization was awarded an international prize, the Gold Mercury, "for its part in developing trade and economic cooperation on an international basis."

Besides sable (marketed under the name Sobol), the Soviet Union produces a number of other furs. Russian broadtail, a beautiful and costly fur that is most often seen in evening pieces, is culled from the stillborn lambs of the caracul, or Persian lamb. White Russian fitch is another gorgeous, expensive fur with striking contrasts of dark and light. Other Russian furs include Siberian squirrel, stone and baum marten, and wolverine.

As in North America, the majority of Russian furs—about 70 percent—are ranched. Russian fur ranches are said to be the largest in the world. One, the Pushkino sable farm near Moscow, has a stock of ten thousand animals. Only 12 percent of Soviet furs come from wild animals, and in fact, the Soviets are said to be far ahead of the West in regards to conservation. Caracul (sold under the name Bukhara) accounts for the remaining 18 percent of total output.

Mink, which is marketed under the name Norka, is also raised in the Soviet Union. While the mink-farming industry had its start in the U.S., the Soviets are the world's largest producers of mink, with an annual production of about 11 million skins as opposed to the 4.5 million produced in the United States. Soviet mink is generally considered to be of slightly lower quality than the Scandinavian and American varieties, although it has won prizes in international competition.

The costliest Russian fur is lynx. The soft, creamy pelts of this distant relative of the American housecat can sell for hundreds of dollars apiece, with the fluffy belly sections worth even more. In 1984, the value of lynx and other Soviet furs imported into the U.S. was $10.2 million. Surprisingly, however, even though Russian furs are sold around the world, the annual value of Soviet-produced furs is only $100 million.

Other Russian furs include kolinsky (a poor cousin of mink, with a strong yellowish cast), ermine, muskrat, weasel, fox, and marten. None of these furs, including Russian mink, is allowed into the U.S., due to an embargo placed on them at the height of the Cold War.

In the Soviet Union the business of fur is very important. The most valuable pelts, including sable and lynx, are sold at the Palace of Furs in Leningrad in three yearly auctions. Buyers at these lucrative events were once wined and dined with the finest vodka and caviar in the best capitalist style, but due to austerity measures introduced by Premier Mikhail S. Gorbachev, excessive spending on public functions has been curtailed, and foreign businessmen must now be content with salmon and Georgian wine.

On the consumer side, Russians, like their North American counterparts, are partial to mink. Fox and beaver are also popular, as well as other furs not seen too often in North America, such as wolverine and weasel. (Raisa Elena Gorbachev, wife of the Soviet leader, has done much for the image of Russian furs—and Russian women—with her fashionable fur ensembles; she seems to favor sable.) A spokesperson for V/O Sojuzpushnina also comments that in the Soviet Union's frigid climate, where winter temperatures often dip below zero, furs are more of a necessity than a luxury.

# FROM CATCH TO CONSUMER

## PRELIMINARIES

What exactly is fur? This question may seem elementary, for hundreds of animals can be classified as fur-bearing, including duck-billed platypi, mice, and kangaroos. Only a small number of these animals, however, are used for fur garments: when's the last time you heard of a platypus poncho or a mouse muffler?

Basically there are two types of fur. The first, which is most often encountered, consists of three parts: the innermost layer, the *leather* (or skin) of the animal, to which is attached the *underfur*, and the outer, or *guard hairs*. The underfiber consists of a dense, dull, very warm mass of fine fiber, which is very similar to wool fiber (by parting the hair of a long-haired dog or cat, you can see an example of it). This layer serves as insulation for the animal in very cold climates.

Growing through this dense mass are the straight, shiny, and usually darker guard hairs. The guard hairs protect the animal from rain and snow. These coarse hairs are at their thickest along the center of the back of the animal, where they form the *grotzen* (a Yiddish word mean-

32

ing *backbone*) that sometimes looks like a short mane. Often the guard hairs are removed in a process called *plucking*, which exposes the velvety underfur. The plucked fur is then *sheared*, or shaved to a soft, even surface, which feels similar to silk velvet. This method is used on the skins of aquatic animals, such as beaver and muskrat, as their underfur is very dense and soft. Mink is sometimes sheared, but usually only on pelts of lesser quality.

The second type of fur consists of hair attached to skin, with little or no underfur. This type includes some un-furlike furs such as calf, pony, and antelope, as well as hair seal.

Whatever the type of fur, however, it must go through certain processes before it is turned into a fur garment. That divine little coat or jacket you've been admiring in the window of your local furrier's, and have been hoarding your subway money for, went through many changes to become a thing of beauty.

The story begins on a fur farm in the U.S., Canada, Finland, or one of the half dozen other countries, where the majority of furs used in garments today come from. From the fur farm, the pelts are sold at auctions in one of the centers of international fur activity. They then travel to the dressing plants, where they are processed, and from there to the manufacturers. The picture now focuses on the designer's workroom, where he or she, keeping in mind the characteristics of the fur being worked with, conceives a design for the garment. Highly skilled craftspersons then take over, cutting, laying out, and sewing the pelts, and after a few finishing touches, the fur coat, jacket, or stole is finally ready to be sold.

It may sound simple, but there's far more involved in the making of a quality fur than meets the eye. Let's take a more detailed look at the evolution of a fur garment.

## FUNDAMENTALS OF FUR PROCESSING

Most of the animals used in the fur industry worldwide—more than 75 percent—are raised on farms. This includes all the chinchilla and lamb, as well as most of the mink, opossum, fox, rabbit, and fitch. Finnish raccoon, which looks quite different from its American relative, is ranched, and experiments are underway to ranch-raise other animals, such as beaver and lynx.

It is very important that the pelts, whether they come from a wild or ranched animal, be harvested at their peak, or prime, when the animal's coat is at its thickest and densest. This factor is especially crucial when it comes to long-haired animals such as fox, coyote, and lynx because furs taken too late will shed excessively. Prime time for fur-bearers used by the industry varies; generally, ranch mink are harvested (pelted) shortly after Thanksgiving, while most North American animals are taken between October 20th and December 20th.

The marketing of most ranched skins is controlled by breeders' associations. Two of the best known are the GLMA (Great Lakes Mink Association) and EMBA (Mutation Mink Breeders' Association), which, in late 1985, merged to form an organizatio The marketing of most ranched skins is controlled by breeders' associations. Two of the best known are the GLMA (Great Lakes Mink Association) and EMBA (Mutation Mink Breeders' Association), which, in late 1985, merged to form an organization called American Legend—The Mink Source (although both EMBA and GLMA still exist as separate legal entities). Scandinavian-bred fox and mink are represented by an organization called SAGA.

Many of these organizations have special trademarks to identify their products. Lunaraine, which describes a color that was developed to imitate the wild mink, is a tradename of EMBA, while the GLMA has copyrighted the name Blackglama to describe a very dark black-brown shade of mink. However, just as we often incorrectly use the trade name Xerox to describe any photocopy, many of these terms are now used in a general sense: Lunaraine, when used by furriers, usually refers to a range of medium to dark brown shades.

Pelts of unranched animals, including lynx, American raccoon, and beaver, are sold through wild-skin dealers, and their trapping is strictly regulated by local, state, and sometimes federal authorities.

The very best skins, be they wild or ranched furs, end up in auction houses in Copenhagen, Leningrad, Montreal, Toronto, Seattle, London, and other cities. Sometimes the pelts are completely dressed, or tanned, before they are auctioned, but usually they are not, except for some preliminary processing that assures that they will not deteriorate.

These auctions are high-stakes affairs, as buyers vie for the choicest skins, which can be very expensive. A single good-quality mink pelt costs about sixty dollars, and as a street-length mink coat requires about sixty to sixty-five pelts, the furrier is making quite a substantial investment. The pelts, which have been carefully presorted according to color, size, and quality, are often bought by secret bidding. Gestures that would go unnoticed by the inexperienced eye—the nod of a head, the movement of a pencil, or some other previously agreed upon signal—often mean that a sale has been made. Smaller manufacturers that cannot afford to attend these auctions use the services of a skin broker, who usually works on either a commission basis or a retainer system. This individual scouts the auctions and purchases skins to the client's specifications. Other manufacturers buy from skin dealers, who purchase large amounts from auctions or directly from breeders and then break these lots up into smaller *bundles*. A bundle contains the amount of skins necessary to make a given garment, be it a full-length coat or a scarf.

Next, the skins must be *dressed*, or tanned. This process turns the raw, stiff, dirty skins into soft, sensuous pelts with creamy, pliable leather and silky fur. It must be remembered that fur is an organic substance, and while the pelt is on the living animal, it is kept soft and healthy by nutrients supplied through the animal's diet—much as your skin, hair, and nails are. The tanning process is crucial, since it prevents the actions of decay-causing bacteria which would cause the pelts to disintegrate. Improperly dressed skins are susceptible to cracking, splitting, and tearing, which cannot be corrected, since the coat is actually decaying.

The fur industry is extremely competitive, so the exact procedures are kept secret, but basically the magic that turns these unappealing pelts into miniature works of art is accomplished in a number of steps. First, in a process called *fleshing*, the tissue is scraped from the pelts. Increasingly, skins are fleshed by mechanical means, but scraping by hand results in a finer, more supple skin.

Then the skins are placed in large vats containing special chemicals. Substances used for tanning skins have included the bark of trees such as hemlock, oak, and sumac, ground insect parts, animal brains mixed with oil, and even animal urine, which was used well into the nineteenth century. Fortunately, modern chemistry has produced more sopisticated and less unsavory solutions.

The cost of this processing varies greatly, according to what must be

> **Fur Facts and Fancies:** *In a throwback to the Middle Ages, there was an attempt in the 1940s to make the fur of domestic felines into a salable commodity. Needless to say, the results were catastrophic.*

done to the pelt to make it salable. Alaska fur seal—which has a very coarse hide, filled with bristly, prickly hairs—must undergo 129 separate steps to make it wearable. Naturally, larger skins cost more to dress than smaller ones. After soaking, the natural oils of the skins, which have been diminished by the potent chemicals, are worked back into the leather. The pelts are then cleaned in huge, revolving, sawdust-filled drums. After this *drumming*, they are beaten and combed to make them soft and fluffy.

## SPECIAL EFFECTS FOR SPECIAL FURS

A variety of processes are employed to alter the appearance of the pelts, the most important being coloring. Coloring processes include dyeing, blending, bleaching, and printing (or stencilling). There are two main reasons for coloring furs: (1) to enhance the fur's appearance, and (2) to imitate other furs.

Furs are dyed in a wide range of colors, including many startling shades such as fuchsia, emerald, violet, and cobalt blue. Sheepskin, rabbit, and other less expensive furs are often dyed, but unusual color effects are not limited to the "poor" furs. At New York's J. Mendel salon, for example, we saw a mink coat, priced in the five-figure range, that had been dyed navy blue and emerald green, with a lining of jade-colored jacquard to match. Other more sedate, but lovely shades have names like curry, shrimp, persimmon, honey dew, butterscotch, champignon, and maple. Such mouth-watering names naturally lead one to wonder whether food or furs are being described.

Furs are also dyed to resemble more costly garments. In the first part of this century, for example, "Hudson seal,"—sheared American muskrat (once known as "the poor woman's mink") dyed black—was the rage. Other "fabulous fakes" such as "chinchillette," "beaverette," and "sealine"—all romantic names for glorified rabbit fur—also became popular with those who had beer budgets but champagne tastes.

The Fur Products Labeling Act of 1952 put a stop to this fanciful selling technique by requiring that the fur's correct name be clearly stated, along with its country of origin, on a tag affixed to the garment. This law also requires that if a fur has been artificially colored in any way, it must be marked on the tag.

*Blending* refers to a process in which color is applied only to the tips of the guard hairs. This is done to give the fur uniformity of color. Blending is also called *tipdyeing*.

*Stenciling*, or printing fur to resemble endangered or rare animals, is also popular. Less-expensive furs, such as rabbit and sheepskin, are often used for this purpose. In past seasons, the fashion world has treated us to cleverly patterned creations that are virtually indistinguishable from leopard, tiger, ocelot, zebra, and even giraffe. In many cases, the markings on these look-alikes are even more distinct than those on the original animal.

*Bleaching* is used to lighten white or pale furs. For example, winter ermine and white fox often have an unattractive yellowish cast. Other furs, such as fitch, sometimes have special brighteners added to heighten the natural pale coloring.

Although natural furs are generally considered more desirable than those that have been dyed, coloring is often used to create unusual effects. In the *degradé process*, pelts are dyed in varying shades of the same color, creating a striking ombre effect. A fur colored in blue degradé, for example, will have tones shading from robin's egg blue at the collar to navy at the hem.

Other furs are colored as a matter of course. Alaska fur seal, mole, and some types of squirrel are almost always dyed, as their natural coloring is unattractive. Black Persian lamb pelts are also, as a rule, dyed in a process called *streaking*, which prevents the white leather (the animal's skin) from showing through. Generally speaking, you can tell a dyed fur by the fact that the leather, underfur, and guard hairs will all be the same shade.

The following chart outlines some of the most common coloring procedures.

## COMMON FUR-COLORING TECHNIQUES*

| NAME | METHOD | PURPOSE | HOW TO DETECT |
|---|---|---|---|
| Dyeing | Total immersion of fur into mordant (fixative) and then into a dye | Change color of entire unit—hair, leather, and fiber | Leather dyed to same, or similar, shade as fur hair and fiber (sometimes singed from over-dyeing) |

*Chart adapted from *World of Furs* by David L. Kaplan.

| NAME | METHOD | PURPOSE | HOW TO DETECT |
|------|--------|---------|---------------|
| Tipdyeing (blending) | Adding color to tip of hair or fiber by feather or air brush | To color only the tip of the guard hair or fiber on all or part of the skin as needed | Color addition on tips can be detected only by close microscopic examination or by experienced furrier |
| Printing (stenciling) | Application of color in some pattern (usually by silk-screen) to prepare hair or fiber | To imitate more expensive product, or to simulate fur of endangered species | Color of pattern penetrates partly on hair or fiber length; pattern crosses seams. |
| Bleaching | Application of dye to part or all of hair or fiber | To lighten part of skin so as to present a different appearance; to whiten all or part of skin as needed | Leather often made unnaturally white (stitching may be weakened as well, if process is done poorly); must be compared with natural or untouched skin to detect difference |

Other techniques used to creatively alter the appearance of fur include *grooving*, which consists of cutting "stripes" into sheared furs such as beaver and nutria, creating an effect similar to corduroy, and *feathering*, in which long-haired fur is cut into shingled layers (somewhat resembling the rows of eyelash fringe on dresses so often associated with the 1920s.

Fur is often dyed and carved to create intricate mosaic, intarsia, and intaglio designs. Ralph Lauren recently designed a jacket of golden-brown sheared beaver with carved intaglio designs in red and white, inspired by the Indians of the American Southwest. Other furs incorporate intarsia techniques, in which designs are actually worked into the fur.

Fur can be woven to produce interesting effects (*left*). With the intarsia method (*right*), complicated designs are actually worked into the fur.

Fur garments can also be beaded and embroidered. American designer Donna Karan, best known for her sportswear, recently created a coat of reversible sheared beaver, with the leather on the *outside*, for Copenhagen-based Birger Christensen. The coat was then hand painted, decorated with multicolored glass beads, and trimmed with Tibetan lamb for an overall "folkloric" look.

## FROM FACTORY TO FURRIER

Behind every quality fur garment, there is a skilled and talented designer. When creating a style, the designer must keep in mind the overall effect he or she wants, the purpose of the garment, and the individual features of the fur that is being worked with. This last factor is very important; different furs have different qualities, and to take full advantage of the beauty of each of them, the designer must understand these characteristics. Mole and chinchilla, for example, possess very soft hair and fragile leather, and are usually made into clothing that will be worn infrequently, such as evening wear.

Only a few very successful manufacturers and retailers can afford to hire full-time designers; others rely on part-time help or freelancers, or they purchase patterns from professional design houses. In this competitive field, a furrier who relies on the same old tired styles year after year is at a distinct disadvantage.

Firms are always looking for new ideas, and many have entered into franchise agreements with top designers of ready-to-wear clothing. These "names" design a few pieces or an entire collection for a furrier, and in return usually receive an initial fee and a percentage of the sales of his or her line. Some of the designers who have taken advantage of these very lucrative deals include Perry Ellis and Jeffrey Banks for Alixandre, Bill Blass for Mohl Furs, Bob Mackie for HBA Fur, Anne Klein for Michael Forrest, and Mary McFadden for Dasa Furs.

A new design is first made up into a canvas, or pattern, and from there it is fitted very carefully to both a mannequin and a live model. It is important that any problems with the design be ironed out at this stage, as mistakes can be very costly.

Now the skins must be cut to conform to the pattern. Before this step, however, the pelts for the garment must be selected. It is important that the pelts are as uniform as possible with regard to height of hair, color, and general quality. Grading the skins is a very exacting task, and workers who are skilled at this job are very well paid. Some firms even hire freelancers to do this.

The pelts are now turned over to the cutter, a highly skilled individual near the top of the hierarchy of fur craftspersons. A skilled cutter can earn over $500 for a thirty-seven-hour workweek—in fact, some earn more than their employers! However, the term cutter is actually a misnomer, since the pelts are never cut with scissors, as this would damage the hair. A sharp razor blade is set in a special holder; this contraption is called a *furrier's knife*. The pelts are then painstakingly sliced, with care being taken not to cut the hairs on the fur side.

There is much more involved to the cutting process than merely placing the pattern pieces on the pelts and hacking away. Since the skins vary so widely as to their different characteristics, there are a number of different layouts that can be used. The three most important are: *let-out, skin-on-skin,* and *pieced.*

## Let-Out Furs

From the leather side, the hundreds of narrow strips that make up a let-out coat make it difficult to see the beauty of the garment. However, let-out garments are generally considered to be the pinnacle of the furrier's skill; the artistry that goes into making a garment of this type is considerable.

For a let-out garment, each presorted pelt is again carefully examined. A fine fur coat will contain minute variations of color since no two skins are exactly alike. But the more closely matched the skins are, the better the quality of the garment.

Each pelt is cut down the center of the *grotzen*, with the left-side skin being used on the left side of the garment, and the other side being used on the right. The halved pelts are then cut out at an angle into very narrow strips—often only one-quarter-inch wide. This was formerly done by hand, but is now accomplished by a machine. Since each fur has a different texture and weight of leather, the machine is adjustable. For example, sable is fuller and denser than mink, with a finer leather, and thus requires a different setting.

The narrow strips are now placed into the hands of another operator, who stitches them together into longer, wider strips with a very sharp needle and thread which is finer than a human hair. The strips are sewn in such a manner that the *grotzen* falls evenly along the length of the long, narrow strip. This laborious slicing and sewing is what is referred to as "letting out."

The long, narrow pieces, which are in turn composed of dozens of let-out strips, are ready to be placed on the pattern, which has been carefully marked on a special board. However, the temperamental skins are wrinkled and puckered, and generally do not conform to the outlines of the pattern. To remedy this, they are brushed with water, and stapled, fur side down, to the board. The pieces are stretched slightly larger than the pattern's dimensions. They are then left to dry for 24 hours, or slightly longer, if necessary.

After the pieces have thoroughly dried, the pattern is carefully marked on the leather side of the fur. The pelts are painstakingly cut to the exact specifications of the pattern in a process called squaring. The squared pieces are hand-taped at the edges to prevent them from stretching out of shape. They are then sewn together.

Why are skins let out? The primary reason is to increase the length of the skins. This letting out process allows the furrier to change the shape of the pelt without reducing the square area. For example, if a pelt contains twenty four square inches uncut, it is still this size after it is let out, but instead of being four by six inches, it may measure two by twelve inches.

This process also creates a more supple, elastic pelt and allows the furrier to achieve the smooth, unbroken line and even coloration characteristic of fine fur coats. Most high-fashion-fur garments are let-out, as this procedure lends itself to complicated design techniques. After letting out, the pelts can be worked in a variety of ways—not only horizontally and vertically, but also in attractive circular patterns, and intricate honeycomb, brickwork, and woven designs.

Even though the let-out pelts are much more elastic than those which have not been treated in this manner, some furriers skimp on skins to save money, stretching them to the maximum. This is commonly done in popularly priced imported coats. For example, a garment that is made in the U.S. by a reputable furrier may consist of sixty let-out pelts, while a lesser quality coat from the Orient might use as few as forty-five. A coat in which the pelts have been stretched will not have the fluid lines that a garment utilizing a greater number of skins possesses, will probably not fit as well, and will be more prone to wear and tear. You can tell a quality let-out coat by the fact that the hem will have a natural scallop—something not found in cheaper garments.

Mink, sable, and fine quality beaver are commonly let out, as are many other skins. Long-haired furs, such as fox, are often *semi-let-out*; this process is similar to the above, except that slightly fewer cuts are made.

## What's My Lining?

The fur is cleaned and fluffed, and before it is *closed*, or finished, it is ironed and steamed to bring out its natural luster. Closing consists of adding all the nonfur parts of the coat, including the buttons or fasteners, pads, etc. The most important steps in this process, however, are the addition of the lining, which is put in last. Sometimes an interlining—usually made of cotton flannel—is put in before the lining to provide additional warmth; however, this is not commonly done.

Choosing a lining for the fur often poses a dilemma, as the fabric used must not only be strong and long-wearing, but smooth and lightweight as well. The fabric that best meets this exacting criteria is silk, which is not only soft and resilient, but tough as well—a thread of silk is actually stronger than a length of steel of the same diameter! Rayon is often combined with silk to make a more durable lining.

More moderately priced garments are lined with a special type of fabric called *Bemberg rayon*. Less expensive fur garments incorporate acetate or rayon/acetate blends. Linings may be of plain or twill weaves, brocaded or in jacquard designs, and can even be silk-screened. Naturally, the fancier the lining, the higher the garment's price tag. In quality coats, the linings are cut and sewn by hand.

Many better coats use what is called a *French bottom* in which the lining is not tacked to the bottom of the coat, but left to hang free. This enables the buyer to actually see the leather side of the garment and thus the quality of its workmanship. An additional length of the lining is attached to the coat at the inside hem, which not only makes for a neater appearance, but also makes the garment more durable.

After the lining is added, the garment is again fitted, and carefully scrutinized. If it passes inspection, there are still a few minor steps to be taken before it is ready for the showroom. One process, called *glazing*, consists of wetting the fur with a special chemical, and then drying it with a steam blower, which makes it fluffy and soft. This process also adds luster to furs with a dull appearance.

## Skin-on-Skin and Pieced Furs

This layout basically consists of cutting the skins into rectangles or other shapes and then sewing them to one another, with the head of one attached to the tail of the adjacent skin. Neither the square area or overall length of the skins is changed. The skins are then wetted and stapled, like let-out pelts, and the closing process is similar.

This layout is most commonly used on fairly large skins, such as beaver, nutria, and opossum. Sheared furs, such as nutria and beaver, can be made using a combination of skin-on-skin and let-out techniques. Skin-on-skin coats are more popular in Europe than in North America.

*Pieced Furs:* This layout is simply what it says: small cuttings from manufacturers are sold to scrap dealers, who in turn send them to Kastoria, Greece, or one of the other centers of the pieced-fur industry. These pieces are then sewn into large sheets, called plates, which are usually made into units measuring about eighteen by twenty-four inches. The plates are then cut like cloth.

---

The plates can be of the same color, or can be multicolored for a harlequin effect. Some coats are even composed of squares of various parts of the pelt, as each part of the fur (such as the paws, bellies, etc.) has a different appearance. Usually, a fur made from specific parts of the animal—in particular, the paws, gills (an area near the neck) and the sides—are less expensive than garments made from whole skins, although this is not always the case. A coat made of the soft, creamy bellies of the Russian lynx, for example, is very costly.

Piecing is often used on very small skins, such as mole, which has a working area of only three by five inches. Rabbit is another fur that is almost always pieced, as are most of the poor furs, although mink and sable are pieced by some European manufacturers. Although pieced coats are usually not as desirable as let-out coats, if the materials they are made from are not scrap, they can be a good buy, although they will not wear as well as let-out garments.

## FROM FURRIER TO YOU

When a fur garment is completed, it is then affixed with the appropriate tags and sent to the stockroom or showroom. Manufacturers display their creations in New York shows during Market Time, which usually starts in late May and lasts until early June, while in Canada and Europe, the shows are held earlier.

These shows are exciting affairs, and the larger firms spare no expense in displaying their creations in the best possible light. One show featured a live mountain lion cavorting about on stage. As the sleek, glamorous models (who are usually clad in simple, dark-colored garments, so as not to detract from the fur creations that are the real stars of the show) glide smoothly down the runway, the "oohs" and "aahs" are audible, and cameras click while pencils furiously scribble down numbers. This scene is repeated all over the world in every center of furdom, from Montreal to Milan.

Roughly speaking, the wholesale price of a fur garment is about one half the retail price. Therefore, a garment that costs the wholesaler $6,000 to manufacture will sell to the consumer for approximately $12,000, although this varies.

What determines the price of a fur coat? In most fine garments, the cost of the skins accounts for slightly more than 50 percent of the price of the garment, while labor accounts for about one third. The other 20 percent or so consists of marketing, promotion, overhead, and other costs.

# THE MASTER FURRIERS

When historians look back at the twentieth century, they will no doubt label it with a name designed to describe the events that shaped its character, much as we call the period from 1400 to 1600 the Renaissance, or the late eighteenth century the Age of Enlightenment.

It would not be surprising if our century were dubbed "The Thirty-Second Century," for almost everything in our lives is concerned with speed and efficiency: we eat at fast-food restaurants, have our clothing cleaned at establishments which promise service in an hour or less, and travel to Europe in less time than it takes to maneuver a mid-Manhattan traffic jam.

Not surprisingly, this concern with speed and efficiency has also hit the fur industry, which has not always been renowned for technical innovations. Machines have taken over many tasks that had been done by hand for centuries, and whereas it used to take two weeks or even longer to make a fur coat, some factories—particularly in the Orient—turn out garments by the dozens every day.

However, there still exists a substantial number of furriers whose *modus operandi* seems more characteristic of the Old World than the twentieth century—people to whom creating fur garments is more of an art than a business. One of these individuals is Ernest Graf of the internationally famous Ben Kahn, Inc., located in the heart of New York's fur district.

In business for over seventy years, the firm is America's oldest existing fur manufacturing house. It was formed in 1913 by Ben Kahn, who came to this country from the Ukraine. Ernest Graf, who is Jewish, is also an immigrant. As a boy in Nuremberg, Germany he wanted to become an actor, but the rise of the Nazi party cut short his plans and, in 1934, the Graf family came to America. Graf, who is married to Ben Kahn's daughter, joined his father-in-law's firm in 1947, after a stint in the U.S. Air Force as a meteorologist. He became president of the firm

---

45

in 1969, and took over the family business in 1979 after the death of his father-in-law.

At Ben Kahn, fur is a family affair. Ernest Graf's daughter Julie, a former magazine editor, handles all in-house advertising and promotion; Mrs. Graf takes care of selling, designing, and accessorizing; and their son Edward, who Graf hopes will succeed him, assists his father in all aspects of the business. Edward has even learned Russian in order to become more adept at dealing with the Soviets, from whom the firm buys top-quality sable, lynx, and other rare and costly furs.

Ben Kahn, Inc. has developed an international reputation for high-quality, exclusive furs which has gained them the patronage of sports stars such as "Dr. J" (Julius Irving) and Reggie Jackson, socialites like Mrs. Norton Simon (née Jennifer Jones), and a host of other celebrities including Cher, Barbra Streisand, and Elizabeth Taylor. Graf even delivered two trunkfuls of capes, coats, and other costly furs to Evita Peron at the rose-colored Argentinian presidential palace in 1950—

A smoky topaz mink poncho by Halston for Ben Kahn.

garments which were then worth more than $100,000. About 65 percent of the firm's business comes from custom-made furs.

Furs from Ben Kahn have also appeared on the silver screen—the company supplied the Canadian lynx coat worn by the Dorothy Michaels character, played by Dustin Hoffman, in the hit film *Tootsie*. Ben Kahn furs have also graced the Great White Way, notably the multicolored coats used in the famous "Emerald City" scene in *The Wiz*. It has been said that "art imitates life," so it was more than appropriate that the glamorous furs worn by Patti LuPone in her starring role in *Evita* were also supplied by Ben Kahn, Inc.

The firm also plans to expand to other "select cities." Recently, Ben Kahn opened a fur salon at Molly Moses, a women's specialty shop located in Pittsburgh's prestigious One Oxford Centre shopping complex.

What should a woman keep in mind when selecting a fur, whether it is her first or fifth? Says the affable Graf, "Fit is all important. A fur should always balance correctly from the shoulders, or it will not fit properly." Other things to keep in mind include the workmanship of the fur. "Many furriers tack the linings to the bottom of the coat, so you can't get a look at the inside," he explains. The reputation of the furrier is also very important, and Ben Kahn's is a sterling one. States Graf proudly, "We have customers coming in here whose mothers, grandmothers, and even great-grandmothers were our customers." Not many businessmen, whether they are selling frying pans or fine furs, can boast of such an accomplishment.

## Gilles Mendel—Fur with a French Flair

Fifth Avenue is home to a number of exclusive stores—Henri Bendel, Cartier, Tiffany—where credit-card-toting sybarites can indulge their wildest dreams. Not the least of these modern-day pleasure palaces is Elizabeth Arden/The Salon, a specialty and cosmetic shop whose presence on the world-famous boulevard is indicated by a door painted in a shade of bright red so unique that it has been patented.

On the store's second floor, fourth-generation furrier Gilles Mendel brings his own special style of Parisian panache to the celebrated J. Mendel Fur Salon. In his late twenties, he is much younger than Ernest Graf, though the two have something in common: a commitment to customer service, coupled with a high degree of technical knowledge and an emphasis on quality furs.

A dramatic fur creation from Gilles Mendel.

Like Mr. Graf, Gilles Mendel did not originally plan to become a part of the rarefied world of *haute fourrure*. Although his family has been connected with the fur trade since the late 1800s (his great-grand-father served as trapper to the czar in prerevolutionary Russia) Mendel originally intended to become a professional skier, having won a French ski championship on his twelfth birthday. However, he eventually enrolled in France's prestigious École Commercial Superiore, and worked as a trader in grain futures before deciding to join the family firm in 1978.

After completing an apprenticeship position with his father at the original salon located on Paris's exclusive Rue St. Honoré, Mendel set his sights on the U.S., and after looking at a number of locations, finally decided to open a fur salon at Elizabeth Arden because of its "chic private atmosphere."

What kind of furs are found at J. Mendel? Garments that combine the highly developed Parisian sense of fashion with the verve and energy that characterizes New York's unique style. Unlike many creators of high-priced furs, Monsieur Mendel is not afraid to experiment with unusual color designs; furs at the salon can be found not only in traditional shades, but in marine blue, emerald green, and blue-violet. The "basic" mink coat is a rarity, as most of Mendel's styles veer toward the unconventional. Says the furrier, "I like outrageous, sexy furs for the American and French ladies, so I leave it to the Americans to turn out the classic, staid mink coat. I am into exotic, creative coats, jackets, and accessory pieces that highlight power and sensuality, garments that always make the woman come on soft and feminine." Recent designs include a cocoon coat, described as "An Ode to Erté," in ermine and fox, a one-armed shawl jacket accented with fox, and fur-trimmed shawls in cashmere and paisley. Many of the furs incorporate complicated, unusual layouts in herringbone, brickwork, and mosaic designs.

Mendel prides himself on treating fur like fine fabric, and when he brings out an inky-dark Blackglama mink for a customer to inspect, it does seem, as the light dances across the coat, that it is made from silk charmeuse or some other fine, costly cloth. Besides the usual mink and fox, Mendel also uses a number of less commonly encountered furs, including ermine, fisher, and bassarisk. In acknowledgment of his design creativity, Mendel was awarded the 1983 SIF D'OR Blackglama Award and the 1984 Emba Award.

Besides his own design staff, the Mendel salon also carries the creations of Parisian couturier Bernard Perris. In addition to ready-to-wear garments, the shop does a thriving custom trade—about twenty-five percent of the garments are made to order. Although all the designing is done at Mendel's New York studio, the coats are manufactured in France; it takes about two weeks for one to be completed.

Although many of the firm's clients are well-known socialites and other women of means, most of whom own a number of furs, Mendel states that many working women also patronize the salon. "Many of these women want a quality fur, and instead of buying a cheaper one, they will save that extra bit of money and come to J. Mendel," explains the dapper Frenchman. "They know they are getting something besides a high-quality coat—personalized service and special attention that would be difficult, if not impossible, to find elsewhere."

# PROFILES OF THE MOST IMPORTANT FURS

## FOUR

Although there are hundreds of species of fur-bearing animals on the earth today, only about fifty of these are of interest to the fur industry, and the types used differ from country to country. In Europe and the Orient, for example, garments of hamster and hare are readily available, while in the United States and Canada, these varieties of fur are rarely, if ever, used.

## HOW TO USE THIS CHAPTER

"Profiles of the Most Important Furs" is intended to familiarize you with some of the most commonly encountered furs and their characteristics. Although furs can differ greatly, even from garment to garment, and nothing can replace the advice of a professional furrier, this chapter will help you make an intelligent and informed decision when it comes to selecting your fur. The following information is included:

*Name of the Fur:* The common English name(s) for the fur.

*Natural History:* Information about the animal in relation to its habitat, size, and appearance.

*Environmental Status:* Whether or not the fur is ranched, wild, or protected in certain locales (which means that the annual take of the pelts is limited by carefully set quotas).

*Durability:* Many factors affect the durability of a fur garment—how the coat is made, for example, and even what manufacturer constructed it. This section will indicate how long a fur should last, with average care and maintenance. Durability is ranked as follows:

>*Perishable:* A fur with very poor durability that is intended primarily for occasional wear.
>
>*Poor:* A fur that will last from five to seven years.
>
>*Fair:* A fur with an average lifespan of six to eight years.
>
>*Good:* A fur that can be worn from eight to ten years with proper care.
>
>*Very Good:* A "workhorse" of a fur that will last for ten to fifteen years.
>
>*Excellent:* A fur with a lifespan of fifteen to twenty years.

*Warmth:* Not all furs are created equal when it comes to warmth. Flat-haired furs, including calf, antelope, etc.—which basically consist of hair on skin—are much less warm than full furs, which have guard hairs growing out of a dense underfur. Curly furs, such as Persian lamb, that have little underfur, are exceptions to the rule, as they are often warm and durable. The furs in this section are rated Not warm, Warm, and Very warm.

*Price:* Although prices do fluctuate somewhat from season to season, prices for fur garments generally fall into five categories:

>*Very Inexpensive:* Fur garments under $1,000. This includes most rabbit, sheepskin, many imported pieced garments, and shorter pieces.
>
>*Inexpensive, or Popularly Priced, Furs:* Garments in this grouping include most poor furs: rabbit, muskrat, squirrel, and skunk; some opossum and beaver; coats and jackets with leather inserts, and many-pieced foxes and mink. Coats in this category cost between $1,000 and $3,000.
>
>*Moderately Priced Furs:* This category includes furs ranging from approximately $3,000 to $9,000; however, since this is such a broad range, it is further divided into low moderate

---

51

($3,000 to $5,000) and high moderate ($5,000 to $9,000). Most sheared furs, coyote, Persian lamb, raccoon, fitch, fox, and some marten fall into this wide category.

*Expensive Furs:* Fine furs—fisher, stone marten, chinchilla, ermine, Russian lynx, and of course, mink and sable—fall into this group. These furs range in price from $9,000 to $15,000.

*Very Expensive:* These haute furs are those over $15,000. Coats in this category can range from $20,000 for a dyed skin-on-skin sable to upward of $150,000 for a white Russian lynx-belly coat.

Categorizing furs according to price is a tricky proposition, as the huge array of furs available to the consumer today differs greatly in quality. A mink garment can claim entries in all five categories. A sporty jacket of mink tails that is ribbed—which means that narrow leather inserts are placed between the strips of fur—can be very inexpensive, while a pieced, imported mink is often inexpensive. The median price for a good-quality, let-out mink coat, however, puts this fur in the high moderate range, while a top-of-the-line mink coat can cost into the five figures. Some mink garments can cost $15,000 or more, although this is the exception rather than the rule.

Some furs are easier to categorize. Rabbit is almost always very inexpensive to inexpensive, having been a poor fur since antiquity, while sable garments have traditionally been very expensive. Generally speaking, however, this category includes the *average* price range for the fur.

*Used for:* Common uses for the fur.

*What to Look for:* Some general guidelines as to what to look for when purchasing the fur.

*Comments:* Miscellaneous comments about the fur.*


*Name of the Fur:* ANTELOPE.

*Natural History:* Varies in size by continent. Usually light brown to gray for blending with the environment—American varieties tend to be brownish, while African types are usually shades of gray.

*Environmental Status:* Protected in some areas.

*Durability:* Perishable (three to five years).

*Warmth:* Not warm.

*Price:* Inexpensive.

*Profiles adapted from *World of Furs* by David L. Kaplan.

*Used for:* Casual coats and other garments. Best manufactured with leather or other durable edging.

*What to Look for:* Although the hair of the antelope is stiff and flat, the skin should be soft and supple. Look for even coloration.

*Comments:* Periodic attempts are made to develop antelope skin as fur by improved processing, especially African subspecies. At present time, infrequently used by the fur industry. *Springbok*, a kind of antelope from southern Africa, is sometimes seen.

*Name of the Fur:* BADGER.

*Natural History:* The size of a medium dog, the badger is almost as wide as it is long. White *grotzen* varies in length and width. Color ranges from pale white to brownish tones, depending on the origin of the pelts:

> Asiatic (China): yellowish-brown underfur and gray guard hair.
>
> Canadian: gray with pale white underfur.
>
> United States: gray guard hairs, creamy underfur.

*Environmental Status:* Protected in some states and provinces.

*Durability:* Very good; leathered varieties, fair.

*Warmth:* Very warm.

*Price:* Inexpensive and up.

*Used for:* Varies greatly with fashion changes. Formerly used almost exclusively as a trim on cloth coats, badger is now seen in coats and jackets. Because it is so heavy, it is often combined with alternating strips of leather to reduce the bulk. As with any fur garment, however, leathering reduces the durability.

*What to Look for:* Pale silvery tones.

*Comments:* This fur is usually unplucked, except for the *grotzen*. Hairs from this area are used to make fine quality paint and shaving brushes.

*Name:* BASSARISK

*Natural History:* The bassarisk is a relative of the raccoon, and it is a brownish-yellow in color, with a very long tail. The *grotzen* is darker in color. Most bassarisk comes from North America, mainly Texas.

*Environmental Status:* Protected in some areas.

*Durability:* Dyed: Poor. Natural: Fair.

*Warmth:* Warm.

*Price:* Inexpensive.

*Used for:* Originally a trimming fur, now sometimes made into popularly priced garments.

---

53

*What to Look for:* Density of fur, strong coloration, interesting markings.
*Comments:* Formerly called rock sable.

*Name of the Fur:* BARONDUKI (also spelled "Burunduki").
*Natural History:* A Russian cousin of the American chipmunk, baronduki comes mainly from Russia, China, and Siberia, and to a lesser extent, India. The fur is gray, with a yellowish tint. The Russian variety, considered the finest, has five dark and four light longitudinal stripes, while Indian varieties have three stripes.
*Environmental Status:* Wild. In limited supply; might become a protected species in the near future.
*Durability:* Poor.
*Warmth:* Warm.
*Price:* Inexpensive.
*Used for:* Because baronduki is not very durable, and the working area is not very large (three by six inches—a little larger than an index card), it is commonly sewn into plates, imported, and made into linings, accessories, and even skirts. It is very rarely used for outerwear.
*What to Look for:* Baronduki is a short, coarse fur. Look for uniform stripes on a yellowish-gray background.
*Comments:* Quite popular in the sixties for so-called fun furs, baronduki is not too common today.

*Name of the Fur:* BEAVER.
*Natural History:* Equally at home in land or water, the beaver ranges in size from two to four feet in length. Best varieties come from the Hudson Bay area of Quebec.
*Environmental Status:* Wild. Ranching has been tried in Canada and the U.S., with little success. Since the beaver was once almost extinct, the trapping of this animal is closely regulated in almost all states and provinces, and the beaver population is now abundant in most areas.
*Durability:* Natural: very good. Sheared: good.
*Warmth:* Warm.
*Price:* Low to high moderate; some may be less expensive.
*Used for:* Fur garments and cloth coat trimmings.
*What to Look for:* Best beaver has subtle, silvery tones. Redness is undesirable in any natural-beaver garment. Sheared beaver should have a smooth, plushlike feel.
*Comments:* Beaver is increasingly used in its natural, unplucked state, which differs considerably in appearance from sheared beaver. Un-

A dyed beaver jacket by
Robert Bernard and Ingrid
Klahn.

plucked beaver is called *spitz beaver*. Sheared beaver is often dyed and
processed to produce a variety of interesting effects. It can be quilted,
corded to resemble fine-wale corduroy, and/or colored in a variety of
shades.

*Name of the Fur:* CALF.
*Natural History:* Young cow, usually mottled brown, black, or russet
with white. Formerly from northeastern Europe, almost all calf now
comes from the United States.
*Environmental Status:* Entirely ranched.
*Durability:* Poor to fair, depending on care given.
*Warmth:* Not warm.
*Price:* Very inexpensive to inexpensive.
*Used for:* Sports garments.
*What to Look for:* Even, attractive patterns. Best types have thin leath-
er, with silky, moiré patterns.

*Comments:* Because the hairs on calfskin are short and brittle and tend to break off, garments made out of calf are not very durable. However, it makes attractive, affordable casual garments.

*Name of the Fur:* CAT LYNX: see *LYNX*

*Name of the Fur:* CAT, SPOTTED.
*Natural History:* Small- to medium-sized spotted cats such as Geoffroy's cat, jungle cat, and wildcat from South America and Asia. Although most are about the size of a domestic cat, these animals have markings that strongly resemble those of the leopard.
*Environmental Status:* After the Endangered Species Act of 1973, replacements were sought for "big cat" coats, and were found in the form of small spotted-cat pelts. Although these animals are now in fairly abundant supply, some environmentalists are concerned that the demand for spotted-cat pelts may prove to be as detrimental to their population as the vogue for ocelot, cheetah, leopard, etc. was in the 1960s.
*Durability:* Fair to good.
*Warmth:* Warm.
*Price:* High-moderate to expensive.
*Used for:* Trims; increasingly used in jackets and coats.
*What to Look for:* Clear, bold markings that strongly resemble leopard.
*Comments:* Spotted-cat coats seem to have filled the fashion void left when the use of big cat pelts was made illegal in the U.S., Canada, and much of Europe. They are much more popular in Europe (where two-thirds of all spotted-cat coats, including lynx, are sold) and the Orient than in North America, where the demand for them is limited largely due to their similarity to leopard, the wearing of which has become socially unacceptable.

*Name of the Fur:* CHINCHILLA.
*Natural History:* Originally wild in Chile, south Peru, and Bolivia, the chinchilla is a small round-bodied rodent, with fur one-half to three-quarter inches long.
*Environmental Status:* Driven nearly to extinction in the early 1900s, chinchilla is now entirely ranched, primarily in the United States. A natural blue-gray in color, mutation shades—including white and beige—have been developed.
*Durability:* Perishable. Generally not a fur for everyday wear.
*Warmth:* Very warm.

A luxurious chinchilla coat.

*Price:* Expensive and up.
*Used for:* Trimmings on cloth coats and other furs, small pieces such as capes and shrugs, as well as jackets and coats.
*What to Look for:* Extremely soft, fine fur of a cigar-ash mottled blue-gray, changing to white underneath. Chinchilla with strong blue tones is the most desirable.
*Comments:* Fur is very soft and fine, and has tendency to mat. Chinchilla is expensive partly because the thin, soft leather and small working area of the pelts make them difficult to handle.

*Name of the Fur:* COYOTE.
*Natural History:* A native of the western United States, the coyote is about the size of a German shepherd.
*Environmental Status:* Varies: while the coyote is considered a pest in some states, particularly those areas with large populations of sheep and beef cattle, it is protected in others. Generally speaking, however, this animal is in fairly plentiful supply.
*Durability:* Fair.

*Warmth:* Very warm.
*Price:* Generally low moderate, although pieced coats and jackets can be found in the inexpensive price range.
*Used for:* Jackets, coats, and trimmings. Popular for sports furs such as ski jackets; a favorite with men.
*What to Look for:* Silky, long fur, pale gray or tan in color, with thick, paler underfur.
*Comments:* Coyote, an increasingly popular fur, makes attractive, casual garments for both men and women. Closely resembles wolf, an endangered species.

*Name of the Fur:* ERMINE.
*Natural History:* Although it is sometimes called the Armenian rat, the ermine is actually in the weasel family. In winter, the fur is white; in summer, a tawny brown. The best grades are from Siberia, Canada, and Alaska.
*Environmental Status:* Wild.
*Durability:* Perishable. Not for everyday wear.
*Warmth:* Warm.
*Price:* Expensive.
*Used for:* In white, used for evening coats, jackets, capes, etc. Summer ermine, less popular than the white variety, is used for more casual garments. Both are high-priced and appeal mostly to the high-fashion customer.
*What to Look for:* White ermine: white, silky pelt, with no yellowish undertones. Summer ermine should be a medium brown with golden undertones.
*Comments:* As white ermine is seldom pure white, it is very often bleached. Summer types are sometimes tipped or dyed to deepen color.

*Name of the Fur:* FISHER.
*Natural History:* A member of the marten family, the fisher is a cousin of the Russian sable. Best varieties come from Western Canada and the U.S. Female skins are smaller, silkier, and more valuable than male.
*Environmental Status:* In scarce supply; protected in many states.
*Durability:* Very good.
*Warmth:* Very warm.
*Price:* Expensive to very expensive.
*Used for:* Traditionally used for now-unfashionable "choker" scarves; frequently used for collar trim, jackets, and coats.

*What to Look for:* Rich, chocolate-brown color with beige tips; dense, silky fur.

*Comments:* Fisher has been called a "furrier's fur," as its durability, luxurious appearance, and beauty make it a favorite of fashion connoisseurs. Because fisher remains in such short supply, it is costly, ranking in price between sable and mink.

*Name of the Fur:* FITCH.

*Natural History:* A member of the weasel family, the fitch is a long, slender animal that resembles its cousin, the ferret. There are several different types, including:

> *White fitch:* White fitch is wild. Best comes from Siberia. Has long, silky guard hairs and woolly, compact underfur.
>
> *Dark fitch:* Comes from Austria, Poland. Has dark stripes interspersed with light. This type of fitch is ranched. Sometimes called black fitch.
>
> *Paradise or yellow fitch:* Comes from Mongolia, possesses strong yellow tones. Most inexpensive types of fitch. Also called Chinese fitch.

*Environmental Status:* Largely ranched, particularly in the Soviet Union and its satellites, as well as Finland, Scotland, the U.S., and other nations.

*Durability:* Good.

*Warmth:* Very warm.

*Price:* Varies. Low moderate and up, depending on type. Best-quality wild white fitch can be more expensive than mink.

*Used for:* Formerly dyed and used as a trimming, now almost always used in its natural color for jackets and coats. Brighteners are often added to reinforce color.

*What to Look for:* The best fitch has long, silky, evenly colored top fur ranging in color from brown to black and dense underfur. Furs with strongest contrast between dark and light shades are considered the most desirable.

*Comments:* Fitch is often worked to create an interesting chiaroscuro effect, with darker top hairs contrasting vividly with pale underfibers. This fur is more popular in Europe than in North America.

*Name of the Fur:* FOX.

*Natural History:* The fox family is a very large one; its members range from the Arctic to Argentina. There are at present thirty-two varieties of mutation fox (often referred to as exotic foxes) in a wide range of shades.

*Environmental Status:* Almost all fox is ranched, with a few exceptions.

*Durability:* Varies. Generally, with proper care, fox will last from eight to twelve years, unless otherwise noted.

*Warmth:* Most fox is very warm.

*Price:* Varies. Red fox, the commonest, is the least expensive, while some of the exotic foxes can cost $20,000 or more for a full-length coat. Generally speaking, however, good quality fox coats fall into the high moderate to expensive category, while some pieced coats and jackets can be inexpensive or even very inexpensive.

*Used for:* Trimmings, coats, jackets, accessories.

*What to Look for:* As fox is a long-haired fur, be on the lookout for dense, full underfur, and soft, silky guard hairs, as well as smooth even coloration.

*Comments:* Some popular types are:

> *Blue Fox:* A darkish blue-brown in winter, more brownish in summer. The best varieties are the palest, with strong blue tones. Variations of blue fox include *shadow blue*, which possesses a lighter tone, or shadow, of this shading. Blue fox is sometimes dyed into high-fashion shades, including *crystal fox*, a frosty-gray fur with orange undertones, and *sterling fox*, which is similar to the above, but with much stronger red-brown coloration. Blue fox is only moderately expensive, very warm, and durable, and should last from eight to twelve years, with care.

> *Corsac Fox:* See *Kitt Fox.*

> *Cross Fox:* Another sport, or mutation, of wild red fox, is red tinged with yellow tones. The name comes from the distinctive darker red cross formed by the dark hair across the shoulders and again just below the eyes and ears. Fur above and below the cross is lighter than the rest of the pelt. Cross fox is a warm, durable, and expensive fur.

> *Gray Fox:* One of the few varieties of fox that is not ranched. The best pelts come from the U.S., mostly the northern states. Once an inexpensive fur, gray fox is now most often found in the low and sometimes high moderate price range. It is gray with strong reddish undertones.

> *Kitt Fox:* Another wild fox, this animal is found throughout North America, but it also occurs in other nations, including

*Above:* Crystal-dyed SAGA fox
jacket by Oscar de la Renta. *Left:*
Gold-cross fox hooded coat by
Fernando Sanchez for Revillon.

the U.S.S.R. and China. North American kitt fox is actually a variety of gray fox. The best kitt fox comes from Siberia, where it is called *corsac fox*. Kitt fox ranges in color from a rusty gray (North American varieties) to a light reddish brown, but always has white or silvery-tipped guard hairs. The fur is short and soft, and is neither as durable nor as warm as other varieties of fox because it has few guard hairs; it will last from five to twelve years. Kitt fox is usually priced at the low end of moderate. It is sometimes also called *prairie fox*.

*Mutation Foxes:* Sometimes called exotic foxes, these are ranched animals that are bred to produce unique colors. There are more than two dozen varieties of mutation fox—Scandinavia is responsible for developing the mutation foxes—and more are being added to the list every year. Here are a few of the more interesting varieties: (1) *Alaska Fox:* A glossy black fox with a dense undercoat. (2) *Golden Island Fox:* A very rare mutation; only a few hundred skins are released every year. This fox is a pale ivory-gold in color, with darker hairs interspersed throughout the fur and a narrow, dark brown *grotzen*. (3) *Lapponia Fox:* A white fox with dense brown underfur. (4) *Northern Light Fox:* A tawny brown fox shading to paler tones near the tail, with a silvery black *grotzen*. Most mutation foxes, like other members of the family, are durable, lasting eight to twelve years, and warm. However, their rarity makes them more expensive than other varieties of fox. Some even surpass top-quality mink in price.

*Platina Fox:* A mutation of silver fox; light platinum-gray in color, it may sometimes be bleached to enhance the pale, silvery appearance of the fur. Platina is one of those furs that falls in and out of vogue. Very popular in the thirties, it is showing signs of coming back. It has always been an expensive fur, but like other members of the family, it is warm and durable.

*Magellan Fox:* From South America, this wild fox closely resembles gray fox in color, price, and durability.

*Prairie Fox:* See *Kitt Fox*

*Red Fox:* Versions of red fox are found on all continents. Red fox comes from both wild and ranched populations. The clearest reds come from the U.S. and Canada; the bright cherry reds come from the Kamchatka region of Siberia. Red fox is a perennial favorite that can range in price from low moderate to fairly expensive. It is a very warm and durable fur. Blue, cross, and silver fox are all color phases of red fox; interestingly, all four color variations can occur in the same litter.

*Silver Fox:* Almost blue-black, with varying degrees of silvery white hairs interspersed throughout the body. The best types have a true silvery appearance. Silver fox has also enjoyed its fashion ups and downs. Once used primarily in trimmings and smaller pieces, it is now found in jackets and full-length garments. Silver fox possesses a dense, silky fur, and is as durable as the other members of the fox family.

*White Fox:* Sometimes called polar or Arctic fox, this is a pure white animal originally found in the subarctic regions of the far north. Today, however, it is almost entirely ranched, particularly in Scandinavia. It is not as durable as other types of foxes (lasting five to ten years), but it is warm. This type of fox was the leading choice of glamorous movie stars of the thirties. Like most other white furs, it was used primarily in evening garments. It has recently come back into vogue for everyday coats and jackets as well. A variation of this fur is *shadow blue fox*, a white fox with a pale blue shading down its spine.

*Name of the Fur:* GOAT, MOUNTAIN.
*Natural History:* Pelt of mountain goat from mountainous regions of North Africa.
*Environmental Status:* Mostly raised in herds; some are wild.
*Durability:* Poor.
*Warmth:* Warm.
*Price:* Very inexpensive to inexpensive.
*Used for:* Often found in shorter pieces, rarely used for full-length coats. Sometimes seen as accent on more expensive furs.
*What to Look for:* A long-haired fur, usually grayish-white in color, sometimes in brownish shades. Although mountain goat is not the softest of furs, the guard hairs should not feel coarse to the touch.
*Comments:* Mountain goat makes attractive, inexpensive, sporty garments. However, it is not very durable, and this should be kept in mind when contemplating a purchase.

*Name of the Fur:* KIDSKIN.
*Natural History:* Kidskin is the pelt of a young goat. Some have marks resembling broadtail lamb; older kidskin has wavy hair. Best grades come from China and are gray with thin, black *grotzen*. African skins

are mottled or colored in combinations of gray, black, or white.
*Environmental Status:* Entirely ranched.
*Durability:* Poor.
*Warmth:* Not warm.
*Price:* Inexpensive.
*Used for:* Jackets and coats.
*What to Look for:* Soft, supple skin, interesting coloration.
*Comments:* Like antelope, calf, and other flat-haired furs, kidskin is not durable or warm, but can make attractive sports garments.

*Name of the Fur:* KOLINSKY.
*Natural History:* The kolinsky is a cousin of the mink—very similar in appearance, but smaller, with shorter hair. It has soft, medium brown guard hair and slightly yellowish fur fiber.
*Environmental Status:* Wild; some is ranched.
*Durability:* Fair.
*Warmth:* Warm.
*Price:* Usually low moderate range.
*Used for:* Coats, jackets.
*What to Look for:* Clear, brown coloring; soft, silky hair (not as fine or soft as mink, however).
*Comments:* Once considered mink's "poor relation," kolinsky was almost always dyed to imitate its higher-priced relative. It is now coming into its own as an attractive, affordable, and durable fur. At present, kolinsky pelts cannot be imported into the U.S.

*Name of the Fur:* LAMB.
*Natural History:* For centuries, the sheep family has been of immense importance to us. Sheep are raised in almost all countries and are extremely numerous—in fact, there are one billion of these creatures on earth, or one sheep for every three human beings! There are about four hundred fifty varieties of domesticated sheep, but only a few are used for their fur. These include: broadtail (Russian- and American-processed), Mongolian lamb, Mouton lamb, Persian (also called karacul, or karakul), and shearling.
*Environmental Status:* Entirely ranched.
*Durability:* Varies.
*Warmth:* Most lamb is warm.
*Price:* Ranges from very inexpensive to very expensive.
*What to Look for:* See individual entries.
*Comments:* Types of lamb include:

Dyed Russian karakul jacket.

*Borrego Lamb:* See *Mouton Lamb.*

*Broadtail Lamb* (sometimes called *Russian broadtail*): From stillborn lambs of karakul sheep. The sheep are *not* killed for their lambs, which is one reason why this fur is so exclusive and expensive. Like chinchilla, the leather and fur of broadtail lambs is soft and fine, making it difficult to work with, which adds to its price. The best varieties come from the Soviet Union. Broadtail comes in a natural gray color, as well as brown; is often dyed black, which is not as durable as naturally colored varieties. The very fine, short hairs should show a moiré or watered-silk pattern. Broadtail, because of its fragility, has traditionally been used for evening wear, including capes, coats, jackets, suits, and even dresses. It is best suited for the woman who has a variety of furs in her wardrobe. It ranges in price from expensive to very expensive.

*Broadtail (Persian) Lamb:* This type of lamb comes from animals one to two days old. The best Persian broadtail has a distinctive "pine tree" pattern with just the slightest suggestion of a curl. Persian broadtail has a slightly heavier leather than Russian broadtail, but is still not very durable, and is usually found in garments that will not be worn too often. It is also high-priced, and at the present time, is not often seen.

*American Broadtail (Processed):* This variety of lamb does not come from karacul, but young Lincoln lambs from Argentina. The skins are sheared near the skin to give the distinctive moiré pattern of natural broadtail. This type of fur is more durable than broadtail, and is most often in the low- to high-moderate price range. With care, it should last from ten to fifteen years.

*Kalgan Lamb:* A white, curly lamb from Argentina that resembles Mongolian lamb.

*Mongolian Lamb:* This type of lamb is very similar to Tibetan lamb, except that the fur is slightly shorter—about one inch. It is an inexpensive, warm, and durable fur.

*Mouton Lamb:* Sheared sheepskin with hair that has been straightened and treated to create a soft, velvety fur. It is often left in its natural creamy color, or can be dyed to simulate Alaskan fur seal. Mouton is also dyed a variety of bright "fantasy" colors, including fuchsia, royal blue, or scarlet. Mouton lamb is very warm, but not too durable, lasting from five to eight years. It is an inexpensive fur, often used for shorter pieces. Mouton lamb from Iceland is called, naturally, *Icelandic lamb. Borrego lamb* is very similar to mouton lamb.

*Persian Lamb* (also called caracul, or karakul): Actually, the name Persian lamb is incorrect, since this type of sheep was never raised in Persia. The name is derived from the fact that the ancient Persians often made their living by trading in this fur. The correct name is caracul, which means "black lake" in the Ubzek language, and the soft, wavy fur of this animal can be compared to the swirling tides of a dark, mysterious river. It comes from sheep that are nine days old. The best types are found in lower central Asia, Mongolia, and Manchuria, as well as southwest Africa. The natural colors are gray, brown, or white, but a variety of interesting mutations have been introduced, including the following: *Sur*, a rich, glossy dark brown with curls tipped in gold or silver; and *Desert Rose*, a soft, medium brown with pink undertones. Darker shades are always colored to prevent the light-colored leather from showing through. The quality of the fur depends largely on the tightness of the "knuckle" curl. Persian lamb is warm, and with proper care, can last from eight to ten years. It is low moderate and up in price. In Europe, Persian lamb is called *astrakhan*. Persian lamb from the Soviet Union is marketed under the name *Bukhara*, and that from Namibia in southwest Africa is called *Swakara*.

*Shearling Lamb:* Sheared lamb, usually from Merino sheep, is often used in its natural off-white color. The fur, or sheared side, is worn next to the skin.

Coats made from shearling are among the world's oldest fur fashions, and garments of this type are still worn today by people in many countries. Today shearling is popular for casual coats and jackets. The outside, or leather side, of shearling garments may be decorated with beads or embroidery, and may also be painted. Shearling garments are very warm and durable, lasting from ten to fifteen years, and range in price from very inexpensive to inexpensive.

*Tibetan Lamb:* This comes from a sheep with long, wavy, shiny hair three to four inches in length. It is usually sold in its natural, creamy color, or is bleached white. A popular choice for sporty garments, it requires special care to keep it from becom-

Reversable Tibetan lamb jacket by David Goodman.

ing frizzy in wet or humid weather. It will last from five to eight years, is very warm, and is inexpensive to low moderate in price.

*Name of the Fur:* LYNX.
*Natural History:* The lynx is a member of the cat family. The four types of lynx used by the fur industry include the following: the bobcat, which is also called the cat lynx, the Montana lynx, the Canadian lynx, and the Russian lynx. The last two animals are members of the same species. All members of this family have soft, spotted dense fur in shades of light brown to cream. Generally speaking, the paler the spotting, the more valuable the fur.
*Environmental Status:* Wild. Trapping of all types of lynx is controlled in most states and provinces. Experiments are underway to raise lynx as a ranch animal. Supply of all types of lynx is limited.
*Durability:* Generally speaking, good. Cat lynx, however, has poor durability.
*Warmth:* All lynx is warm.
*Price:* Moderate to very expensive. White Russian lynx is currently the costliest fur in the world.
*Used for:* Coats, jackets, trimmings.
*What to Look for:*

> *Bobcat* (cat lynx): A close relative of the coveted Russian lynx, the bobcat gets its name from its short, bobbed tail. It is about three-quarters of the size of the true lynx, with spotted markings that are much more sharply delineated than those of the former. This fur is reddish black, fading to spotted white on longer belly hairs. The best grades come from the U.S. and Canada. Although bobcat is the least costly member of the lynx family, it is not inexpensive, usually falling into the high moderate category. It is not quite as warm as the other members of the family, nor is it as durable. Like all long-haired furs, it tends to shed, and needs regular care to keep it in good condition. Look for long, silky fur, soft underfur, and strong, interesting coloration.
>
> *Canadian Lynx:* This type of lynx resembles Russian lynx, except that the markings have a bluish tone. It is very warm, durable, and expensive. The best types come from the Hudson Bay region of Canada.
>
> *Montana Lynx:* Midway in price between Canadian lynx and bobcat, its markings are slightly darker than those of the Cana-

dian lynx, but more subtle than those of the bobcat. The best quality comes from the western states. It is warm, soft, and durable, and is high moderate and up in price. The fur is thicker than that of the bobcat.

*Russian Lynx:* Along with sable, this fur is considered the *crème de la crème* of furs. Its supply is strictly controlled by the Russian government, and coats of the soft, creamy underbellies have been sold for more than $200,000 (coats of full skins are about half as much). The best quality lynx is creamy white, with very subtle markings—the paler the fur, the better. It should not have a "stripey" appearance. Soft and fluffy, Russian lynx is as warm and durable as the other members of the family, and when taken prime, will shed very little.

*Comments:* Lynx, like other long-haired furs, has enjoyed a resurgence in popularity. Lynx population is limited, while popularity of spotted-cat coats keeps increasing (particularly in Europe); the rarity keeps prices high.

*Name of the Fur:* MARMOT.
*Natural History:* The marmot is a large rodent with coarse, sparse hair. It is unique among fur-bearing animals because the flow of the hair goes toward the snout. The brown fur is bluish in tone before the animal hibernates and yellowish afterward.
*Environmental Status:* Wild.
*Durability:* Fair.
*Warmth:* Warm.
*Price:* Inexpensive.
*Used for:* Coats and jackets, as well as trimmings on popularly priced cloth coats. Occasionally dyed in a striped pattern to imitate more expensive let-out furs.
*What to Look for:* Soft bluish tones. Although the guard hairs are coarse, the fur itself tends to be thick.
*Comments:* There are eight to sixteen species of marmot. The best known American varieties are the woodchuck and chipmunk, neither of which are used for fur.

*Name of the Fur:* MARTEN.
*Natural History:* There are several varieties of marten; only three are used by the fur industry: the American marten, the baum marten, and the stone marten.
*Environmental Status:* Wild. Trapping controlled in many areas.

*Durability:* Good to very good.

*Warmth:* All marten is warm.

*Price:* High moderate and up.

*Used for:* Marten, once used almost exclusively in now-unfashionable "chocker" scarves, is common in coats and jackets and is also used as a trimming.

*What to Look for:*

> *American Marten:* A cousin to the Russian sable, it has fine dense underfur and guard hairs as long as those of a fox. It varies in color from blue-brown to chocolate-brown, and pale brown to yellow with orange tones. Whatever the color, however, the fur should be clear and even. American marten is the least expensive type of marten, as it is not as fine or soft as other varieties of this animal. It is moderately priced and can last from eight to ten years with care. American marten can be worked in a variety of ways, and is sometimes dyed to resemble other furs. As with other martens, look for soft, dense, silky fur.
>
> *Baum Marten* (also called pine marten): Native to Northern Europe, Asia, and the Himalayas, it is usually brown, but can also be gray in color. Baum marten fur is softer and silkier than American marten, and is durable, lasting from eight to ten years. It ranges in price from high moderate to expensive, and is sometimes dyed to resemble more costly furs, such as sable.
>
> *Stone Marten* (also called beech marten): This animal is found from the Baltic Sea to the Mediterranean and eastward to the Himalayas and Mongolia. It is the most desirable type of marten, with very fine brown fur with a soft bluish cast and whitish underfur. Stone marten is very warm and soft, and is slightly more durable than its less expensive relatives. The very best qualities of stone marten are costlier than prime mink, although it generally falls into the expensive end of the moderate category.

*Comments:* Marten is an attractive fur that is increasing in popularity.

*Name of the Fur:* MINK

*Natural History:* A small, fierce creature, the mink is currently the most important animal used by the fur industry.

*Environmental Status:* Mink is almost entirely a ranched animal; very little wild mink is used nowadays.

*Durability:* Mink is among the most durable of furs, lasting up to twenty years with proper care. Pieced minks, however, are not as sturdy, lasting only from five to eight years.

*Warmth:* All mink is very warm; pieced mink a little less so than ranch or mutation mink.

*Price:* Mink can be very inexpensive to very expensive, but generally, good-quality mink garments fall into the high moderate to expensive range.

*Used for:* Everything from coats, jackets, stoles, and hats to earmuffs and eyeglass cases.

*What to Look for:* In all varieties of mink, soft, lustrous guard hairs, silky dense underfur. Types include:

> *Natural Ranch Mink:* As most mink is ranched, this term can be confusing. Generally, however, it refers to a group of colors ranging from a rich brown to a deep brownish black. The guard hairs should be soft, lustrous, and silky, while the underfur should be dense, compact, and paler in color than the guard hairs.
>
> *Mutation Mink:* Mutation mink comes in a wide variety of colors, ranging from the palest white to a very dark brown, with many shades in between.

A full ranch mink jacket.

71

*Wild Mink:* Wild mink is rarely used by the fur industry, as farmed mink is superior in quality. Wild mink is costly and not quite as durable as ranch and mutation mink. There is, however, a ranch-raised color known as Wild Type produced in Scandinavia which imitates the red-brown of wild mink.

*China Mink:* This is another term for the fur of the weasel.

*Comments:* Russian mink is marketed under the trade name *Norka*, while Canadian mink is sold under the name *Majestic*. American mink is marketed through cooperatives such as American Legend (an organization combining the members of the GLMA and EMBA), and Amerimink. The finest quality Scandinavian mink is sold under the SAGA label.

*Name of the Fur:* MOLE.

*Natural History:* One of the smallest animals used for fur, with a working area about the size of a three-by-five-inch index card. Most varieties come from Scotland, the Netherlands, Belgium, and Denmark.

*Environmental Status:* Wild.

*Durability:* Perishable. For occasional wear only.

*Warmth:* Warm.

*Price:* Usually inexpensive, sometimes low moderate and up for high-fashion pieces.

*Used for:* Jackets, coats, costumes. This very fine, soft fur drapes like fabric, and is made into plates and cut like cloth. Mole is always dyed, often in high-fashion colors.

*What to Look for:* Dense fur with very soft, velvety texture. Skins should be well-matched.

*Comments:* Queen Alexandria of England wore the first garment made of Scottish moles. She was successful in her objective of starting a fashion trend, which also helped relieve Scottish farmers of a pest.

*Name of the Fur:* MUSKRAT.

*Natural History:* The muskrat is a large rodent that inhabits marshy areas throughout the U.S., and gets its name from musk glands near its tail that give off an odor. Musk oil is used in perfumes and cosmetics. It is dark brown in color, with golden brown side backs and silver flanks. Northern muskrat is usually plucked and sheared; southern muskrat, which is used for natural or unplucked coats, comes from Louisiana, Texas, and other southern states. Jersey muskrat, the finest and most costly, is almost black in color, with a dark *grotzen*, or black stripe, and paler beige sides. It is also usually plucked and/or sheared.

*Environmental Status:* Wild. So numerous in some areas that it has become a pest.
*Durability:* Good; Jersey variety is the most durable.
*Warmth:* Very warm.
*Price:* Inexpensive to low moderate.
*Used for:* Muskrat is used for a wide variety of garments and trimmings. It is particularly popular for men's garments and, when plucked and sheared, is often used as a lining for reversible coats and jackets. Coats made from the various parts of the animal, such as bellies, sides, flanks, have a different appearance from garments made from entire pelts. These three sections may also be worked in sequences of light to dark lines in an ombre effect. Sides and bellies of silver shades in northern muskrat are often worked skin-on-skin; very fine pelts are let out in Europe.
*What to Look for:* Jersey and northern muskrat: density of fur and well-matched skins. Southern muskrat: flat, glossy fur with little underfur, pale color, and uniformity of guard hairs.
*Comments:* In Europe, muskrat is called musquash.

Natural beige nutria jacket trimmed with bleached nutria by Robert Bernard and Ingrid Klahn.

*Name of the Fur:* NUTRIA.

*Natural History:* Another "swamp thing," the nutria originally hails from Argentina, Brazil, Uruguay, and Chile. It was imported for ranching to California in 1954 and also introduced to the wetlands of the United States in an attempt to reduce the muskrat population, as these animals are natural enemies.

*Environmental Status:* Increasingly ranched, mostly in South America; some nutria is still trapped. Can become a pest if numbers are not controlled.

*Durability:* Natural (unplucked): good. Sheared: good.

*Warmth:* Very warm.

*Price:* Inexpensive to low moderate.

*Used for:* In plucked, sheared form, traditionally used for quality garments, also for fur-lined and reversible garments. Unplucked natural skins now used for casual men's and women's coats, parkas, linings.

*What to Look for:* Nutria ranges in color from cinnamon brown to brown with gray stripes, and fur should be similar to that of the beaver, although it is not as glossy, lustrous, and thick. Underfiber is sepia brown. Ranched varieties are bluish beige in tone and slightly coarser.

Sheared types should be even in height and color and have a velvety texture, although sheared nutria is somewhat lighter in weight than sheared beaver because the nutria is about half the size of the beaver.

*Comments:* Nutria is the Spanish word for otter.

*Name of the Fur:* OPOSSUM.

*Natural History:* The opossum is a long-haired marsupial, meaning that it carries its young in a pouch like a kangaroo. There are many different varieties; the four principal types used in North America are:

> *American Opossum:* The American opossum is an unattractive creature with beady little eyes and a head like a rat's.
>
> *Australian Opossum:* Looks somewhat similar to American opossum.
>
> *New Zealand Opossum:* This animal looks quite different from the other varieties of opossum, being a rich tawny brown in color.
>
> *Tasmanian Opossum:* From the island off the coast of Australia, this animal is protected and is not often seen in North America.

*Environmental Status:* Mainly wild. Some varieties of opossum are ranched, mainly American.

*Durability:* American: good. Australian: good. New Zealand: good. Tasmanian: fair.

*Warmth:* All varieties are warm.

*Price:* Most opossum falls in the inexpensive to low moderate range.

*Used for:* Coats and jackets. Only the finest Australian skins are let-out; most opossum is worked skin-on-skin. It may also be worked in a variety of interesting patterns, and can be dyed, sometimes to imitate more expensive furs such as fitch.

*What to Look for:*

>*American Opossum:* Long, straight guard hairs, silvery gray in color, with thick, black-tipped underfur. The fur should be soft and thick. It can be colored or plucked and sheared for a variety of fashion effects.

>*Australian Opossum:* This variety of fur looks similar to its American cousin, except that it is silkier and thicker. It has more of a plushlike feel than the aforementioned type. The best type is a rich blue gray in color. It is the longest-wearing variety of opossum, lasting up to fifteen years with proper care.

>*New Zealand Opossum:* Should have silky, dense fur with an even tawny brown color. It is often used as a lining in raincoats and sport jackets.

>*Tasmanian Opossum:* This looks quite different from the other three varieties, being a rich chestnut brown in color. It is the least durable type of opossum, lasting five to eight years with care.

*Comments:* Opossum makes an attractive, moderately priced garment. It is particularly popular for sports furs.

*Name of the Fur:* OTTER.

*Natural History:* The otter is a sleek-bodied, water-loving mammal ranging in color from a rich, dense, lustrous mahogany brown to a light fawn.

*Environmental Status:* The sea otter, formerly called the *Kamchatka beaver*, was nearly hunted to extinction, and is still an endangered species. The otter used by the North American fur industry is the American and Canadian inland river otter, which is generally in abundant supply. However, trapping is controlled in some areas.

*Durability:* Excellent. Otter is considered the most durable fur for its weight and thickness, and can last twenty years with proper care.

*Warmth:* Very warm.

*Price:* Low to high moderate.

*Used for:* Coats, jackets, trimmings.

*What to Look for:* Otter is a flat, lustrous fur, the most desirable being a blue-brown in color. It has black guard hairs and fur fiber which is slightly lighter, with the base being gray to white in color. The best qualities come from eastern Canada. Otter may also be dyed, sheared, or plucked, but should always possess a smooth feel and a soft, attractive sheen.

*Comments:* Another "furrier's fur," otter is popular for both men's and women's garments. Although it has not been very popular in recent years, otter is an extremely durable fur which, like fine linen, actually improves in appearance with age.

*Name of the Fur:* PAHMI (Asian ferret badger).

*Natural History:* A smaller edition of the badger, this lean, narrow-bodied animal comes from China and India. The fur ranges in color from brown to silver gray, and is considerably darker than the dense orangish-yellow underfur.

*Environmental Status:* Wild.

*Durability:* Fair.

*Warmth:* Warm.

*Price:* Inexpensive.

*Used for:* Jackets and coats, trimmings on popularly priced men's and women's cloth garments.

*What to Look for:* Clarity of color. Fur ranges from brown to silver gray over orange-yellow underfur.

*Comments:* Pahmi may be sheared, plucked, or dyed, and makes an attractive, reasonably priced garment. Like skunk, however, it can develop a disagreeable odor when wet.

*Name of the Fur:* PONY.

*Natural History:* Skin of wild pony from Russia, Poland, South America, Denmark, and other countries. The best varieties come from the Volga region of the U.S.S.R. Skins from Iceland have long, wooly hair.

*Environmental Status:* Wild.

*Durability:* Perishable.

*Warmth:* Not warm.

*Price:* Inexpensive.

*Used for:* Casual coats and jackets. Skins are usually dyed.

*What to Look for:* Like other furs with flat, stiff hairs, pony tends to wear easily. For this reason, the leather should be as soft and supple as

possible. Fur has a wavy appearance, like a moiré ribbon.
*Comments:* Pony, which was very popular in the 1920s and 1930s, is not commonly seen today.

*Name of the Fur:* RABBIT.
*Natural History:* Once wild, rabbit is now almost entirely ranched. In its wild state, it is usually brown, but ranching has developed colors that range from white to almost black.
*Environmental Status:* A farmed animal; very little wild rabbit is sold.
*Durability:* Poor, slightly better for some fine ranched rabbits.
*Warmth:* Warm.
*Price:* Rabbit is usually very inexpensive to inexpensive.
*Used for:* Coats, jackets, earmuffs, novelties. Rabbit fur is popular for children's garments.
*What to Look for:* Rabbit could be called "the great imitator" because it can be bred and/or processed to resemble almost any other fur. For example, "chinchilla rabbit" has the soft, mottled blue gray of the more expensive article, while "rex rabbit" is a mutation that "feels like chinchilla and looks like sheared beaver." Rex rabbit occurs in fifteen natural colors. Rabbit is generally long-haired, although some varieties may be shorter.
  Rabbit is often dyed, and can also be sheared or grooved. The fur should be silky, and the color uniform. Ranched skins are more durable than wild pelts. Lapin, or French rabbit, is a type of imported rabbit that is supposedly of better quality than other types.
*Comments:* Rabbit, which since antiquity has been considered a poor fur, is not very durable, and with the best of care lasts only three to five years. Long-haired rabbit is notorious for its tendency to shed. With the exception of "chinchilla rabbit"—a very fine ranched fur that can be expensive—it is definitely not an investment fur, but might be a good choice for a casual garment.

*Name of the Fur:* RACCOON, American and Finnish.
*Natural History:* There are two varieties of raccoon used in North America. The American raccoon is a long-haired animal with dense brown underfur and silvery guard hairs with black tips; the gray sides shade to black along the middle of the back. Finnish raccoon differs considerably in appearance from its American cousin. It is bushier than American raccoon and resembles tanuki, being yellowish in color.
*Environmental Status:* Finnish raccoon is ranched in Scandinavian countries, and sold by SAGA under the name finnraccoon; the Ameri-

can variety is wild. Russian furriers are reported to be experimenting with raising the American variety on ranches.

*Durability:* For both varieties, durability is good to very good. With care, this is a sturdy fur; some coats from the 1920s are still in existence. Sheared and plucked types, however, are not as durable.

*Warmth:* Very warm.

*Price:* Low and sometimes high moderate; some grades hover at the higher end of the inexpensive category.

*Used for:* Trimmings, jackets, coats. Both varieties of raccoon can be plucked, sheared, dyed, or otherwise processed for a variety of effects. Distinctive ringtails of this animal are often used for trimmings on coats and accessories.

*What to Look for:* American: silvery cast, long, luxurious guard hair with dense underfur. Plucked, sheared varieties closely resemble sheared beaver. Finnish: thicker than the American type, and should be soft, supple, and bushy, with yellowish undertones and even coloration.

*Comments:* Raccoon is a fur that enjoys periodic swings in popularity. Most people associate raccoon coats with the long-haired garments worn by college men of the twenties; similarly styled coats were also worn by women, and are popular with both men and women today.

*Name of the Fur:* SABLE.

*Natural History:* Sable has long been one of the most sought-after furs. A small, ferocious member of the weasel family, the sable lives in the frigid forests of the U.S.S.R., and because of the intense cold, the sable grows a magnificent coat of thick, dark, soft fur. Although sable is also indigenous to Canada, China, and Japan, the Russian variety is universally considered to be the best.

*Environmental Status:* The U.S.S.R. is the only country in the world where sable is ranched. Some animals are left to run semiwild in preserves.

*Durability:* Natural sable is very durable; the Russian type will last fifteen to twenty years with proper care. Dyed as well as Canadian and Oriental types are less sturdy.

*Warmth:* Very warm.

*Price:* Expensive to very expensive. Some commercial quality Japanese and Chinese types are moderately priced.

*Used for:* Coats, jackets, scarves. Tails often used as trimmings.

*What to Look for:* Soft, deep fur in dark, lustrous brown, with silky

*Above:* Natural Imperial sable blouson
jacket. *Right:* Natural Imperial sable
great coat. Both by Evelyn Paswall.

guard hairs. The most desirable type is rich brown with a blue cast, and silvery tipped guard hairs. Ranched sable is significantly darker in color than wild sable. Canadian and Oriental types, although similar in appearance, will not be as lustrous or fine as Russian. Golden sable is less expensive than the darker variety, although it is by no means an inexpensive fur. Look for rich, clear amber coloration.

*Comments:* Because of their scarcity, the best qualities of Russian sable are considered to be, along with Russian lynx pelts, the most valuable furs in the world. Russian furriers are said to be experimenting with mutation colors, including black.

*Name of the Fur:* SEAL.

*Natural History:* There are over ninety varieties of seal; the two main varieties used today are the Alaska fur seal and the hair seal. The Alaska fur seal lives in herds on the Pribilof Islands and other Arctic areas; hair seal comes from the hooded blueback seal, ranger seal, and other varieties.

*Environmental Status:* The Newfoundland harp seal, the round-eyed "whitecoat" which aroused so much controversy in the late seventies, was *not* used by the American fur industry. Because of worldwide pressure, however, the harp seal hunt has been all but discontinued. Limited harvest of Alaska fur seal by Aleut Indians was, until 1984, controlled by the U.S. government, and the animal is still the center of controversy. Some environmental groups have petitioned to have the Alaska fur seal listed as a threatened species.

*Durability:* Alaska fur seal is among the most durable of furs, lasting up to twenty years with proper care. Hair seal, while not as sturdy, is the most durable of all the flat-haired furs, and can give from eight to ten years of service.

*Warmth:* Fur seal is very warm. Hair seal is the warmest of all the flat-haired furs.

*Price:* Alaska fur seal is low moderate and up in price; hair seal is less costly, falling into the inexpensive and up ranges.

*Used for:* Coats, jackets; hair seal often seen in sports furs.

*What to Look for:* Alaska fur seal is always plucked in order to remove the bristly guard hairs and then sheared. It is always dyed. Some colors include *Lakoda,* a dark brown, *Matara,* dark brown female skins, and *Kitovi,* plum, as well as high-fashion shades.

*Comments:* Although both Alaska fur seal and hair seal make attractive and durable garments, neither are very popular in North America

# MINK AND FOX: TWO POPULAR FURS WITH VARIETY AND STYLE

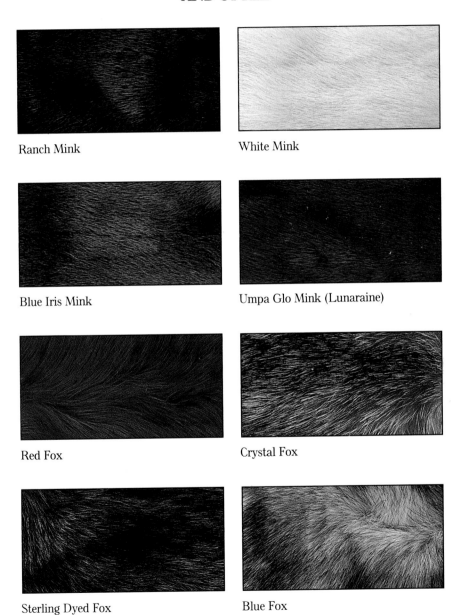

Ranch Mink

White Mink

Blue Iris Mink

Umpa Glo Mink (Lunaraine)

Red Fox

Crystal Fox

Sterling Dyed Fox

Blue Fox

# FUR GLOSSARY: SELECTIONS FROM THE WORLD OF FUR

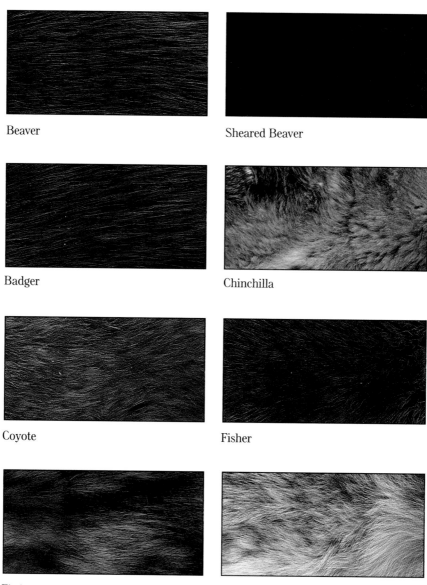

Beaver

Sheared Beaver

Badger

Chinchilla

Coyote

Fisher

Fitch

Canadian Lynx

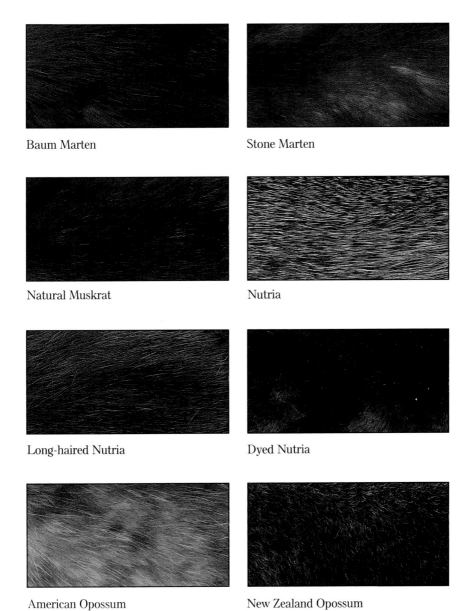

Baum Marten

Stone Marten

Natural Muskrat

Nutria

Long-haired Nutria

Dyed Nutria

American Opossum

New Zealand Opossum

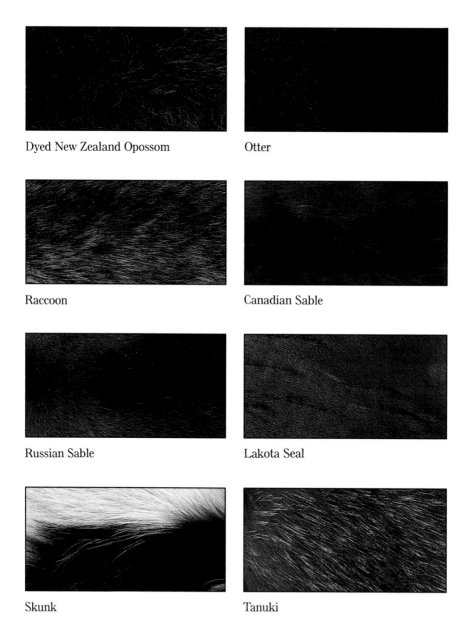

Dyed New Zealand Opossom

Otter

Raccoon

Canadian Sable

Russian Sable

Lakota Seal

Skunk

Tanuki

today, due to fashion changes and unfavorable publicity generated by the harp seal controversy.

*Name of the Fur:* SKUNK (zorina).
*Natural History:* The skunk, a member of the weasel family, is found in both North and South America. The North American variety is blackish brown in color, with a distinctive white stripe down its back, which is bisected into a V formation. Some skunks, however, may be entirely black in color. The South American variety, called a zorina, is smaller, with softer leather and hair. The best skunk comes from the Dakotas and Minnesota.
*Environmental Status:* Wild. Ranching was attempted in the 1940s, when the fur was popular.
*Durability:* Good.
*Warmth:* Warm
*Price:* Inexpensive.
*Used for:* Trimmings, parkas, jackets, and coats.
*What to Look for:* Fur can be worked with or without stripe. Best skunk is blue-black in color, rather than brownish. Look for soft, glossy fur and even white markings if stripe is used.
*Comments:* Once very popular, skunk is rarely seen today, although it makes an attractive and slightly unusual garment. Skunk coats once tended to develop an unpleasant musty odor when wet, a problem that has largely been eliminated.


*Name of the Fur:* SQUIRREL.
*Natural History:* Squirrel is another animal found throughout the world. There are fifty-five varieties; however, only the Siberian, which is blue-gray in color, and the Canadian, which is brownish, are used for fur. Only the best blue-gray Siberian squirrels are used without dye.
*Environmental Status:* Wild.
*Durability:* Fair, more durable than commonly thought. Can last up to eight years if worn infrequently. Generally, however, not a fur for everyday wear. Squirrel is often used for linings in fine raincoats.
*Warmth:* Warm.
*Price:* Generally inexpensive to low moderate; some quality garments fall into the high moderate range.
*Used for:* Coats, jackets, sometimes children's garments. Sold only in plates.
*What to Look for:* Siberian: clear, blue-gray color, with dense fur and

silky texture. Other types are usually dyed.

*Comments:* Squirrel is one of the softest furs, feeling very silky to the touch.

*Name of the Fur:* SUSLIK.
*Natural History:* The suslik, a close relative of the squirrel, lives throughout Europe. The best type comes from Russia. It is a natural yellowish-gray.
*Environmental Status:* Wild.
*Durability:* Poor.
*Warmth:* Warm.
*Price:* Inexpensive.
*Used for:* Jackets, coats, trimmings on cloth coats.
*What to Look for:* Silky, yellowish-gray fur with soft guard hairs.
*Comments:* Suslik, never a major fur, is seen rarely. It is not very durable, which limits its use.

*Name of the Fur:* TANUKI (pronounced ta-nuck'-ee).
*Natural History:* The tanuki is a Japanese relative of the American raccoon.
*Environmental Status:* Wild.
*Durability:* Good.
*Warmth:* Very warm.
*Price:* High moderate and up. Best quality tanuki coats are expensive.
*Used for:* Coats, jackets, trimmings.
*What to Look for:* Color is more similar to cross fox than American raccoon. Look for clarity of color and dense, full texture.
*Comments:* Once dyed to resemble other furs, such as cross fox, tanuki is increasingly being valued for its own beauty and is becoming more popular.

*Name of the Fur:* WEASEL.
*Natural History:* The weasel is found throughout Europe, Asia, and North America.
*Environmental Status:* Wild.
*Durability:* Poor.
*Warmth:* Warm.
*Price:* Inexpensive.
*Used for:* Trimmings, jackets, some coats.
*What to Look for:* Weasel varies in color, depending on a number of factors, including the season in which it is caught. Generally, it ranges

from creamy white to yellowish brown in color. Fur resembles mink, although it is slightly shorter and not as soft and silky as this fur.
*Comments:* Weasel is usually dyed to resemble more costly furs. Some year-round brown weasel is mistakenly called "summer ermine." Sometimes referred to as China Mink.

*Name of the Fur:* WOLVERINE (also called a glutton).
*Natural History:* The wolverine, a small, fierce dynamo of an animal, resembles a miniature bear, and is found throughout cold areas of Europe, Russia, and North America. The largest member of the weasel family, the underfur is thick and dense, with the guard hair varying from dark brown to yellowish. The wolverine has yellowish stripes along the side of its body.
*Environmental Status:* Wild, protected in some areas.
*Durability:* Excellent. One of the most durable of furs.
*Warmth:* Very warm.
*Price:* Usually low moderate.
*Used for:* Trimmings and jackets. Because it is so heavy, it is almost never used for full-length garments.
*What to Look for:* Thick, dark brown underfur, with guard hair varying from dark brown to yellowish.
*Comments:* Wolverine, an extremely durable fur, is unique in that it does not attract frost, a fact that was discovered by the Eskimos. For this reason it is often used as a face edging on cold-weather garments.

# T CLOSEUP
# THAT TOUCH OF MINK

Perhaps no other type of fur has captured the acceptance and imagination of the fashion-conscious public than mink. The mink is a member of the weasel family so ferocious that it literally must be handled with kid gloves, even in captivity. From its status in the 1950s as the fur of choice for upwardly mobile "organization wives" to its position in the 1980s as *the* yuppie fur, mink has reigned supreme, capturing about 60 percent of total American fur sales. To many people, the word fur *means* mink.

Mink has even become part of popular culture. One punk rock group made a song entitled "Don't Mutilate My Mink," while Lou Reed chronicled the life of a lonely film star in the tune "What Becomes a Legend Most?" And comedienne Joan Rivers parodied the slogan of the famous Blackglama advertising campaign with her record album, *What Becomes a Semi-legend Most?*

## The Mink Mystique

Why the fascination with mink? In practical terms, it is one of the most durable and versatile of furs. It is popular with both men and women, and full-length coats can be found for even the tiniest toddler. Mink is not only made into coats, jackets, and fine linings for raincoats; it can also be found in ponchos, sweatshirts, earmuffs, and, for people with more money than brains, diaper covers. Mink also lends itself to a variety of intricate special effects—it can be woven, sheared, knitted like fine silk yarn, and "tweeded," or combined in two-tone color effects. Ranched shades of mink range from white to black, with many shades of beige and gray in between, and it also can be colored in a mouth-watering palette of nonfur shades (one furrier has even dyed mink yellow and green to match the colors of his clients' cars).

The "What Becomes a Legend Most?" advertisements for Blackglama, a very dark brown fur produced only by the members of the Great Lakes Mink Association, have done much to promote the mink mystique. The brainchild of advertising executive Jane Trahey, the campaign was conceived in the early seventies, when mink—and all fur sales—had plummeted, largely because of the ecology movement. In addition, mink was seen as an "old lady" fur, and younger women who dared to be seen in fur at all would not be caught dead in it.

The campaign made mink glamorous, fashionable, and exciting again with its clever use of celebrities from every conceivable field. Actress/singers Diana Ross and Lena Horne, playwright Lillian Hellman, diva Leontyne Price, even ballet dancer Rudolf Nureyev, all smiled for the camera for the not inconsiderable compensation of a free Blackglama mink coat, worth about $10,000 or so. (To date, the most popular "legend" has been Ann-Margret. Requests for reprints of the poster featuring the Swedish-born star have outstripped those of the former favorite, Barbra Streisand.) The photos for the advertisements—many which were taken by famed celebrity photographer Richard Avedon—graced the pages of such upscale publications as *Harper's Bazaar, Town and Country, Vogue,* and even the staid *New York Times Magazine*. Public interest in the "What Becomes a Legend Most?" advertising campaign, which still continues, was so great that a book about it was published—titled, of course: *What Becomes a Legend Most?—The Blackglama Story*.

Not to be outdone, EMBA ran its own series of similar ads, featuring glamorous, mink-clad models snuggling up to male celebrities such as Henry Winkler and Jack Klugman. The tagline? "Wrap yourself in something special." Although these two groups have merged to form one organization—American Legend, The Mink Source—they will continue to exist separately on paper, largely to protect their trademarks. One wonders what enterprising adpeople could come up with if they decided to merge the two slogans: how about "Wrap Yourself in What Becomes a Legend Most"?

*Good Sports*

Mink's broad palette of natural colors makes it a favorite of both consumers and furriers, as it comes in more natural shades than any other animal. However, like a true blue rose or a bright red canary, pure black mink was once nonexistent. Even today, much of the black mink you see is actually a very dark brown, because pure black mink is one of the most difficult shades to breed successfully.

Mink did not always come in such a wide variety of colors. Wild mink, which has fallen out of fashion due in part to its strong, unattractive yellowish tones, was once the only type around. The first ranched animals were also varying shades of brown. In the 1930s, mink breeders began to notice that kits were turning up in various litters whose color, size, and sheen was markedly different from their parents and siblings. Early biologists called these mutations "Wasserman Sports"—an educated way of dismissing a phenomenon without knowing why it happened.

Breeders soon began to put two and two together, literally, and a whole new world of high-fashion shades was made available to the fur-buying public. Some of these colors are trademarked, including, of course, Blackglama. EMBA has two categories for its mink: Royal and Rare quality. Royal quality mink is described only by color, while Rare quality is given such fanciful names as Arcturus (lavender-beige), Jasmine (white), and Tourmaline (pale beige). Mink in a shade paler than the designated color is described as being a Breath of Spring. For example, a coat of Breath of Spring Lutetia would be slightly lighter than the fur's usual gunmetal gray.

Although the Scandinavian countries and the Soviets produce greater quantities, American mink is also considered among the finest. American mink "receive the finest quality diet of any mink in the world, ensuring that the American rancher produces the finest mink available. American mink is world-famous for this unique combination of light, flexible, and luxuriant fur." Canadian mink (Majestic) is also considered top quality, while mink produced in the Soviet Union (Norka) is not as highly thought of. The highest quality mink from the Scandinavian countries is marketed under the SAGA label.

# HOW TO SELECT AND BUY THE RIGHT FUR

## FIVE

When it comes to choosing a fur garment, the average consumer is likely to go into a state of pleasant shock: there are so many options to choose from, and all of them are appealing. There are traditionally styled garments and new-wave fashions in brilliant colors, ankle-sweeping greatcoats and waist-hugging bomber jackets, and specialty furs that are redefining just what a fur is. There are coats and jackets of every type of fur from fitch to fox, and rabbit to raccoon. Lingerie designer Eve Stillman has even come out with a line of fur-trimmed underwear.

Besides the obvious consideration of price, a number of other factors come into play in the decision-making process: *function* (lifestyle considerations), *fashion* (the many styles available), and *fit*.

# FUNCTION

More than anything else, a fur coat should reflect your particular lifestyle. A busy working mother who needs a coat that can go to a board meeting as well as a school play would find a fragile fur such as chinchilla very impractical; instead she might want to choose one of the versatile sheared furs, such as beaver or nutria, which can be dressed up or down according to the occasion. The woman who chooses to stay at home with her family needs a fur suitable for everyday wear as well as social occasions.

The price-conscious high school student or college coed, who is probably purchasing a fur garment for the first time, probably would not buy a "serious" mink for campus wear (it would suit neither her lifestyle nor her budget), but would choose a fur such as opossum or muskrat, or even mouton, all of which have a more casual look but can be styled to go with ease from football games to informal school dances. The woman with an active social life, for whom price is not a major consideration, has different needs altogether—she might want to add an elegant broadtail suit with mink a collar to her already extensive fur wardrobe, or an item that combines luxury fabrics and semiprecious stones as well as fur into a one-of-a-kind garment.

Whether you spend your winters skiing in St. Moritz or shoveling your driveway in Milwaukee, here are some pointers to keep in mind in deciding which fur best suits your lifestyle:

■ *When will the fur be worn?* To work? On social occasions? Or both? The majority of fur buyers expect their coats to be versatile enough to wear from nine to five and beyond. A fur that is very casual, such as a shaggy Tibetan lamb vest, or one that goes to the other extreme, an ermine jacket trimmed with white mink, would obviously be poor choices.

■ *Where will you wear your garment?* If you take public transportation frequently, you might consider buying a jacket instead of a full-length coat, since these are cumbersome on crowded buses or trains. Sheared and flat-hair furs might also prove to be more comfortable than long-haired, bulky furs.

The woman who travels a great deal by car might want to consider a shorter piece, too, as the constant friction of the bottom of the coat rubbing against the car seat can be detrimental to the fur.

■ *What sort of climate do you live in?* Those who live in parts of the

"Movie star" jacket in
Natural Imperial sable by
Evelyn Paswall.

country where winter temperatures are cool but rarely below freezing,
such as San Francisco and some parts of the Pacific Northwest, might
want to avoid very warm, very heavy furs such as long-haired beaver
and raccoon; these might prove to be just too much fur. Lighter garments, even shorter pieces such as ponchos and shawls, however,
might be ideal.

Conversely, residents of Canada and the chilly Frostbelt regions of
the U.S. would probably find that furs such as broadtail or mole, both
of which are lovely but not truly warm, would not provide enough
coverage.

This brings us to an interesting question: why would a woman in a
warm area of the country, such as southern California or Texas, need a
fur coat at all? One answer is that nighttime temperatures in such
places are fairly cool, and while a fur might not be a necessity, it cer-

tainly comes in handy as a luxury. Also, many women today travel extensively; bicoastal lifestyles are not uncommon. The executive who goes coatless in Dallas may freeze half to death in Detroit.

A good choice for the woman who travels a great deal would be a raincoat with a removable fur lining. The shell can be made of silk poplin, wool gabardine, tweed, or specially treated, moisture-impermeable cotton. The lining may be made of squirrel, sheared beaver, nutria, mink, or a number of other furs.

Another alternative is a reversible coat, which is available in as many combinations as fur-lined garments. A reversible garment offers a number of fashion options: it can be worn on the cloth side for a more casual look, and on occasions when a more formal appearance is desired, it can simply be turned inside out. Coats of both types offer a variety of exciting looks, and are usually not as costly as full, fur-side-out coats.

## FASHION

### Type of Fur

What type of fur should you buy? This is a very personal matter. Some may like the rugged appeal of spitz beaver; others may find the off-beat charm of tanuki irresistible.

Your lifestyle should have a bearing on the type of fur you select. When shopping for a fur, try to envision yourself wearing the garment in a variety of different situations. Some unplucked furs, such as raccoon and nutria, might have too casual an appearance to work as all around furs; while you might be uncomfortable walking your dog in a sable or Persian lamb coat. When shopping for a fur, try to envision yourself wearing the garment in a variety of different situations.

### Long vs. Short

Should you select a short- or long-haired fur? Short- and medium-haired furs are generally easier to care for than long-haired garments, with the exception of sheared types, which tend to mat when exposed to excessive amounts of rain or snow. All long-haired fur will shed, but this generally subsides after a year. Rabbit sheds the most; Russian lynx, the least. Generally speaking, the poorer the quality of the fur, the more susceptible it is to shedding.

Longer-haired furs are subject to more extreme changes in fashion than other varieties. Fox was "in" during the 1920s and '30s, particularly silver fox, but by the 1950s, shorter-haired furs such as mink had come into style, causing many fox farmers to go bankrupt. Long-haired furs are very popular now, but who is to say this will be the case by the year 2000? Whether or not a particular fur has the blessing of the fashion world should not be of concern, unless you are extremely fashion conscious. You should buy a fur because you like it, not because someone else says it's "in."

Long-haired furs have a built-in drama that is not for everyone. They seem to say "look at me!" which causes some women to tire of them rather quickly.

If you are thinking of purchasing a long-haired garment as your first fur, consider this question carefully: will you be as happy with it in two months or two years as you are now, or will the novelty have worn off? Furs range in length from very short (mole) to very long (coyote). Some furs fall in between, such as mink, which is classified by some furriers as short and by others as medium haired.

## SHORT-HAIRED FURS

| | | |
|---|---|---|
| Alaska Fur Seal | Calf | Mole |
| Baronduki | Chinchilla | Nutria, Sheared |
| Beaver, Sheared | Ermine | Otter |
| Broadtail, American | Kid | Squirrel |
| Broadtail, Russian | Lamb, Persian | |

## MEDIUM-HAIRED FURS

| | | |
|---|---|---|
| Beaver, Spitz | Marten, Stone | Muskrat, natural |
| Fitch | Mink | Nutria, natural |

## SEMI-LONG-HAIRS

Fisher      Sable

## LONG-HAIRED FURS

| | | |
|---|---|---|
| Coyote | Lamb, Tibetan | Lynx |
| Fox | Raccoon, Finnish | Opossum |
| Lamb, Mongolian | Raccoon, Japanese | |

Even among specific categories of furs, there are differences when it comes to length. For example, red fox is not quite as fluffy as silver fox, which in turn is a bit flatter than blue fox. Among sheared furs, beaver is a little longer than nutria.

## Style

When it comes to style, there is an enormous range of furs to suit every taste, from the urban clotheshorse to the conservative Midwestern matron. There is a variety of choices as to type of sleeves, collars, and back treatments. A fur coat is the sum total of its parts, and a good designer will attempt to create a fur garment in which all the components add up to one harmonious whole.

The first-time fur buyer would probably do well to stick with classically styled garments. While you may be tempted to buy that green, pink, and blue sheared mink, think again—how many places will you be able to wear it, and how long will it be before you get tired of it?

A classic garment incorporates clean, simple styling and uncluttered lines to create a subtle but lasting impression. It should serve as an extension of your personality without overpowering it. Think of styles that have stood the test of time: Coco Chanel's cardigan suits, for example, will probably look as fresh and contemporary in the twenty-first century as they did when first introduced in the 1920s.

## Length of the Fur Garment

Although a majority of the furs sold in North America are full-length coats, jackets and other pieces such as vests and ponchos are also popular.

Most furriers feel that a full-length coat—one that covers the hem of your longest day dress, generally about forty-eight to fifty inches—is the most versatile, as it can go with almost all the clothing in your closet, including suits, pants, and skirts. Other lengths include the following:

■ *Stroller:* A term that can mean a number of things, generally used to describe a longer jacket.

■ *Three-quarter length:* A garment that covers three-quarters of the garment worn beneath it, generally about thirty-six inches long.

■ *Seven-eighths length:* a coat that conceals seven-eighths of the dress or skirt worn under it; about forty-two inches long.

---

Fur garments range from (*clockwise*) waist-skimming boleros to chic seven-eighths length and ankle-grazing great coats.

Beside being fashionable, hooded coats and jackets add a bit of extra warmth on *very* chilly days

■ *Nine-tenths length:* A fur about forty-five inches in length, one-tenth shorter than the garment it is worn over.

■ *Greatcoat:* Like "stroller" this is another loosely defined term, but generally, it is an ultralong, full-length coat, loosely cut, that is fifty-two to fifty-four inches in length. Some greatcoats, though, graze the ankle.

## The Long and the Short

Jackets are another alternative that are warm and attractive as well as versatile. Some women prefer them to full-length garments.

Says Sandy Blye, executive director of the American Fur Industry, a trade organization consisting of manufacturers, retailers, and other individuals prominent in the industry, "If you grew up thinking a jacket was just the first step on the way to a full-length fur coat, think again.

---

So easy to throw over everything from pants to party clothes, a fur jacket makes great fashion sense for today's woman . . . with a jacket you can indulge your taste for drama, especially for formal wear. Nothing else creates the classic silhouette over long dresses and evening pants."

Jackets come in every style from ultrashort, sexy boleros to high-fashion numbers that skim the hips. With one exception, the most flattering jackets are finger-tip length—approximately thirty-two to thirty-six inches, covering the widest part of the derrière. This length not only makes fashion sense, but is energy-efficient as well: for maximum warmth, a fur coat should cover the kidneys, as a goodly amount of body heat can escape through this area if it is not properly protected.

## Sports Furs

So-called sports furs are those garments that are strictly for casual and active wear. This category includes furs designed specifically for active sports such as skiing, skating, tobogganing, etc. and those that just look as if they could be used for these activities. This type of fur jacket is often styled like its fabric counterpart: fur parkas usually have hoods and zip fronts, but are much warmer and, unlike cloth, will not absorb moisture.

Many members of the lamb family—including Tibetan and its slightly shorter Mongolian relative, as well as shearling—have a casual look that's just right for sportier pieces. Otter, a short-haired, glossy fur, is popular for men's sports garments, and both sexes find spitz beaver and unplucked nutria ideal for the active life. Coyote, badger, and wolverine are also used for sporty styles, as are some types of fox—particularly the red variety. But any fur can become an active-wear fur, depending on the way it is styled, even mink. For the sportsman, or woman, who has everything, how about a sable ski jacket?

In areas that are not too cold in winter a vest can be an inexpensive and fashionable option. Vests come in shearling, long-haired lamb, nutria, and a host of other furs. They can be worn by themselves on crisp fall days and, later on, layered over a sweater. Remember, however, that this is a look that is informal and probably too casual to be worn to work.

For those with a flair for the dramatic, fur capes, ponchos, ruanas (another type of poncho), and shawls are a fashionable option. A fur shawl can be worn not only by itself in mild weather, but over other coats—both fur and cloth—as well.

A sporty mink sweater by
Pierre Balmain.

## FIT: A SHOULDER'S STORY

■ *A fur garment must hang properly* from the shoulder area, or it will
not fit correctly. A good furrier will tailor your coat so that the bulk of
its weight is supported at the level of your collarbone, where you won't
be able to feel it. When you try on a well-constructed fur garment, even
one made out of a bulky fur such as spitz beaver, it should not feel
extremely heavy. If it does, you're looking at a poorly made garment.

■ *A fur coat should not make you look fat* if you aren't.

■ *Your fur coat or jacket should be roomy enough to allow you to move
around freely in it.* Even a fitted fur coat should not be tight. This is
because fur, unlike fabric, has no "give," and coats that are too snug
will sooner or later rip in strategic areas such as the underarm or shoulder area.

■ *Don't worry if a sleeve or hem is a little too long, or a hook seems out of place.* Most furriers will cheerfully make minor adjustments to your garment free of charge.

## FURS FOR EVERYBODY

Not every fur garment is flattering to every body type. Choosing the right *style* and *type* of fur for your figure is very important.

Three popular sleeve styles; bell (*left*), batwing (*right*), and set-in (*middle*).

The wing (*left*), cross-cut (*right*), and saddle (*middle*) are just three of the collar options available to today's fur buyer.

## The Tall Figure

Women who are five feet seven inches and over are lucky, as they can carry off any fur, especially the more dramatic styles and the longer-haired furs, such as fox and lynx. The newer lengths, such as seven-eighths, are also ideal. Tall women can wear horizontally and circularly worked furs that are off limits to most women.

Just be careful not to go overboard; exaggerated, "costumey" furs with excessive detailing look just as silly on tall women as they do on shorter ones.

## The Average Figure

If you have an average figure, meaning that you are about five feet four inches to five feet seven inches in height and your weight and measurements are fairly proportionate, you can wear a wide variety of furs with a broad range of styling. If you wish to appear taller, look for garments with long, vertical lines.

## The Petite Woman

If you are five feet four inches or under, you are not alone—there are approximately twenty-seven million women in this country who can be called petite. In fact, according to the National Bureau of Standards, the *average* height of the American woman is five three and a half, not five five or five six, as is commonly believed.

Once *persona non grata* in the fashion world, petites have emerged as a force to be reckoned with. Many well-known designers have created lines of clothing and furs especially for smaller figures. With a bit of foresight and fashion savvy, there's no reason why a shorter woman can't look just as sensational in a fur coat as Jean Harlow (5′2″) and Joan Crawford (5′1″) did in the movies of the thirties.

What works.

What doesn't.

## Types of Fur

*Best Bets:* The best types of fur for the petite woman are the shorter-haired varieties, such as lamb (Persian, broadtail, and mouton), seal, and the sheared furs. Among the medium hairs, mink is an excellent choice, as it can be styled to suit the smaller figure.

Many fashion authorities feel that sable is absolutely the longest-haired fur that petites can get away with. Others say that fox can work, as long as it is fashioned in a manner that does not add unwanted bulk to the figure.

One alternative for the shorter woman who craves a long-haired fur is lynx. This is because the hairs lie *flat* instead of standing away from the body. With any long-haired fur, make sure that the coat is a let-out, vertically worked one. Coats with horizontal and circular layouts are almost *always* wrong for petite figures.

*What to Avoid:* Stay away from Mongolian and Tibetan lamb, as well as natural beaver and raccoon. Coyote and opossum would also be poor choices.

## Fur Styles

■ Look for furs that were specifically created with the petite figure in mind. A cut-down misses size simply will *not* work.

■ Avoid double-breasted coats. They tend to be too overwhelming for small frames.

■ Stay away from coats with wide, double-notched lapels. Mandarin, wing, and narrow shawl collars are good choices, as is a modest tuxedo collar. Collarless cardigan styles will add an elegant, elongating effect.

■ Short women often have short necks. Look for a coat that has a clean neck and shoulder line. Hooded coats should be avoided.

■ Avoid extreme sleeve styles—bell sleeves, those with wide turn-back cuffs, and extremely puffed sleeves. A blouson sleeve tapered into an elasticized wrist is not warmer than other types, but emphasizes a slender wrist.

■ Belted coats generally cut shorter women in half, and are best avoided. However, if you like the extra shaping that a belt provides, try a half belt, which ties in front of the garment and leaves the back of the garment free. The belt can be slipped off for an easy unbelted look.

Jackets *can* be worn by shorter women. The two best lengths are waist-length (if you're short and heavy, however, you'd best stay away from this style). The other ideal length is a jacket that stops not at the hips, but *at the hipbone*. The shorter your jacket, the longer your legs will look.

However, if you prefer a longer jacket, make sure that it stops within a half inch to an inch past your buttocks.

## The Full-Figured Woman

Although fashion designers seem to believe that women who weigh over 100 pounds are nonexistent, thirty percent, or more than twenty million American women, wear a size 16 or larger.

More and more clothing manufacturers are discovering that "plus size" women are interested in fashionable clothing instead of the frumpy styles usually designed for them. Fur coats are increasingly becoming available in larger sizes as well.

What works.

What doesn't.

## Types of Fur

*Best Bets:* Much of what is advised for petites also goes for larger figures. Full-figured women should stick with flat, short-haired furs. Mink, which is a little longer than these types, could be a good choice, depending on the way it is worked. Other medium-haired furs that might work include marten, fitch, sable, and fisher.

*What to Avoid:* Larger women should stay away from bulky and long-haired furs, including natural nutria and spitz beaver.

## Fur Styles

Fit is very important for you. In fact, if you can't find a fur that suits you, you might want to consider having your fur custom-made. Here are some hints to make your shopping easier:

■ Avoid huge "greatcoat" styles—they will only make you look larger. Double-breasted coats are also a no-no.

■ Let-out garments, with their smooth vertical lines, create the illusion of slimness. Horizontally or circularly worked garments are not for you.

One feature sometimes found in fur garments is the "sunburst" back. This layout is done by using the slim, darker necks of the pelts up near the shoulder line, graduating to lighter skins at the hem. Coats with this type of patterning are very flattering to the fuller figure.

■ Avoid furs with complicated collar treatments. Cardigan, wing, and shawl collars are good choices. A modified notched collar is also an option.

■ Blouson and bell sleeves will only make heavy arms look heavier. You may also want to steer clear of coats with tightly fitting set-in sleeves, as they create a shoulder to shoulder expanse that is broadening. A sleeve set into a square armhole or a modified dolman or raglan sleeve would be better choices.

■ Although it's often been said that dark shades make one look slimmer, don't feel that you should stick to basic black. You can wear anything from dark ranch mink up to the medium tones, although you might want to stay away from very light shades. Avoid coats with fancy two-tone treatments.

■ Full-length coats are more flattering to the larger figure than shorter pieces, but a well-fitted, well-proportioned jacket that covers the widest part of your body is also an option.

■ Capes are an area of contention—while some furriers feel that they are ideal for the fuller figure, others say that they only make full-figured women look larger. Much depends on the way the garment is executed—a sweeping cape of white mink dripping dozens of white fox tails probably won't be flattering, while a conservative style in a darker color may be perfectly suitable.

## Other Special Figure Types

### Heavy Lower Body

If you have what is sometimes called a pear-shaped figure—meaning that most of your weight is distributed below your waist and your hips/tummy/thighs and/or derriere are large in proportion to the rest of

What works.

What doesn't.

your figure—you had best stay away from long-haired furs.

In your case, the style of the fur garment is more important than the type of fur. Full-length garments are best, but if you want to wear a shorter piece, make sure that it is at least fingertip-length. Avoid hip length and above the waist styles, as they are probably the least flattering to this type of figure.

Also to be avoided are patch pockets, wide belts, and other details that will draw attention to the area around your waist. Any detailing on a fur garment should be around the shoulder line; the eye will be drawn upward and away from your problem area. Coats with extended shoulder lines and hoods are ideal.

The best all-around coats for this type of figure are easy, unbelted styles in body skimming A-line or tent shapes.

What works.                    What doesn't.

## Short Waist/No Waist

If your upper torso is short in proportion to the rest of your body, it would be wise to stay away from horizontally or circularly worked garments and those with chevron patterning. Your goal is to create a more balanced silhouette, which is best achieved with the same fur shapes as listed above. Watch for coats with shoulder interest.

For those with little or no waist, avoid tightly fitting straight furs, as these only accentuate the lack of contour. To create the illusion of a waistline, stick with loose A-line or wrap-around styles.

Both short and no-waisted women can wear capes and ponchos, as these types of garments cover up the middle area completely—out of sight, out of mind.

What works.

What doesn't.

# CUSTOM-MADE COATS

If you can't find a coat that suits your fancy, you can always have one made. A custom-made fur offers many advantages, as in effect you are the designer: you can choose the exact length, sleeves, collar, and color you want. You may even choose to combine the collar on one coat with the sleeves of another. Inspiration can come from many sources, including books, magazines, and even your own sketches. Surprisingly, custom-made furs are roughly equal in price to ready to wear garments.

You may want to have your coat made during the spring and summer months, as most furriers are busy from fall to late winter. Custom-made furs are not for everyone, as the measuring and fitting process can be time-consuming.

# FUR, COLOR, AND YOU

Fur comes in a wide array of natural colors, from creamiest white to the deepest, most mysterious black. With so many options, it might be difficult to select the right shade for your complexion. Sandy Blye, Executive Director of the American Fur Industry, offers these words of advice: "A woman should select the color of her fur with as much care as she uses in picking the tones of clothing she wears. When selecting a fur in terms of color, look for shades that provide some contrast to your complexion instead of blending in with it. Your goal should be to select a fur that *complements* your skin and hair coloring instead of competing with it."

Here are some hints for selecting the right shade of fur for your complexion:

## Blondes

Blondes, very light brownettes, and fair-skinned women in general, should stay away from very pale shades. "White and other light-colored furs tend to wash blond skin tones right out," explains Ms. Blye. Black and other very dark colors, however, may provide *too* harsh a contrast.

Fair-haired women look best in medium brown shades, such as Lunaraine mink. Stone marten, with its soft palette of browns, would also look striking against paler skins. Furs with golden undertones will bring out the highlights in fair hair—golden sable, summer ermine, and Golden Island fox, with its warm shadings of gold and ivory. Red fox is also flattering.

## Brownettes

Women with light to medium brown hair and medium complexions are lucky, because they can wear an almost unlimited selection of furs, including most shades of mink, raccoon, tanuki, and lynx. Once again, however, avoid furs that blend in too much with your skin and hair tones.

## Brunettes

Women with dark brown to black hair and eyes and darker complexions also have a wide variety of choice. Lynx, with its various interesting shadings, is a good choice, as is silver fox, many shades of Swakara, raccoon, and red fox. The gray furs, such as chinchilla, are also a possibility. Fitch, with its interplay of dark and light tones, looks particularly attractive on brunettes, as do paler furs. You might want to avoid very dark furs.

## Redheads

Redheads can wear a variety of gorgeous furs in the earthy brown shades, such as sable (both golden and the darker variety), stone and baum marten, and many shades of mink. Crystal fox would also be a good choice. Sterling fox, with its orange undertones, would bring out the highlights in sandy or auburn hair. Gray fox, which has ochre undertones, is very flattering. White and pale furs might also be considered, but they do little to complement this complexion type, since most redheads are fair-skinned as well.

## Asian Complexions

Asian women, who usually have strong yellowish tones to their skin, look best in light to medium brown shades, which include pastel and Lunaraine mink, stone and baum marten, and sable (except golden sable) as well as lynx. Darker shades are also a possibility, including ranch mink. Avoid furs that might not provide enough of a contrast to be interesting, including any furs with strong golden tones.

## Brown and Black Skin Tones

Since black skins come in such a wide array of colors, it's hard to pinpoint which shades suit them best. Generally speaking, though, dark skins can wear many colors well, including red fox, raccoon, fitch, and tanuki. Silver fox is one fur that seems tailor-made for black and other dark-skinned women.

*Very* dark-skinned women should avoid pale or white furs that create too harsh a contrast. Similarly, very dark or black furs against dark skin blend in too much with the complexion to be really complementary.

## Gray, White, and Silver-Haired Women

This type of hair coloration looks best in fur that brings out the silvery highlights in the hair, including raccoon and silver and crystal fox. Best avoided are furs with a great deal of gray, such as chinchilla.

White-haired women should follow the advice listed for blondes and stay away from very light or very dark shades.

## WHERE TO BUY YOUR FUR

Now that you've thought seriously about what kind of fur you want to buy, the next step is to decide where the best place is to buy your fur. Since even a moderately priced fur is an important investment, you'll want to choose the furrier you will be dealing with very carefully.

## Finding a Furrier—What to Keep in Mind

### Reputation of the Furrier

Whether you choose to purchase your fur from a large department store, a chic specialty shop, or a small, family-run firm, the reputation of the individual or company you are dealing with is very important. After all, would you buy a car or a house from a person or firm you knew nothing about? Of course not!

One way to find a reliable establishment is to ask the advice of a friend, relative, or acquaintance whose judgment you trust—and whose fur you admire—where he or she bought the garment. Chances are if they walked away a satisfied customer—you will too!

### Does the Furrier Stand by What He Sells?

This is very important. Suppose, for example, after several wearings, you are dissatisfied with your purchase for some reason or other—the coat seems to shed more than it should, it develops tears in several strategic areas, or after being caught in a downpour it looks like a completely different coat from the one you bought! You should be able to take it back to the shop and have it replaced or repaired.

### Does the Establishment Have, or Offer, Its Own Alteration, Repair, Storage, and Cleaning Facilities?

Minor adjustments are usually made free of charge, but what if you rip a foot-long gash in the sleeve of your mink jacket six months after you bought it? The vast majority of furriers offer these services—but some of them do not.

### What Kind of Rapport Do You Have with the Person Who Is Waiting on You?

This can only be judged after you've actually started shopping for your fur, but it's important that you feel comfortable with the people you are dealing with.

Beware the intimidation factor. We have all been in stores that look as if one has to be a millionaire or a celebrity to be able to shop there and where the clerks act as if they are doing you a favor by waiting on you.

There is one simple way to solve this problem—if you feel uncomfortable in a particular store, or dislike the treatment you are receiving, ask to see the store manager. If the situation isn't resolved, you have another option—simply leave.

## Shopping Options

Not so long ago, a woman in the market for a fur was more or less limited to the traditional fur salon, especially if she lived in a small town or city. The coat or jacket was usually paid for by cash or check.

This situation has changed drastically. There are almost as many places to buy a fur as there are types of fur. Says Sandy Blye, "Furs were traditionally sold in elegant 'salons,' with plush carpets and crystal chandeliers. They were beautiful, but also a bit intimidating. You couldn't just browse." Adds Ms. Blye, "Today's shopper won't put up with that. She's grown up shopping in malls . . . she likes to browse and see everything before even deciding to try something on."

In response to this new, younger, and more independent customer, fur retailers have taken a closer look at the way their product is being presented to the public, with the result that furs are increasingly being sold in nontraditional outlets. Affordable furs of respectable quality can now be found in the coat departments of major department stores, small boutiques, leather stores, and even bridal shops. These-so-called "bridge" furs span the price range between very expensive coats and

SAGA mink coat by Oscar de la Renta.

lesser-quality garments, taking furs off their high horse, so to speak, and making them accessible to everyone who wants them.

The operation of a fur facility—whether it is an exclusive salon or a large wholesale outlet—is a complicated and risky business, so specialty shops and department stores usually lease space to independent furriers. Thus, while the fur department is a part of the store, it is at the same time a separate entity, often with its own sales stall and advertising and promotional budget. Examples of this type of arrangement include Bloomingdale's Northern Lights salons, which are leased and operated by The Fur Vault, and the Carol and Irwin Ware Fur Collection at Chicago's I. Magnin. At other establishments, the fur salon is as much a part of the store as any other department, and is not operated by any outside agent.

The changes in the marketing of fur have not been limited to *where* furs are sold; they include *how* they are sold as well. Garments can be bought on a lay-away plan, and many stores have flexible payment plans. Anticipating the woman with more than one fur in her future, the New York–based Furs by Antonovich, which claims to have the largest fur inventory in the world, even issues its own credit card.

Each type of establishment has its advantages—and disadvantages—depending, to a large extent, on who the customer is and what she wants. The older, more quality-conscious consumer may not find the informal atmosphere of the huge fur warehouse to her liking, preferring to take her business to a more personalized fur salon, while the woman for whom cost is a primary consideration may find such an upscale shop intimidating and pricey.

Let's look at some of the advantages—and drawbacks—of dealing with each type of establishment, including fur salons, department stores, specialty stores/boutiques, manufacturer/retailers, mail-order firms, and a few others you may not have thought of.

Canadian coyote and Arctic fox coat.

Fisher coat by Ben Kahn.

## Fur Salons

It has been estimated that more than half of all fur retailers are small, family-run businesses that employ fewer than twenty people. This is the type of establishment that the older, more conservative customer often chooses to visit when making a fur purchase.

*Advantages:* The advantages of a fur salon are many. Most have highly trained salespeople, many of whom have been with the firm for years and are knowledgeable about fur garments and how they should fit. Most salons have a reasonable selection of basic types and styles of furs in a fairly broad price range.

*Disadvantages:* Smaller fur salons may not be the best choice for the woman who wants a more avant-garde fur. The intimidation factor may also come into play in some cases, particularly since many fur salons are operated by older men who might find it difficult to develop a rapport with the younger, more informal customer. Generally, most fur salons do not carry a wide selection of very inexpensive to inexpensive furs—a definite drawback for the price-conscious shopper.

## Department Stores

Department stores sell everything—linens, china, furniture, appliances. With the increasing popularity of fur garments, many have added fur to their inventories. Reasonably priced furs, as well as garments incorporating fur (leather or cloth jackets lined with such pelts as rabbit, New Zealand opossum, or even mink), can even be found in nonfur sections of many of these stores, usually in the coat and sportswear departments.
*Advantages:* Most department stores offer fur garments in a variety of price ranges, the majority of which fall into the inexpensive to moderate price range. Few carry the very expensive furs.

Service varies, but many have convenient plans that stretch out payments over a period of time. A woman can put her fur on layaway in June and have it well before January winds begin to blow.
*Disadvantages:* Customer service is where some department stores receive failing marks. (This is usually not true of leased departments, most of which train and hire their own staffs.) Many women find that the salespeople in the fur departments of large stores are poorly trained and, even worse, uninterested. Comments one furrier (who chooses to remain anonymous), "They'll pull someone out of better blouses, put her in the fur department, and expect her to be able to sell mink coats—it just can't be done!"

One woman tells of a shopping trip to the fur salon in one of New York's major department stores, where the clerks casually stood talking to one another, arms folded across their chests. They sighed in annoyance whenever they were asked for assistance, especially when this involved unfastening the padlock attached to one particular fur so that the customer could try it on. Finally, the woman left in irritation, vowing never to return.

## The Fur Department Store

Our unique concept in selling furs is the independent fur department store where a wide variety of fur garments of every type, style, and price range are sold.

The pioneer in this new type of fur retailing has been the New York–based Fur Vault, which operates three of these "stores of the future." At the Paramus, New Jersey location, the firm has gone through great

---

114

expense in creating a shop that combines the atmosphere of a fine furrier with the convenience of a shopping mall.

The Fur Vault has utilized the store-within-a-store concept—one that has been successfully employed by many of the country's exclusive specialty establishments—with a series of boutique-type shops that are strategically arranged around the edge of a spacious, sparkling white atrium that is washed in the sunlight which beams down from a sixty-foot domed skylight. The garments are segregated by type, from casual jackets in the lower price ranges and fur-leather combinations to a superluxe shop complete with its own customer lounge. Separate shops containing petite, long, and large sizes are also included, as well as boutiques selling nonfur accessories such as boots, leather goods, and handbags. The store has about three thousand furs in stock.

The Fur Vault features kitchen facilities equipped to wine and dine up to 150 people when fashion shows are staged in the atrium. Antique furs are also displayed in glass cases in the same area. The fur depart-

Canadian silver fox coat.

ment store even includes color TV sets where Fur Vault chairman Fred Schwartz, known for his flamboyant marketing techniques, states that "husbands can watch the football game on Sunday while their wives shop."

Says Schwartz of the shop: "It is not a store in the strict sense of the word. It is an environment. We sought to complete the circle: from the comfort and convenience of easy shopping, to separate shops and boutiques, to a place where fashion shows can be staged and could reflect the craftsmanship of fur and the elegance and joy connected with the purchase of fur."

### Specialty Stores/Boutiques

Located mainly in larger cities, specialty stores sell high-quality, high-priced garments and accessories, many with designer labels. The garments in the fur departments of specialty shops will usually reflect that store's fashion philosophy: if the establishment itself specializes in costly, avant-garde fashions, the furs carried by that store will be of the same ilk.

Boutiques are usually small shops that are similar to specialty stores, except that they often carry hard-to-find, one-of-a-kind pieces—with corresponding price tags. The furs they carry usually fit in the same category.

*Advantages:* Like fur salons, many of these shops have well-trained and helpful sales personnel, although others are closer to department stores in the way their staff is trained. Unlike salons, though, they usually specialize in furs that appeal to the fashion-forward customer rather than the woman who is looking for a basic mink.

*Disadvantages:* This is probably not the right place for the first-time fur customer to shop, unless she is looking specifically for something out of the ordinary. Prices are usually high, so if cost is an important consideration, it might be best to plan on shopping elsewhere. Stores of this type can and do offer inspiration for the woman who eventually wants to trade up to a more expensive fur, but the intimidation factor may also be significant.

### Manufacturer/Retailers

In recent years many manufacturers, mostly in the New York area, have begun selling to the public, with great success. In 1985, sales from this type of activity totalled about $200 million.

*Advantages:* Manufacturer/retailers probably have a wider range of types and styles of fur than any other type of establishment. If you live in an area where one is located, by all means visit it, if only to get an idea of the many types of fur available. The main selling point of manu-facturer/retailers is price: since they actually make their own fur garments, their prices are usually low.

*Disadvantages:* Some women do not like the no-frills environment of this type of establishment, preferring the more luxurious surroundings of a salon or boutique. Although service is usually good, it can be rushed and impersonal. The reputation of the manufacturer/retailer is also very important—be wary of buying from someone you have never heard of.

## Mail-Order Firms

This is a relatively new area of fur retailing. In 1982, furs by mail accounted for $140 million in sales, a small portion of the $40 billion Americans spent on mail-order products annually. However, the number of furs sold by mail is increasing every year. In addition to the companies that offer a fur or two in their catalogues every year, there are firms such as Spiegel which in its *Ambiance* catalogue offers a number of furs, most in the moderate price range.

*Advantages:* Buying fur by mail is very convenient. Many busy women, particularly working mothers, simply do not have the time or the inclination to spend hours shopping for a fur. For those who live in isolated areas where furriers are in short supply, a mail-order catalogue may be the best solution.

When dealing with reputable mail-order firms, customers who are dissatisfied with their fur purchase can usually send it back with few problems. In addition, many mail-order catalogues have toll-free numbers where a customer who has questions about a particular garment can have them answered.

*Disadvantages:* Many women are leery of buying fur by mail, not only because of the expense, but because many feel that fur is a sensual item that must be touched and seen in order to be truly appreciated. In fact, according to one retailer, mail-order furs are bought by consumers who are less knowledgeable about the product and would feel intimi-dated walking into a fur salon. Cleaning, storage, and repair may also present problems when you order your fur by mail. Plan ahead by checking out the fur storage facilities nearest you. You should also be wary of dealing with mail-order firms you are not familiar with.

Even though the above guidelines can give you a good idea of what to expect from certain types of establishments, it's important to keep an open mind when shopping for furs. Don't feel that just because you have only a limited amount of money to spend, or you are looking for a particular type of garment, that certain shops are out of your league. Make a point of visiting as many stores as possible, just to get an idea of the wide range of fur types and styles available. It may turn out that a shop you have never considered patronizing will have just the fur you're looking for.

## Other Options

### Close-out Sales

Many who live in smaller towns and cities have probably noticed advertisements in the paper for fur sales held at large hotels, convention centers, and similar places. These sales are held by manufacturers who travel around the country with their wares, most of which are left over from previous seasons, or were left for storage or cleaning and never claimed.

Prices advertised at these events—most of which last only for one or two days—are very low. In one such advertisement, a mink coat, originally retailing at $6,000, was advertised for $1,500.

Although bargains can be found at sales of this type, the buyer should be wary and cautious. If the coat or jacket is not satisfactory after a few weeks, there will be no way to return it.

### Buying a Fur Overseas

Many women are eager to purchase furs during their travels to foreign countries, particularly if they are available at "bargain" prices.

You may not come out ahead by buying a fur abroad. Although European women tend to buy more high-fashion garments than Americans do, the furs are basically the same, in terms of raw material, in every country. This is because the fur industry is an international

---

**Fur Facts and Fancies:** *When the first shipment of platina fox— a strain of the silver variety—arrived from Norwegian fur farms in 1939, skins sold for as much as $10,000 apiece. One of the first platina fox garments was made for the Duchess of Windsor.*

---

one, where pelts are bought every year at auction by individuals from all over the world.

Remember also that you must pay a duty on all products over a certain amount that you bring into the U.S. Since the duty on a fur coat may be as high as 30 percent of the total price of the garment, you may end up paying more for a foreign fur than an American one. If you are not perfectly satisfied with your purchase after bringing it home, there is no way you can return it. You will also have to consider where you will have the coat cleaned, stored, and repaired. In addition, products made from animals that are classified as endangered species cannot be brought into the country. Even though leopard, cheetah, and other garments made from endangered species can legally be sold in some parts of Europe and the Orient, they cannot be brought into the U.S. or Canada. If you attempt to bring an ocelot-skin coat, for example, into North America, it will be confiscated, and you won't be compensated for your loss.

Natural Russian golden sable "steamer" coat by Ben Kahn.

# HOW TO SELECT AND BUY A FUR

The best way to pick out a fur is to look at as many as possible. After you have gone to a number of establishments, you will begin to get a better idea of what the different types of fur look like, the differences in quality among the various furs, and what you want.

## Size

Start out by telling the salesperson what type and style of fur you had in mind, as well as your size. Remember, however, that few people are strictly one size. As the cut and style of fur garments varies, you may find that you are able to fit into a number of different sizes. One woman—usually a size twelve—found that she could fit into a size ten mink, and even a size eight evening cape of golden sable.

You should also be aware that the fashion industry is moving toward a more conceptual attitude when it comes to sizing clothing, including furs. You will find that some furs—mostly unconstructed pieces such as ponchos, capes, etc.—come in small, medium, large, etc.

## Read the Label

According to the Federal Fur Products Labeling Act of 1952, every fur product costing more than five dollars must have a tag affixed to it that states the name of the fur, its country of origin, and how it was processed. This information must also be used on invoices or bills of sale, and also in advertising.

### Name

In the past, many of the "poor" furs were processed to resemble more expensive ones and were called by a variety of fanciful names. Thus, rabbit became "sealine" or "chinchillette," while specially processed muskrat was called "Hudson Bay Sable."

The Federal Fur Products Labeling Act requires that fur products be labeled according to their true English name, which must be preceded by the phrase "fur origin" or "country of origin." If two different furs are used in one garment, each must be correctly identified. This law also requires that the name must not be combined with another fur name, even to explain a color—muskrat dyed to resemble mink must still be called muskrat, *not* mink-dyed muskrat. Trade or coined names describing fictitious furs—such as those described above—are also forbidden, except in a few cases of legally accepted terms, such as "American broadtail, processed lamb."

---

## Origin

This tells you what country the fur comes from, and must always be indicated on the label. A fur from the United States, however, may say nothing at all.

Some furs will have two countries of origin indicated. This happens when the pelts came from one source, but the coat itself was made in another nation. This is particularly true of Soviet furs because of the embargo on seven types of Russian pelts: ermine, fox, kolinsky, marten, mink, muskrat, and weasel. Finished garments made from these furs can be imported, but the raw pelts cannot. Therefore, you will see a coat made from one of these types of furs with two countries of origin listed: the first, the source of the pelts themselves, and the second, where the garment itself was made.

In addition to informing the shopper exactly where the fur came from, the country of origin sometimes has a direct bearing on the quality of the fur, and the well-informed consumer should be aware of this. For example, Siberian squirrel is softer, fuller, and is considered to be of finer quality than the Canadian variety. Similarly, if you see a label on a sable coat that lists the Soviet Union as the country of origin for the pelts, you know that you will be getting the finest sable available. Russian lynx is also considered to be of higher quality and, consequently, is more expensive than Canadian lynx.

## Processing

This refers to what has been done to the fur, aside from the tanning and dressing. It usually refers to how the fur has been changed in texture, color, or both.

A fur that has not been altered in any way will be called *natural*. Other furs may be dyed, blended or tipdyed, or bleached. On bleached furs, the leather will look unnaturally white; on dyed garments, the leather and the fur will be the same color, with the exception, of course, of those that have been tipdyed.

Sometimes you will see a particular term that refers to a method of coloring that you may not be familiar with. For example, if the label says *greigé degrade*, it means that the fur has been colored in various shades of beige-gray. If you have any questions about the labeling, ask your salesperson.

A fur must also tell you whether whole, partial, or pieced skins have been used. This term also refers to specific processes such as plucking, shearing, cording, or feathering. If the fur is used or secondhand, that fact must also be indicated on the label.

Although it is not required by law, the tag may also tell you if a coat is made from male or female skins, particularly expensive garments made from fine furs such as fisher and mink. Female skins are smaller than male skins (a male mink is twice as large as a female mink) and also lighter and silkier. A coat made out of skins from female animals uses about 25 percent more skins than one made out of male pelts, and is subsequently more expensive.

## Price

When it comes to cost, the question most often asked by consumers is: what determines the price of a fur garment? Fur prices are governed by the simple laws of supply and demand: the scarcer the fur and the higher the demand for it, the more costly it will be.

Take, for example, the Canadian lynx. In the sixties, the fur of this animal was not in high demand, and in fact, it was considered a pest. Canadian pelts could be bought for as little as $40.00.

With the increased interest in long-haired furs in the late seventies and early eighties, however, demand for the fur skyrocketed. Ironically, this came at a time when the Canadian lynx population was dwindling. The decrease in population was a part of a natural chain of events that occurs about every ten years, and is not due to interference from man.

Snowshoe hares, the lynx's primary food source, live off woody plants. When the hares become too populous and start to overgraze, the plants produce chemicals which cause the hares' fertility to decline. As a result of this reduced food supply, the female produces smaller litters, and eventually stops breeding altogether. The cycle reverses itself when the hares', and subsequently, the lynx's, food sources recover.

As a result of the reduced population of Canadian lynx, trapping restrictions were tightened and strict quotas were introduced. Correspondingly, the cost of lynx pelts skyrocketed: fine female skins were sold for as much as $1,000 apiece. The situation was much the same for the even rarer Russian lynx.

Ranched furs also fall prey to the dynamics of supply and demand. The Soviet Union keeps sable prices high by limiting the number of pelts sold at auction to no more than 150,000 or so annually, and forbidding the exportation of breeding stock.

Although fur garments are considered to be expensive luxury items, their average price has changed surprisingly little over the years. This is because the cost of the raw materials that go into the garment—namely, the pelts—remains relatively constant from year to year. In fact a fur garment is one of the best bargains around because its price has only increased by about 10 to 15 percent over the past twenty years.

An advertisement for a mink sweater coat in a February 1965 edition of *The New York Times* is listed for sale at a reasonable $4,000—which is comparable to the prices asked for similar garments in many of the nation's stores twenty years later—while a "roomy studio apartment," advertised in the same issue, was renting for a shockingly low $149 a month!

When shopping for furs, give the salesperson some idea of how much you want to spend. Do try to be flexible—a coat in a range slightly above or below what you were originally prepared to spend might be the one you've been looking for. However, Edythe Cudlipp cautions, "If looking at furs out of your price range will make you unhappy, stay away from them. You'll find a big enough selection in the range you can afford."

## Making a Compromise

If you have your heart set on a certain type of fur, but can't afford a full-length coat, why not try a jacket? Shorter pieces are usually less expensive than longer ones, and offer a number of fashion options. If a jacket of your fantasy fur is still out of your price range, an accessory made of the fur—a sable fling, a lynx hat, or even a pair of mink earmuffs—will add a touch of luxury to all your outfits.

This brings us to a very important point: *Buy the best quality fur you can afford*. This means deciding what price you can afford and then buying the best quality fur in that range. Although you might have your heart set on mink, if you can only afford a poorer grade of this fur, you'd be better off purchasing a good-quality beaver or muskrat. Similarly, if your budget allows you to purchase only a middling grade of sable, it would be wiser to buy a top-quality mink.

Remember that if you are buying a second fur, many furriers will take your old garment as a trade-in. The price is usually applied to that of the new coat, which should save you some money.

## Let the Buyer Be Wary

Unless you are the type of person who buys on impulse—and usually doesn't regret her decision—you'll want to take your time when looking at furs. Don't be pressured into buying a garment you don't really like—or one that is way beyond your price range—just because the salesclerk or manager thinks it looks good on you.

Don't be afraid to ask questions. The old adage—"if you don't know furs, know your furrier!"—should be heeded. If the salesclerk you are dealing with can't or won't answer your questions, ask to see the manager. If he or she offers little help, it's probably best to visit another establishment.

Remember that you don't have to put up with rude, indifferent, or hostile salespeople. You also don't have to settle for a fur you do not like, or buy one in an establishment where you are made to feel uncomfortable. The better the reputation of the furrier, however, the less likely you are to run into this problem. Today's furriers know that many women are interested in owning not one fur, but a whole wardrobe of them. The wise furrier hopes that the woman who buys a sheared muskrat today will trade up to a mink or perhaps even a fisher or sable tomorrow. That's why establishments that sell fine furs work hard to maintain good customer relationships.

Many women ask if it's advisable to take a friend or spouse along when shopping for furs. That depends: while a friend may have a more objective view of what suits you and what doesn't, and can offer valuable suggestions and advice, his or her taste may be very different from yours. If you're shopping with someone who doesn't like fur jackets, and you're in the market for a shorter piece, you may run into problems. On the other hand, don't let a friend pressure you into buying a garment you don't like. You will end up regretting your purchase, and resenting your friend as well.

## Actually Buying a Quality Fur

Let's assume now that you've found the coat or jacket of your dreams and are ready to plunk down your hard-earned money. Now is the moment to pause, clear your head, and assess your prospective purchase from every possible angle: is this *really* the right fur?

What determines a quality coat? There are three important factors to remember and to consider: (1) it should be made of fine fur; (2) the workmanship should be of a high caliber; and (3) it must fit properly.

You already know that more than 50 percent of a fine fur's value is determined by the quality of the pelts that go into it. A mink of top-quality pelts will cost considerably more than one of average skins. Although it takes a highly skilled individual to determine the nuances that makes one skin worth much more than another, after looking at many coats you will be able to see why a $2,000 mink differs from a $20,000 coat: the less expensive garment will not have the luster, softness, and beauty of the costlier fur.

Workmanship is also very important. Naturally, the $2,000 coat will not have as high degree of craftsmanship as the costlier garment. Both the quality of the fur and the manner in which it is made will determine the performance and durability of the fur. A manufacturer can do a number of things to save himself money, but the result will be a poorer-quality garment. Check the inside of the coat carefully: if you examine the inside of the cheaper garment, you will often find hairs caught between the seams of the let-out strips, something that doesn't occur in quality garments.

When you actually wear the coat, how will one differ from the other? If you were to wear the cheaper coat in a heavy rain or snowfall, you would notice after the coat has dried that it's shape is not quite the same as before. The fur will not swing and drape as it did when the coat was new. Perspiration, heat, and moisture will also gradually cause the fur to change shape. None of these factors will affect a high-quality coat to any great extent. Although it is likely that, with good care, a quality fur will last a decade or more, the cheaper coat will have gone the way of all flesh (or fur) long before then.

When checking the workmanship of your dream coat, remember that in quality coats, the lining is not tacked to the bottom. There are exceptions, however: it would be foolish to have an unattached lining on a reversible coat, and on some garments with unusual hem treatments, it would be impossible. And just because a garment has a tacked hem does not mean it is of poor quality. Generally speaking, though, the finest furs have free-hanging hems, often with French bottoms.

The importance of a proper fit cannot be overemphasized. Poorer-quality garments will not fit quite as comfortably as better coats and jackets, whether they are rabbit or sable. That is why it is so crucial to buy the best fur you can afford.

But what about the woman with a muskrat budget who has mink on her mind and won't settle for anything less than a full-length coat? If it's what you really want, go ahead and buy that inexpensive mink—but remember, it won't last as long or look as good as the coat of your dreams. Make sure you wear it as often as possible, too—enjoy it while you can!

Review the terms and information contained in these guidelines for determining quality, and use these terms when examining the coat and questioning the salesperson.

■ *Let-out coats* are generally considered the crème de la crème of furs. A let-out coat should have graceful, flowing lines, and the leather should not be visible where the strips are joined together.

■ *Skin-on-skin coats*—in which pelts have been sewn together, usually head to tail—are not as costly as let-out garments, although they can be of good quality. The same is true of garments made of partial skins. The seams in both skin-on-skin coats and those made of the latter type of fur should not be visible on the outside.

■ *Pieced garments* are the least durable of the three major types of layouts. The seams in this type of garment should always be reinforced with tape or nylon; otherwise in a short while the garment will literally fall to pieces.

■ The *guard hairs*, particularly on long-haired furs, should be lustrous, silky, and uniform. The underfur should be soft, compact, and dense.

■ *Sheared furs*—as with skin-on-skin coats, there should be no sign of where the pelts have been joined. The shearing should be uniform, and the coloration even.

■ *Patterned furs*, such as Russian broadtail or Swakara, should feel smooth and silky. Look for beautiful, interesting patterns.

■ Generally speaking, in most natural furs, a bluish cast to the skins indicates high quality, while a reddish tint is a sign of inferior quality.

Regardless of how they are processed, all furs should have smooth, even coloration. Unless it is part of the pattern, one pelt should not be noticeably darker or lighter than another. Even if a coat has been dyed or bleached, the dyeing and bleaching should be uniform. No matter if the fur is muskrat or mink, the skins should be soft and supple.

## When to Buy Your Furs

For bargain hunters, August and January have traditionally been the best times to purchase furs. Many attractive pieces are available at 10 to 20 percent off retail prices. Some prefer to purchase their furs in August, before things start to get busy, as there is a wide choice of garments available and the sales personnel, being less rushed, are more likely to give the customer personal service and attention. Besides, you'll want to get your fur before cold winds start to blow!

In recent years, however, year-round off-price promotions have become common in the fur industry. In many medium to large cities, it is not unusual to find furs advertised at 40 percent or more off regular prices in all seasons of the year.

This price-cutting has caused concern among many furriers, who feel that some of these price reductions are not legitimate. Many think that price wars are cheapening the image of the fur industry, causing many consumers to adopt a "let the buyer beware" attitude. Some furriers even believe that the Federal Trade Commission should start investigating the claims of these advertisements.

Are these drastically reduced prices legitimate? It seems that in some cases, they are not. One industry executive tells of a raccoon-paws coat advertised by a Chicago retailer as being reduced from $1,995 to $995. He commented that the same fur in his own store's stock was regularly priced at $695.

What's a customer to do in the face of such claims? Your best defense is to be well-informed. *Why* are the furs being sold at such reduced prices? Are they last year's styles? Is the furrier trying to clear the way for new merchandise? Are the goods damaged? Or are they simply of inferior quality and workmanship? Once again, the reputation of the furrier is very important. Even though most quality establishments do offer sales, they usually do not engage in continuous, extensive price cutting.

Even if you are very cost-conscious, it's still important to think of the value of the fur you're getting. If a fur looks unappealing and fits poorly, even if it's priced very low, you're not really getting a bargain. With fur, as with anything else in life, you get what you pay for.

It's also wise to think twice when purchasing a garment marked "final sale" because even if they are damaged, they cannot be returned.

## IN CONCLUSION: IT SHOULD BE FUN

Buying a fur is a highly personal experience. It involves a lot of decision-making—where to buy your fur, who to buy it from, and what type of fur to buy. Although even a moderately priced fur is a major investment for most individuals, remember that a fur, whether it be a simple hat, a modest rabbit jacket, or a full-length sable greatcoat, represents much more than warmth—it is luxury, fantasy, and glamour all rolled into one. Buying a fur should be a joyous, sensual experience, not a chore. So when looking for your dream coat—or hat, or jacket, or boa—remember to be serious-minded about evaluating your purchase—and have fun doing it, too!

## S CLOSEUP
# SPECIALTY FURS

In the past ten years, the fur industry has seen the emergence of a new type of customer—the fashion-forward woman who wants something a little different, something that goes beyond that basic "dumb" fur coat. For this woman, a specialty, or novelty fur might be the answer.

What are specialty furs? Their very uniqueness defies description. They can be furs dyed in an array of brilliant colors, coats that pair fine wool fabric with fur, or furs that are knitted or woven like cloth. Loved by some, panned by others, but ignored by few, specialty furs are making their mark in the world of fashion. Some authorities even feel that in the near future they may account for 25 percent of the entire consumer market.

Let's take a look at a trio of talented young women who design these very special furs:

### Marilyn Blumer: A Way with Wovens

Although Montreal native Marilyn Blumer has a background in the fine arts, she began her fashion career as a textile designer. Her woven creations were used by some of the most prominent names in the Canadian fashion world, but like many in the design field, she eventually felt the urge to go out on her own.

The petite, black-haired designer manipulates fur in an unusual manner. Although she is reluctant to divulge exact details of her process, which took a great deal of time to develop, she reveals that it

A unique woven fur coat from Marilyn Blumer Designs.

basically involves incorporating such furs as raccoon, muskrat, rabbit, and blue fox into her hand-woven cloth. "The fur does not rest on top of the fabric," she explains, "but is completely integrated into it." Ms. Blumer designs all the fabric used in her creations.

At first, her designs were so unusual that some retailers were reluctant to carry them; fur designers, says Ms. Blumer, "thought I was crazy!" But all this is past history. Her creations can now be found at such prestigious stores as Bloomingdales and, in Canada, Eatons. Ms. Blumer's designs have been worn by the scheming Alexis Colby on the top-rated show "Dynasty," and also by Jamie Lee Curtis in the hit movie "Trading Places."

Although the Toronoto-based designer uses a variety of natural furs, the innovative use of color is a Blumer trademark. A world traveler, she is fascinated by the rich colors contained in medieval tapestries in museums such as New York's Cloisters and the Cluny in Paris. One fabric, which she terms her "Byzantine mix," contains at least twelve shades, including brilliant ruby, royal purple, rust, orange, black, fuchsia, and evergreen. One of her pieces, a full-length reversible coat made of this multi-hued cloth, combines black Mongolian lamb with rabbit dyed in red, purple, and a multitude of other shades for a truly eye-catching look.

Ms. Blumer likes to combine a wide array of colors and textures including cloth, leather, and fur, in a single garment. She comments, "I try to create clothing that is elaborate and intriguing to the eye . . . what I am striving for is a garment that is unique without being outrageous . . . art that can be put on your back."

The designer's creations are much lighter than traditional garments, but she insists they are just as warm. "The loose spaces in the weave of the cloth allow air to circulate," she explains. "This means in cold weather, my garments keep the wearer warm, while in more temperate areas of the country, heat can escape easily."

Ms. Blumer finds that many women who already own a fur garment will purchase one of her coats or jackets. "I am seeing a different type of customer who likes fur, but isn't attracted to the more traditional type of garment," she says. "She is looking for more than just a fur coat; she wants something young and different. I look at my designs as a whole new way of wearing fur."

## Kip Kirkendall: A Certain Style

One of the rapidly rising stars in the world of design is a young woman by the name of Kip Kirkendall. Although not yet thirty, the Portland, Oregon, native is already carving out her own niche in the exciting world of specialty furs. The Kirkendall collection is carried by Giorgio and Neiman-Marcus, and her creations have been featured nationally on "The Today Show."

In her designs, which include coats and jackets, dresses, sweaters, and coordinated separates, Ms. Kirkendall effectively combines a number of furs, including sable, tanuki, fox, chinchilla, sheared beaver, mountain goat, and Swakara with hand-woven fabrics such as raw silk, mohair, alpaca, and angora. Materials such as snakeskin, suede, leather, and silver bullion ribbon are also used. She comments: "I see my creations as 'tapestry pieces' that will never go out of style . . . I like to think of them as being the new classics."

Ms. Kirkendall also uses a variety of distinctive minerals and semiprecious stones in her creations—malachite, Austrian crystal, jet, lapiz lazuli, and stalactite chips. "In my designs, I try to capture the

A distinctive ensemble from Kip Kirkendall.

universal spirit of woman, which is very powerful, but at the same time, very feminine," she states. "Natural materials that come from the earth help to express this feeling."

Kip's designs range from a full-length white mink coat combined with cowrie shells, Austrian crystal, black jet beading, and snakeskin inserts to a chic dinner suit of American broadtail embellished with fox tails. Many of her pieces have their own accessories, including cocktail hats of lace and fur and stone-embellished turbans. Countering criticism that her creations are perhaps a bit too elaborate for everyday wear, she states, "I think of my designs as being jewelry for the body. Women wear semi-precious stones around their necks; why not on their clothing?"

The normally softspoken designer becomes adamant when speaking of the old-fashioned attitude prevalent among today's furriers. "In regard to design, the fur world has become stagnant," she proclaims.

"Today's fur customer is an independent and self-confident woman—a leader, not a follower. The woman who buys my furs has a certain sense of style...she doesn't want the same sort of fur that her mother wore." Mr. Kirkendall adds that "This doesn't mean that my furs couldn't be worn by women of all ages—grandmothers have bought my designs and tell me that they feel wonderful in them!"

### Paula Lishman—Knit Picks

A textile artist by training, Paula Lishman started designing clothing out of necessity: she could find little that would fit her six-foot-three-inch frame (she models many of her own designs). She began her commercial career as a leather designer, and soon began knitting the leftover strips together because, she explains, "I just can't stand to waste anything." She soon transferred this idea to fur, knitting it exactly as if it were yarn.

This is accomplished by a patented process in which the pelts are scored into extremely thin, continuous strips with a very sharp knife,

in much the same way as apples are peeled. These strips are then knitted into a variety of garments by skilled needleworkers in the town of Blackstock, Ontario. Each creation takes from sixty to eighty hours to make.

Although her garments are soft and very lightweight, Paula Lishman maintains that they are warm in winter, as the fur is worn directly against the skin, with no woven lining blocking air or free movement. "I come from Labrador, a very cold region of Canada where fur garments are more of a necessity than a luxury," she explains. "However, people up there wear their furs with the texture inside, against the skin, which is much warmer than the other way around. In fact, if you wore a fur-outside garment in Labrador, you'd probably be laughed off the street." The furs are also ideal for milder climates because the knit furs "breathe," with no woven lining blocking air or free movement. Lishman also states that her garments are "much easier to live with" than traditional furs, as they travel well and can even be stashed in a suitcase.

The Lishman line includes hats, jackets, sweaters, and shawls that are sold throughout the U.S., Japan, and Canada. The designer gets her inspiration from a variety of sources including traditional Indian motifs, nature, and even sports (her "curling" sweaters are modelled after those used in a Scottish game called curling which is played on ice). Because knitted fur does not lend itself well to full-length coats ("they tend to sag in the bum," Ms. Lishman comments), her longer garments combine knitted fur with fabric.

What kind of woman buys a knitted fur garment? Ms. Lishman states that her customers fall into two categories: the woman who already has a basic fur or two in her closet and wants something different, and the woman who is purchasing her first fur and wants something that looks "glamorous without being ostentatious." Ms. Lishman also designs a line of jackets for men—in fact, her first knitted fur garments were created for her two young sons.

# FUR AND THE WORKING WOMAN

## SIX

Although women entered the labor force in substantial numbers after World War II (between 1940 and 1973, the number of females in the work force increased by 173 percent), it is only recently that many have risen to prominent positions in the worlds of business, science, and the arts. Women have shown that they can become vice-presidential candidates, astronauts, electricians, and Supreme Court justices—and that they can do all this and more without compromising their femininity.

More than thirty-one million of these working women fall into the twenty-five to fifty-four age bracket (the time of life when earnings for both sexes are at their peak), and according to the U.S. Census Bureau, this number is expected to grow to forty million by 1990.

Even though many women are still concentrated at the lower end of the pay scale, the disposable income per capita of this group of females has increased from $7,250 in 1979 to over $10,000 in 1984. What are these newly affluent wage-earners doing with all their money? They are buying everything from condominiums to common stocks, from fine art to fur.

## DRESSING FOR SUCCESS

A fur coat is the new symbol of affluence for the working woman (especially those in the under-thirty-five age group), whether she is a secretary or a surgeon. Fully 60 percent of the fur garments sold in this country are bought for working women *for* themselves, *by* themselves. Says Ernest Graf of Ben Kahn, "In 1947, the average age of women buying mink was fifty and the woman's husband or boyfriend bought it for her. Today, she's thirty or under and buys it for herself with her own money." Fred Schwartz of The Fur Vault adds: "These women are conscious of the competitive nature of their work. A fur lets a woman reaffirm her femininity, yet represents achievement."

Carol Teitelbaum, treasurer of Bernard Teitelbaum, Inc., which specializes in long-haired furs, also notes that many of her customers are working women. She says, "This trend is not limited to single women; those who are married are also coming in to buy coats and jackets with their own money."

A fur garment has become the new symbol of achievement—the working woman's reward to herself for a job well done. And the phenomenon is seen all across the board—from the executive secretary who is buying her first fur to the bank president who already has three or four furs in her closet.

The fur industry has also taken notice of this new trend, realizing that a majority of their sales come from this new, independent customer. Some firms have even started to hold seminars for women who are interested in purchasing fur garments, but whose exposure to them has been limited in the past.

## BUYING A "WORKING FUR"

As a busy career woman, you'll want to purchase a fur that will do double—or even triple—duty both for your on and off hours. As few of us are wealthy enough to purchase a new fur every season, here are a few tips for smart shopping:

■ As many working women live multifaceted lives, a *versatile* coat is a

---

135

must. Although many fashion authorities feel that a full-length coat is a good investment, the woman who goes to many evening parties— or takes public transportation a great deal—may find that a fur jacket is more practical.

■ Buy the *best quality* fur you can afford. Remember that whether you are an attorney or an administrative assistant, your image is important—*nothing looks cheaper than a cheap fur coat!*

■ Stick with classic styles that will not go in and out of fashion quickly. This advice has been repeated in so many fashion guides that it has become the Golden Rule of dressing well. This rule means that you should AVOID:

> • *Garments in bright or unusual colors.* Neutral tones, such as brown, gray, or black work best. Don't think that neutral means boring. Furs are available in so many shades that the choice is almost limitless. A brown fur, for example, could mean an earth-dark ranch mink, a cinnamon-colored sheared nutria, or natural blush mink in rose-kissed cafe au lait.
>
> White is one of the newest neutrals. Once exclusively for evening wear, paler furs are increasingly being seen in the daytime, and are a good choice if you're willing to give them the bit of extra care they need.
>
> • *Tightly fitting garments.* A coat for everyday wear should be generously cut to allow for maximum comfort.
>
> • *Coats with too many details, such as belts, bows, and buckles.* Excessive detailing cheapens the look of a coat, and one year's "look" is usually outdated by next season.

Another thing to keep in mind when selecting a fur is your work environment. Obviously you will not wear a glamorous blue fox to work if you are the director of an anti-poverty program, but in most fields, women have great leeway when it comes to what they wear. Individuals employed in the so-called glamour industries—those having to do with art, theater, cosmetics, advertising, and certain aspects of communications—are allowed to be a bit more flamboyant than those in more staid fields, such as law, banking, and insurance. Dressing conservatively is important for those whose professions fall in the latter category, but if you work in an environment where dress codes aren't rigid, you can afford to be more extravagant.

## THE WORKING FURS

What furs do the experts recommend for the working woman? Not surprisingly, the hands down winner is mink. Says Barry Novick of Evans, Inc., "Mink is probably the most versatile fur available. Its durability and beauty make it the best all-around fur for the working woman." Other furriers, however, list other choices. Says Carol Ware of Chicago's I. Magnin, "Sheared beaver is a very good choice for the working woman. It's warm, soft, and can be worked in a number of ways." Fred Schwartz of The Fur Vault recommends New Zealand opossum. He states: "Mink is a bit too serious for a lot of women—opossum is a young fur that's growing in popularity."

Here are some of the furs most often mentioned as being good choices for the career woman. Price ranges quoted are for quality full-length garments; naturally, jackets and more commercial grades are less expensive.

## FURS FOR THE WORKING WOMAN

| Name | Price | Advantages | Disadvantages |
| --- | --- | --- | --- |
| Beaver, sheared | Moderate | Thick and luxurious, appropriate both day and evening | Fur mats when wet; needs care in damp climates |
| Beaver, long-haired | Low moderate | Very durable and warm | Heavy |
| Coyote | Low to high moderate | Warm, durable, and luxurious | Long hair is more fragile than short with tendency to shed like most long-hairs |

| Name | Price | Advantages | Disadvantages |
|------|-------|------------|---------------|
| Fisher | Expensive | Very warm, durable, and luxurious | Expensive; a high-fashion fur that might not be for everyone |
| Fox, red | Low to high moderate | Soft, warm, luxurious, a glamorous look | Fox tends to shed, although this usually stops after the first year; long-haired, fluffy fox furs may be too overwhelming for petite and fuller figures |
| Fox, silver | High end of moderate to expensive | Same as above | Same as above |
| Fox, blue | Same as above | Same as above | Same as above |
| Lamb, Tibetan or Mongolian | Low moderate | Warm, fairly durable | May be too casual for evening wear; hair frizzes when wet, needs special care from furrier |
| Marten, American | High moderate to expensive | Warm, soft, durable, and stylish | Some types (stone marten in particular) can be expensive; American marten is not as durable as the other types |
| Marten, baum | High moderate to expensive | Same as above | Same as above |
| Marten, stone | Expensive to very expensive | Same as above | Same as above |
| Mink | High moderate to expensive | Very versatile, durable, and warm | None |
| Muskrat, sheared | Low moderate | Soft, warm, durable | See *Beaver*, sheared |

| Name | Price | Advantages | Disadvantages |
|------|-------|-----------|---------------|
| Muskrat, long-haired | Low moderate | See Beaver, long-haired | See *Beaver*, long-haired |
| New Zealand Opossum | Low moderate | Warm, soft, fluffy, durable | Sheds; may be too casual a look for some situations |
| Nutria, long-haired | Low moderate | Versatile, warm, and attractive | See *Beaver*, long-haired |
| Nutria, sheared, let-out | High moderate; skin-on-skin: low moderate | See Beaver, sheared | See *Beaver*, sheared |
| Persian Lamb (caracul) | Low to high moderate | Warm, soft, attractive; increasingly worked in exciting, fashionable styles—no longer is Persian lamb an "old lady's fur!" | Some coats can be heavy; if not properly cared for, leather will split and crack |
| Rabbit | Very inexpensive to inexpensive | Soft, attractive, can be worked in a variety of interesting ways and inexpensive; good for the woman on a budget | Usually sheds a great deal; perishable, does not have a long life; many rabbit coats look "chintzy" |
| Raccoon, American | Low to high moderate | Warm, durable, very attractive | Can be heavy; some shedding |
| Tanuki | High moderate to expensive | Very warm, attractive, durable | Some shedding; best tanuki is expensive |

This list is by no means exhaustive. Other furs suggested for the working woman include sable and lynx (if you can afford them!), fitch, and Finnish raccoon. The best way to select a working fur—or any fur, for that matter—is to look at as many garments as possible and consult a knowledgeable furrier with whom you feel comfortable.

## OTHER OPTIONS

There are times when a fur garment may not be the best choice for the working woman. Consider the following story:

Laura G. is a middle manager at a very conservative Fortune 500 firm in the equally conservative Midwest. After receiving a substantial raise, she rewarded herself with a costly coat of Finnish raccoon. Says Laura,

> *Although I felt fantastic in my coat, and had received compliments from many of my friends and relatives, I knew after the first week that wearing it to work was a mistake, as the city where I live and the firm where I am employed are both very conservative. I am one of only two women in my department, and many of the men I work with seemed to look on a fur as something for suburban country club wives, not serious professionals. I also experienced resentment from some of my co-workers, who seemed to feel that I was "showing off," and I would often hear remarks like, "here comes the fur!"*
>
> *I was reluctant to get rid of that gorgeous coat, because not only did I feel terrific in it, it was the warmest thing I've ever owned, and believe me, winters in this city are bone-chilling . . . A friend suggested that I sell the raccoon and buy a reversible garment. I found a coat of this type, at a good price. It's a shell of silk poplin lined with sheared beaver. It's turned out to be a good investment. Not only do I feel more comfortable in the coat, but I actually have received compliments on it, not only from my co-workers, but from my superiors as well. I also find that it's very versatile—I can wear it to work with the poplin showing and, for social occasions, I can turn it inside out. I strongly advise any woman who works in a conservative, male-dominated field, such as manufacturing, to consider buying a coat like this instead of a traditional one with the fur outside. She'll probably find that's she's made a wise decision.*

Laura's words of wisdom may be advice well taken if you live in a conservative area of the country where fur garments are still considered suitable only for dressy occasions. But whether you live in Baltimore or Buffalo, it's a fact that in some areas of endeavor, fur garments, while not exactly frowned upon, are just not part of the corporate culture. Says one senior editor at a leading New York publishing house, commenting upon the lack of interest in fur garments by her

> **Fur Facts and Fancies:** *For the woman who has everything, The Fur Vault offers a genuine mink "Freddy Bear," named after the firm's flamboyant chairman. The bear even has a diamond belly button!*

co-workers: "Many people in this field seem intent on maintaining a 'grubby' or owlish appearance...fur just isn't part of the image they want to project."

Another instance where a woman might not want to wear a fur garment is to a job interview, particularly if it's for her first position. Comments one industry executive, "If a young woman is going to be interviewed for a legal position and she dresses in a mink coat, she'll never get beyond the first secretary." And a woman politician who wears a fur coat will probably not be taken very seriously.

All things considered, however, fur has earned its rightful place in the wardrobe of today's dynamic career woman. Whether your taste runs to a luxurious lynx, a classic mink, or a nutria-lined trenchcoat, there is a fur for your lifestyle, budget, and image.

## CLOSEUP
# THE LOOK OF LUXE

What is a luxe fur? More often than not, it is a fur that is so rare and exclusive that it is off limits to all but the wealthiest, most discerning customer. According to the American Fur Industry, "Like perfect pearls and old Orientals, the fewer there are, the more they're valued."

In a broader sense of the term, however, a luxe garment is one that incorporates these three ingredients: high-fashion styling, quality skins, and five-figure price tags. It can mean a jewel-embellished jacket or a classic, floor-length opera cape.

Beyond that, luxe dressing is an attitude, a way of life for the woman who has long since graduated from her basic "dumb" fur coat. A recent article in *Fur World* claims, "The modern, moneyed fur customer is younger, fur-savvy, and more inclined to make a statement by way of a chic, expensive fur garment...What women want now, say designers and furriers, are dynamic, strong furs which, by their very nature, make the woman feel and look moneyed."

Two designs by Carolina Herrera for Revillon: *above*, Natural Barguzin Russian sable three-quarter length coat; *right:* white mink dinner jacket.

## The Image-Makers

A whole new group of designers is meeting this special customer's need for special furs. One of these individuals is Neiman-Marcus's house designer, Jerry Sorbara. Sorbara, a master craftsman, says in regard to fit: "Fur has more body than fabric and therefore should be fitted even more precisely than a dress or suit." Although Sorbara has several collections, including Sorbara Sport, which appeals to the younger, more price-conscious consumer, he seems to be at his best when working with exclusive, expensive furs including mink, fisher, sable, and lynx. Comments Sorbara, "I generally like to put a coat together with pelts assembled from more than one auction over a period of time. That way, the woman who understands pricey fur realizes she's getting a collector's item and not just another coat. She's making a statement then and that becomes her way of individualized dressing."

Venezuelan-born socialite-turned-couturiere Carolina Herrera, who was recently named one of the world's ten most elegant women by *Elle* magazine, is another designer who caters to the carriage trade with her simply cut, low-key creations for Revillon. In both her daytime and evening fur collections, Ms. Herrera strives for a look of understated chic.

No discussion of fur trend-setters would be complete without mentioning Fendi of Rome. Since 1925, this Italian firm has been turning out furs known all over the world for their uniqueness and fashion flair. The five Fendi sisters—Franca, Paola, Carla, Alda, and Anna—are the third generation of Fendis to run a fashion empire that includes leather and ready-to-wear as well as furs. Best known for their avant-garde designs and use of luxe furs such as Russian ermine, they also have the knack of turning poor furs such as weasel, generally shunned by the North American industry, into high-fashion items with the innovative use of color and special layouts. One of their recent collections included batik-dyed squirrel coats.

## The Entrance-Makers

When thinking of exclusive, expensive furs, Russian sable immediately comes to mind. This luxurious fur has been highly coveted since the days of the czars, when it was the exclusive province of the royal family, hence the term crown or Imperial sable. The best variety of this fur comes from the Lake Baikal region of Siberia—a heavily wooded, sparsely populated area—and is called Barguzin sable.

Although sable is usually left natural, it is sometimes dyed. André and Lisa Bisang, a young Swiss couple who are making waves in the fashion world with their luxurious fur creations, have succeeded in bleaching this fur to a pale ivory white.

Sable is fuller and softer than mink and is amazingly lightweight. According to Evelyn Paswall of Martin Paswall Furs, Inc., a highly respected manufacturer of sable garments, a full-length, let-out coat of prime quality sable weighs only about five pounds.

Russian broadtail, another product of the Soviet Union, also falls into the luxe category. This elegant, silky fur has an intriguing moiré pattern and is so soft and supple that it is often cut and used like fine wool cloth. Designers such as Bob Mackie, John Anthony, and Bill Blass have taken advantage of its suppleness by tailoring it into elegant little cocktail suits and separates, including blazers and even halter tops.

Although not as rare and costly, another type of sheep, Persian lamb, is nearly as soft and drapeable as Russian broadtail. It is often made into suits and hats, leg-warmers, and other accessories as well as coats and jackets. One Italian firm even showed a wedding gown in natural white Swakara that was trimmed with beads and lace.

Pale, silky soft Russian ermine has been associated with royalty for centuries. Although this beautiful fur is rarely seen today, it is sometimes used in glamorous full-length coats as well as jackets and muffs, or paired with other white pelts, and with fabrics.

Chinchilla has traditionally been used for evening wear. Like ermine and sable, at one time it was a royal fur, its use restricted to members of the Inca nobility. Chinchilla is the oldest fur known to man, and in earlier times the pelts were cut into strips and woven into fabric. Like squirrel, it is extremely soft, and is often worked horizontally in capes and jackets.

Lynx, a truly glamorous fur, has increased in popularity in recent years. Although the Russian variety is considered the most desirable, the Canadian type is almost as pricey. Fragile lynx is a high-fashion fur whose appeal is mostly limited to the tall, slender woman, who is best able to carry off this long-haired fur.

Fisher is fur that appeals mainly to the rich, fashion-forward customer. According to the American Fur Industry, "Fisher is known for its superlative richness of color and silkiness of texture. Durable, warm, and totally luxurious, it's a fur that lends special drama of its own to even the most basic fashion silhouette." Because of its limited

Ranch mink evening jacket with gold, silver, and semi-precious stone detailing.

quantity, fisher is expensive, surpassing fine mink in price.

Then, of course, there's mink. Although this fur is certainly not in scarce supply, a mink coat of the very finest quality is a work of art. Because of its versatility, mink is often shaped and cut into unusual designs. From up-and-coming fur designer Adrienne Landau comes a cardigan jacket in dark sheared mink. The sleeves and hip band are trimmed with pavé diamonds, emeralds, and amethysts overlaid on fourteen-karat gold and sterling silver—yours for about $30,000.

For the woman who desires something special that expresses her own unique style, the luxe furs are ideal. But even if you can't afford a full-length sable or lynx, remember that a hat, scarf, or collar of any of these furs can give you that look of luxe without emptying your bank account.

# WEAR, REPAIR, AND CARE: MAINTAINING YOUR FUR

## SEVEN

It has been said that two sure signs of having made it are a Rolex watch and a mink coat. While the former is supposedly so well constructed that it will last a lifetime with little or no maintenance, a mink coat—or any other fur for that matter—needs some tender loving care to keep it in working order.

## NO MORE WIRE HANGERS, OR EVERYDAY CARE

How should a fur garment be cared for on a day to day basis? Here are some DOs:

---

■ DO store your garment in a closet where it will have plenty of room and enough space to allow air to circulate around it freely. Jamming the coat in an area where it will be crushed against other garments will cause the tips of the hairs to bend back; eventually they will break off.

■ DO hang your garment on a wide-shouldered, padded hanger. This will help distribute the weight of the garment on the hanger evenly and avoid putting stress on certain spots, primarily the shoulder area. Never use wire hangers; they may leave rust stains or indentations on the lining of the coat and probably aren't strong enough to support the garment anyway. In fact, wire hangers aren't really good for any clothing. Replace them with wood, padded, or even plastic ones when you can.

■ DO turn the collar of the coat *up* before hanging it. As fur-on-fur flattens the hairs, this is necessary to keep both the underside of the collar and the shoulders full, soft, and lustrous.

■ DO wear a scarf, muffler, or other neck accessory when wearing your fur, particularly if you have long hair. A scarf prevents oils from your hair and neck, as well as makeup, from getting on the collar.

■ DO touch your fur the way a furrier does—in the direction it grows. And be gentle! Rubbing fur briskly creates friction that will eventually cause the hairs to break off.


And now for some DON'Ts:

■ DON'T store the coat in a plastic bag! Fur is an organic, porous substance, which means that it has to "breathe." Plastic inhibits this process by cutting off air, which in turn dries out the leather and causes the fur to shed. You can purchase fabric garment protectors for your fur, or can even construct your own. An old terry-cloth bathrobe could be called into service to cover a full length coat; for a jacket, a man's shirt will do the trick nicely.

■ DON'T use perfume near a fur, as the chemicals in it cannot only damage the leather, but harm the hair. Colognes and toilet waters contain alcohol which can dry out the leather, while perfumes, which are more concentrated, are full of hard-to-remove oils. Apply perfume *before* putting on your fur, or better yet, dab some scent on a cotton ball and tuck it in your bosom.

■ DON'T smoke near your fur, or at least keep this to a minimum. Eventually the fur will pick up the scent of the smoke, which may be difficult to remove.

■ DON'T store your coat near a source of light or heat. Have you ever placed a pair of good leather gloves near the radiator? The result is similar to a piece of beef jerky. The same thing can happen to the leather of a fur garment if it is continuously exposed to heat or light. This is because the leather of the garment consists of three layers: the curl layer, which is closest to the fur, the sponge layer, and the back layer. What happens when leather dries out is that the top layer peels away from the middle layer, so that the leather cracks and splits.

However, if you must hang your coat near a strong light source (many women work in offices where dark, cool closets are at a premium!) try to cover it with an old sheet or cloth fabric protector.

■ DON'T brush or comb furs, particularly when they are wet. You may inadvertently pull the hairs out. This is particularly true with long-haired furs. When good-quality furs begin to look "tired," all they need is a good shaking. Not only will this fluff out the fur; it will remove any excess dirt or debris.

■ DON'T hang your fur on a hook, as this places undue stress on the garment. However, if this is unavoidable, have your furrier attach a chain to the coat.

■ DON'T wear heavy jewelry where it can rub against fur. This applies to rings, bracelets, and heavy chains. Put it on *after* your coat, or carry it in your purse until you reach your destination.

## OTHER PROBLEMS

### Oxidation

Despite the best of care, all furs will eventually change color, or oxidize. Dark furs will turn lighter, while pale furs will turn yellow. This is a natural process caused by the fur's exposure to light and air, much as bronze develops a greenish patina over time. An oxidized fur will have a yellowish or reddish tint. An oxidized fur can be recolored, but the oxidizing process itself cannot be reversed. Dyed furs will generally oxidize at a quicker rate than naturally colored furs.

Although oxidation cannot be entirely prevented, if the proper procedures for fur care are carefully followed, it should not prove to be a major problem.

## Insect Damage

Many women worry about insect damage to their furs, but if fur garments are stored during the summer months, when insect damage may occur, this should not be a major concern.

Commercial moth repellents should *never* be used on fur garments; they contain chemicals like paradichlorobenzene, which are not good for either you or your fur.

## Weather Damage

What should you do when you and your fur get caught in a rain or snowstorm? Furs from animals with long guard hairs, such as sable, natural beaver, and muskrat, you can simply shake the excess moisture from the coat. If the fur is thoroughly soaked, however, you may want to take it to your furrier. In the meantime, dab off [do not rub] excess moisture with a clean towel, and hang coat well away from direct heat.

## Safety Precautions

One question that frequently arises is what to do with one's fur while at a restaurant, the theater, or some other place where the garment will be out of sight for long periods of time. Many fur owners are understandably reluctant to leave an expensive fur coat in the care of a coat-check person, no matter how reliable he or she may be. One solution is to carefully drape your coat or jacket over an empty chair. (One wealthy woman even went so far as to reserve a first-class airline seat for her fur *and* her dog when traveling abroad.) Some women have started carrying leather or cloth tote bags to hold their coats while dining or at the theater.

Women in urban areas have expressed concern about the advisability of wearing their furs on the subway and in other public places. Fur is a symbol of affluence; they fear that it may make them a prime target for muggers and other street criminals. The rule of thumb here is to use your own judgment.

Women who work in offices should take precautions against hanging their furs in closets (or on doors) which are accessible to outsiders. If you own a costly fur, you might want to have it insured against theft.

In many cases you can have a rider added to your homeowner's policy—check with your insurance agent. Generally, this costs about $10.00 per every $1,000 of value; hence a $10,000 mink will cost approximately $100 a year to insure.

## WEARING YOUR FUR

Some furs are much more fragile than others, but whether you own a garment of sable or squirrel, you can increase its lifespan with a few simple precautions:

■ DO take off your coat when going on a long trip, and hang it up or drape it over the back of your seat. Continued exposure to surfaces such as car, plane, and bus seats will only cause the fur to wear away.

■ DO be careful with fur garments that have zippers, as many sports pieces do. If the fur should get caught in a zipper, work it free by gently tugging, *not* pulling. The same thing that happens to fine cloth when caught in a zipper can happen to fur!

■ DO open your coat when traveling. Reaching for straps on the bus or subway puts strain on the underarm seams of your garment; opening the coat reduces this strain. By opening the garment while driving, you will reduce strain on the back and shoulders of the coat.

Here's what *not* to do when wearing your fur garment:

■ DON'T pin jewelry or corsages to fur garments. Although you may have seen this done in high-fashion magazines, this puts holes in the leather, weakening it and making the coat more susceptible to tears.

■ DON'T wear a shoulder bag with a fur coat. The constant friction of the strap causes the fur to flatten and eventually wear away. However, as we all know, clutch-type purses are not always practical. If it is absolutely necessary for you to carry a purse with a strap, alternate shoulders, or try wearing the bag *under* your coat.

---

**Fur Facts and Fancies:** *In the mid-1800s, Victor Revillon designed and patented the first cold-storage facility for furs.*

---

# CLEANING AND STORAGE

## Cleaning

Furs should be cleaned once a year by a professional furrier. Due to the nature of fur, it is cleaned by abrasion, not by immersion (as cloth is).

How are furs cleaned? Basically, they are tumbled in a drum with sawdust that has been soaked in a specially formulated solution. The sawdust removes the dirt and oils which have accumulated in the fur. The garment is then glazed to bring out the fur's luster and sheen and to make it soft and fluffy.

Some furs may require additional procedures to rejuvenate them. For example, flat, curly furs such as Russian broadtail are pressed with a special type of waxed paper to give them added sheen.

You should *never* attempt to clean a fur garment at home, nor should you use any commercial dry cleaners or solvents on them. Even if you spill some strong substance on your fur, such as an alcoholic beverage, it's best to just dab, *not* rub, the excess moisture away, and leave the rest to your furrier.

## Storing Your Fur

Since fur garments, like wool, are susceptible to insect damage, it is necessary to have them stored in a climatically controlled storage vault during the insect season. Professional storage also protects your garment from heat damage. You should have your garment stored as soon as you stop wearing it which, in the Northeast, is usually in late March or April.

While some may argue that a cool, dark cedar closet will work just as well as a furrier's vault, this is simply not the case. Fur vaults are climatically controlled, with the temperature set at about forty degrees and a relative humidity factor between 45 and 55 percent. Storage usually costs between $30 and $50 per season, depending on where you live.

Furriers do not, as a rule, make much money from this service; fur storage is an expensive proposition for a variety of reasons. The construction of such a facility is costly, and once a fur is in the furrier's hands, he or she is responsible for any damage or loss that occurs through negligence, whether it be from moths or mildew. This is why fur vaults must be insured, and this insurance is granted only after a rigorous examination by a trained inspector. Although the majority of fur vaults are insured, some are not; make sure that the place where your garment is stored has this type of coverage.

Many furriers cannot afford to maintain their own vaults, so they rent space in huge fur-storage warehouses. This is why it might take several days to retrieve your fur once it is taken out of storage in the autumn. The average notification time is about three days.

What should you do when you cannot take your garment to a furrier? (Say you live somewhere in Booniesville County and the nearest furrier is 500 miles away, and can only be reached by seaplane.) While home storeage is *not* advised for any fur, if absolutely necessary, smaller pieces such as hats and gloves may be placed in the refrigerator (*not* a freezer)! Cover coats and jackets with some type of cloth, and then— cross your fingers and hope for the best!

## SPECIAL FURS NEED SPECIAL CARE

Some furs require a little more extra care than others. These include sheared furs, specialty furs that are embroidered, beaded, or otherwise embellished with nonfur; white or light-colored furs, frizzy furs, fur-trimmed pieces, and accessories.

Sheared furs have had their guard hairs plucked, and are then shaved to a uniform texture. This makes them susceptible to matting, particularly if they are worn often in heavy rain or snow. Give the garment a good shaking; if the problem persists, take the coat to the furrier.

As we've discovered, hand-painting, embroidery, and beading are becoming increasingly popular additions to many fur garments. A decorated fur can be cared for just like any other, except that it might have to be repaired more often—even the smallest loose bead should be taken care of by a professional. You should also be careful storing them in your closet; it is important that these fragile furs have their own cloth protectors.

White furs, such as white mink, fox, chinchilla, and ermine present some special problems. Everything that's been said about protecting furs from light goes doubly for garments in this category. Natural sunlight in particular adds an unattractive yellow tint to white furs and this can also happen with some light-colored furs. To remedy this, white furs can be bleached and pale furs brightened, although this will weaken the leather over time.

Mongolian and Tibetan lamb, both curly furs, tend to frizz when very wet. This is a problem that must once again be brought to the attention of a professional—never try to iron fur yourself.

Fur-trimmed garments should be treated like furs, and cleaned only by a furrier. This is also true of accessories, such as hats, boas, ponchos, etc. The cloth shell of a garment with a removable lining must be dry-cleaned, while the liner must be fur-cleaned.

## REPAIR AND REMODELING

### Repair

Even furs that are very well taken care of are subject to the snags and tears of outrageous, or even everyday, misfortune—three-year-olds tugging on sleeves, linings that are caught on rings, and despite our best intentions, hips and derrieres that spread. What do you do when your fur coat is in need of some major—or minor—surgery?

Remember that all tears and other minor damages should be taken care of by a furrier. Even if you or someone you know is handy with a needle, repairing fur garments is not like mending cloth coats. More often than not, repairs that are made from the outside are only temporary; to do a good job, the fur coat must be opened. Bring even the smallest damages to your furrier's attention as soon as possible; even tiny rips and tears in fur garments tend to grow.

Most furriers do minor repairs on the garments they sell as a courtesy. Major repairs, however, can be costly, particularly when part of the fur is worn away and a whole section has to be replaced.

### Remodeling

One fashion advantage of fur garments as opposed to those made of cloth is their adaptability. An older style can be updated, and a full-length coat can be made into a jacket, or even a stole, muff, or hat.

However, even a simple remodeling job is fairly complicated. In many cases, a new pattern must be constructed and fitted, which means that the old coat must be taken apart. The unusable fur must be discarded and the usable fur completely reworked to fit the new pattern. In many cases, new fur must be added to the garment—which, of course, has to be carefully matched with the original pelts.

If you would like to have your fur garment remodeled, you should seek the advice of a reputable furrier who handles this type of work. Here are some things you should take into account when considering a remodeling job:

***

A fur coat can be re-styled into a jacket.

■ *Age of the garment*. Although a good fur is still a good fur, regardless of how old it is, an older garment is a poorer candidate for remodeling than a newer one.

■ *Type of fur*. Generally, popularly priced furs, including rabbit, muskrat, etc., do not warrant remodeling, unless they are of very fine quality. Some expensive furs, such as chinchilla and Russian broad-tail, also do not lend themselves to remodeling because of their fragility.

■ *Lay-out*. Pieced furs are usually easier to remodel than let-out furs. In the case of the latter, each tiny seam holding the skins together, as well as some of the let-out strips themselves, must be reopened. In addition, even more cuts may have to be made, which is a time-consuming and complicated process, whereas, in pieced coats, the sections can often just be taken apart. Garments with unusual or highly complicated layouts are poor candidates for remodeling.

When deciding whether or not to have your fur garment remodeled, you must take into account the cost-utility factor—that is, the potential usefulness of the garment weighed against the cost of the remodel. A coat whose original cost was $8,000 may warrant a $1,500 remodel, while one whose original investment was $800 may not be worth the $200 it would take to remodel it. Once again, it's best to consult a furrier whose judgment you trust when it comes to remodeling.

One method of remodeling a fur garment is to lengthen it. This is usually accomplished by adding a border of matching fur. *Shortening* is a popular and relatively uncomplicated way of giving a coat a new look; the garment is merely cut to the desired length and the ends finished. The worn edges on many furs can be re-edged with matching fur or leather.

Another way to give a fur a new lease on life is to restyle the sleeves, collars, or other sections. Such remodels are usually not too expensive, but should only be attempted by a skilled craftsman.

### Fur-Lined Cloth Coats

One very practical way of recycling fur is to have it made into a fur-lined or reversible garment. David Goodman of Gus Goodman, Inc., offers this comment: "Many younger women will come to us with a fur that belonged to their mothers or grandmothers and will want it made into a fur-lined or reversible coat. Many times the customer has developed an attachment to the fur—she sees it as a kind of security blanket. Sometimes she'll even want us to save the monogram from the old coat and put it in her new one." This kind of remodeling job is usually complicated, and should only be attempted by a professional.

### Things to Keep in Mind

In conclusion, whether you want a collar replaced or your whole coat restyled, here are some things to consider when having a garment remodeled:

■ Choose the furrier who will remodel your coat with as much care as lavished on a new coat. If your furrier does not do remodeling (most of them do), ask him or her to recommend someone reliable. Word of mouth is the best advertising; ask a friend with a "born-again" fur where he or she had the job done.

■ Have in mind a rough idea of what you want done with your fur. Clippings from magazines and newspapers, or even rough sketches, might help.

■ Get a price estimate of the job. That way, you won't get any unpleasant surprises—or a heart attack—when the bill comes. If you feel that one firm's services are priced too high, do not hesitate to seek out another one. But remember that remodeling is a highly skilled task, and a good job cannot be done inexpensively.

■ No matter how good your fur looks after it has been restyled, don't forget that it is still an older fur. Says Edythe Cudlipp, "Remember, if you do have a coat remodeled, you are not getting a new coat . . . remodeling is like a face lift. Although the fur, like you, looks better and younger, nothing can actually make either one of you younger. If the fur is eight years old, it's still eight years old after remodeling. You'll get a lot more wear out of the fur, yet not the same wear you would with an entirely new fur coat."

The following chart lists some things you should know about the care, repair, and remodeling of fur garments. However, it must be stressed that nothing can take the place of an experienced and knowledgeable craftsman—if you don't know furs, know your furrier!

## CARE, REPAIR, AND REMODELING OF FUR GARMENTS*

| Name | Care | Repairability | Remodeling |
|------|------|---------------|------------|
| Antelope | Normal; edges wear quickly | Not advised, except for re-edging involving no additional fur | Not advised |
| Badger | Strong fur; normal care and cleaning | Cannot be patched; matching added fur is almost impossible | In trimming, slight changes are possible, if similar pattern; in garment form, not advised |

*Chart adapted from *World of Furs* by David E. Kaplan.

| Name | Care | Repairability | Remodeling |
|------|------|---------------|------------|
| Baronduki | Occasional wear only | Edges only, if not badly worn; advise covering with suitable edge binding rather than attempt to repair poor edges | Not advised |
| Bassarisk | Not for everyday wear, especially if dyed; if plucked, do not allow hair to become matted | Not particularly difficult, so long as only edges are involved | Not advised |
| Beaver | Has tendency to mat; requires annual treatment to separate and fluff out fiber (called electrifying) | Usually good; easier on dyed than on natural sheared | When let out, remodeling involves stripes, etc., and therefore is costly |
| Calf | Hair stiff, will break if subjected to abrasion; not an everyday fur | Edges, if slightly worn; otherwise, bind with suitable edging | Not warranted because of cost-utility ratio |
| Cat, spotted | Normal | Fair | Only if fur and leather are fairly new and change is limited; strong pattern is a drawback |
| Chinchilla | Obviously for occasional wear; do not allow to become matted | Edges repairable if condition of fur and leather is good enough; fine, weak, remodeled garment should be stayed | Warranted if condition of fur and leather is good enough; fine, weak, remodeled garment should be hand-stayed |

| Name | Care | Repairability | Remodeling |
|---|---|---|---|
| Coyote | Normal | Fair | If in garment form, may be warranted |
| Ermine | Keep white ermine out of sunlight, preferably in dark place when not using | Fair; avoid attempting to replace for matching—material not easily available | Cost of fur warrants reuse if leather and fur are in good condition; should be reinforced (*Note:* Reblending or rebleaching will weaken leather and stitching) |
| Fisher | Normal; strong fur | Some re-edging possible | Throat coloration, plus neck and shoulder formation, limits remodeling in order to leave this area unchanged; pattern must be selected with care |
| Fitch | Normal; must be cleaned regularly to conserve whiteness; Garments more than five years old may need slight bleaching | Edging possible; sharp color variants prevent patching | Warranted when fashionable, but color and horizontal layouts limit pattern changes to length of skin |
| Goat, mountain | Normal for long-hairs | Fair | Fair, but usually not warranted in this inexpensive fur |

## *The Fox Family*

As most members of the fox family are long-haired, they will shed when you first get them. In good-quality coats, this should level off after twelve months. Regular cleaning is important. If your fox should become matted, *do not* attempt to untangle it with a comb or brush—leave this to a professional.

| Name | Care | Repairability | Remodeling |
|------|------|---------------|------------|
| Blue fox | Keep fur fluffy by regular cleaning | Fair; edges wear if fur is matted, as with most foxes | Slight changes only; coloration and size, also possible leathering inserts limit changes; never on old pieces |
| Corsac Fox: See *Kitt Fox* | | | |
| Cross fox | Normal fox care | Normal for foxes | Coloration a drawback |
| Gray fox | Normal fox care | Normal for foxes | Not advised, except especially fine pieces |
| Kitt fox | Normal for foxes | Fair | Probably not warranted |
| Mutation fox | Normal for foxes | Normal for foxes; material for patching may be difficult to obtain | Strong coloration of some exotics may be a drawback |
| Platina fox | Normal for foxes | Fair | Not too difficult to rework if leather is in good condition; an expensive fur that usually warrants remodeling |
| Red fox | Will not stand much friction; keep fur fluffy | Fair; edges can be reworked and some patching possible | Possible with conservative changes; not too practical for radical styling, either block or let-out |
| Silver fox | Normal for foxes | Fair when new | Full silver not too difficult to rework if leather is in good condition; depends on price structure |

| Name | Care | Repairability | Remodeling |
|---|---|---|---|
| White fox | Susceptible to rubbing wear; clean and fluff out | Good | Good—monotone color lends itself to manipulation |
| Kidskin | Not for daily wear; avoid friction | Required often; edges can be cut down | Questionable in view of cost versus potential use; multicolored types difficult to handle in remodel |
| Kolinsky | Normal; needs to be kept fluffy | Fair; will take re-edging | Difficult to secure added material if needed |

## The Lamb Family

| Name | Care | Repairability | Remodeling |
|---|---|---|---|
| Broadtail, American (processed) | A fragile fur—not for everyday wear | Fair | Good |
| Broadtail, Persian or Russian | A fragile fur—not for everyday wear | Fair | Fair; soft leather makes extensive restyling costly |
| Kalgan lamb | Normal | Fair | Usually not warranted on this inexpensive fur |
| Mongolian Lamb | Normal. Fur tends to "frizz" in very wet or humid weather | Fair | Usually not warranted |
| Mouton | Normal | Poor re-edges and repairs will show seams | Not difficult, but cost may not warrant expense of remodeling unless fur is in excellent condition and is made into a small garment |

| Name | Care | Repairability | Remodeling |
|------|------|--------------|------------|
| Persian lamb (caracul) | Normal | Best of all furs | Additional material easily added and areas can be removed without difficulty; only when fur starts to peel is it too old for remodeling |
| Shearling | Fur may mat | Poor re-edges and repairs will show seams | Probably not warranted |
| Tibetan lamb: see *Mongolian lamb* | | | |
| Lynx (all varieties) | Requires care to prevent loosening of hair; Russian lynx sheds the least of all the long-haired furs | Fair if no material is needed | Can be shortened or reworked as a trimming, within limits; otherwise strong coloration pattern is drawback |
| Marmot | Subject to hair breakage due to friction | Fair; if in dyed and striped form, problems similar to real let-out garments | Leather has tendency to soften as it ages; in general, radical, expensive remodeling not warranted |
| Marten, American | Fair | Needs to be kept unmatted and fluffy | Usually in let-out form, in which case has usual drawbacks; remodel costs warranted because of value of fur |
| Marten, baum | Same as American marten | Worn sections can be cut away on large garments needing re-edging | Same as American marten |

| Name | Care | Repairability | Remodeling |
|------|------|---------------|------------|
| Marten, stone | Avoid matting; clean when flat matted hair areas show | Edges repairable on garments | White patching at throat limits flexibility of change through this area, otherwise presents same problems as do all let-out garments; warranted if fur and leather is in good condition |
| Mink | Requires normal care; should not be subject to friction of metal bracelets, etc; regular cleaning will prolong life and looks | Excellent; edges and worn spots can be repaired, but pieced minks sometimes more difficult, especially if boldly patterned | Mink garments can be remodeled to any reasonable change, if fur and leather is in good condition (leather often dries up and disintegrates when wet if too old; fur can be added, color restored by blending; good remodel is expensive |
| Mole | Not for daily wear; avoid excess friction | Poor; best to remove skin if replaceable, but not always possible; edge repair limited because of short hair | Questionable unless almost new. Leather not strong, has tendency to dry out |
| Muskrat | Leather has tendency to dry up with age and disintegrate when dampened; therefore, proper storage is very important | Excellent; will accept edging well and patching not too difficult if material available | Bold patterns require careful handling; avoid expensive remodels on older fur |

| Name | Care | Repairability | Remodeling |
|------|------|---------------|------------|
| Nutria | Sheared types mat easily and require attention (unplucked form needs less care); storing is important | Excellent in both forms | Leather is spongy and has tendency to weaken with age, as with muskrat; fine nutria can be remodeled with care if in good condition |
| Opossum | Australian types mat easily and have tendency to develop wave which requires periodic attention | Normal | Not warranted on worn American, New Zealand, or Tasmanian types; acceptable on Australian if in excellent condition |
| Otter | Minimal, a strong fur | Excellent, except for very flat sheared varieties | No patching possible, as with Alaska fur seal |
| Pahmi | Plucked forms may mat and rub; requires regular care | Good | Limited by cost— avoid elaborate remodel |
| Pony | Vulnerable to hair breakage due to friction if rubbed against hair flow | Poor, especially if edges are worn; binding advised rather than cut-away repair | Pattern of skin may be deterrent; addition of material will make job too costly |
| Rabbit | Some natural, poorer skins wear away at edges after one full season of wear while others last three to five years; normal care required | Excellent; can be re-edged easily in most cases | Only salient factor is cost versus use after remodel; usually not warranted, except for fine sheared skins, because of high labor costs |

| Name | Care | Repairability | Remodeling |
|------|------|---------------|------------|
| Raccoon, American | In sheared form, will mat; needs periodic ironing to restore fluff | Excellent; accepts re-edging well on all phases | Excellent on long-haired types if not let out; sheared and let-out types more difficult; leather is weaker if skin has been bleached |
| Raccoon, Finnish | Normal | Same as American | Good; strong coloration may be a drawback |
| Sable | Needs blowing out to keep from matting | Excellent; edges repair well | Always worthwhile if fur and leather is in good condition; can be reblended if color has faded |
| Seal, Alaskan fur | Normal. A strong fur | Excellent; can be re-edged and repaired | Traditional difficulty with remodels that may involve adding width across shoulders or through top front; skins cannot be patched or stretched in any prominent areas, but fur amenable to reworking otherwise; color can be redone |
| Seal, hair | Most hair seals have stiff hair, prone to wear; daily wear not advised; normal care | Fair; edging limited by prominence of pattern; dyed types easier to repair | Limitations of skin design and size to . new pattern prevent radical style changes without adding full skins; matches difficult—may not be warranted with average worn coat |

| Name | Care | Repairability | Remodeling |
|---|---|---|---|
| Skunk | Normal; fur develops slight musty smell when wet that disappears when dry and may be objectionable | Excellent; can be re-edged without any trouble | Rare problem these days, as let-out garments are usually not made; not too difficult on full-skin garments with pattern; cost versus utility must be compared |
| Squirrel | Because of extreme softness, fiber will wear if it becomes matted—must be kept fluffy to prevent wear at fiber base from friction | Edges and fur in general not difficult to repair | Easy to reshape because of the elasticity of the leather and not too difficult to add fur if needed; only best natural grades warrant remodel |
| Suslik | Not durable, must be worn accordingly | Fair | Probably inadvisable except if labor cost is minimal |
| Tanuki | See *Raccoon*, Finnish | | |
| Weasel (China mink) | Probably not useful for daily wear; normal attention required | Fair | Probably not advisable, except for fine grades of skin |
| Wolverine | Normal | Excellent; re-edges well | Warranted if in garment form; fur durable and can be worn a long time |

# ARLETTE SMOLARSKI, FUR CRAFTSWOMAN

Although fur garments are versatile enough to be restyled in a number of ways, a ho-hum fur coat will become a run-of-the-mill jacket in the hands of an uninspired furrier. The woman who desires to turn an old "dumb" fur into something a little bit different should seek out a furrier who is an artist as much as a craftsperson. One such individual is New York's Arlette Smolarski.

Ms. Smolarski, who originally began as a manufacturer of inexpensive fur garments, has been remodeling fur garments since 1979. From her loft in the heart of the city's wholesale flower district, Ms. Smolarski, a native of Paris, creates one-of-a-kind designs for her customers, most of whom come to her by word of mouth. Her work has been featured in such publications as *The New York Times* and *New York* magazine.

A "furrier by family tradition, but also an experimental artist by school training," Ms. Smolarski works exclusively on a one-to-one basis with her clients. Says the dark, intense, thirtyish Frenchwoman, "My clients come to see me by appointment. I then suggest possibilities to the customer based on the size and age of her coat and decide with her on a style most suitable to her personality." She then creates a prototype in canvas, which is fitted to the customer. "At the time of the fitting," she adds, "I work out the final touches which I find most important, such as buttons, linings, and trimmings." Each job takes from two to three weeks and costs anywhere from $300 to $2,000.

Ms. Smolarski uses a variety of techniques and materials to create her originals, which are mostly hand-sewn. Hand-painting, textiles, leather, and even lace are combined with fur. For example, a mink coat was turned into a roomy poncho with panels of flowered chintz and panne velvet in dusty rose. Another mink was made into a coat lined with Belgian linen painted with multicolored tulips, which Ms. Smolarski states, "took away the seriousness of mink."

Ms. Smolarski travels extensively, and in 1983 she took a long trip through Japan, Thailand, the People's Republic of China, and a number of other Asian countries. She comments, "I closely observed the traditional culture of the countries and how it is reflected in their clothes." Oriental influences can be seen in a number of her designs, including a coat of Mongolian lamb which reverses to rough canvas boldly painted with black I Ching characters, a traditionally styled Chinese jacket lined in raccoon, and even a mink kimono with sleeves that can be zipped off.

Ms. Smolarski advises against remodeling inexpensive furs such as rabbit. Muskrat is a particularly poor candidate for restyling, as the skins tend to dry out. Which fur is the easiest to work with? "Mink," she replies promptly. "Sable also lends itself well to remodeling, but it is so expensive that many people are afraid to work with it!"

# PREVIOUSLY OWNED FURS

## EIGHT

There comes a time in every woman's fashion life when she feels the need for more than one fur. Like a famous brand of potato chips, it's hard to stop with just one! What does the savvy shopper do when her spirit is willing but her checkbook is not? The answer may be to buy a pre-owned fur.

Several decades ago, purchasing used furs was frowned upon, but like many such dictates—such as not mixing silver and gold jewelry, or wearing white in winter—this rule has fallen by the wayside.

Although incredible bargains can be had by purchasing used furs, the woman who shops in secondhand fur stores is not always a budget watcher. Many who prefer to buy older furs could well afford to purchase them brand new. Increasingly the used-fur customer is more value-conscious than price-conscious; she is an intelligent, well-informed consumer who realizes that she can get more for her fashion dollar by purchasing an older garment. A used coat in good condition is an excellent way to fill any gaps you might have in your fur wardrobe; for example, the career woman who owns a sporty coyote coat might want to purchase a dressy mink jacket for evening wear at less then the price

A fur style from the 1940s.

of a new garment. Buying a used fur also allows you to change fur coats more often than if you were purchasing a new coat. Whatever your reason for going the secondhand route, however, you'll want to select your used coat with as much care as a new one.

There are a number of good sources for used coats, including auctions and private sales; however, probably the best bet is a secondhand store that specializes in such apparel, as most furriers do not handle older garments. Secondhand fur establishments range from holes in the wall that should pay *you* for buying their merchandise to quality establishments with national reputations. An example of the latter kind of store is New York's Ritz Thrift Shop, which has been in business for over fifty years.

## PUTTIN' ON THE RITZ

The Ritz Thrift Shop, with its thick carpets, crystal chandeliers, and triple mirrors, has the aura of an expensive first-sale salon, rather than a secondhand fur store. On the same block as such well-known spots as the Russian Tea Room and Carnegie Hall, the Ritz has five thousand square feet of selling space and stocks a wide variety of garments ranging from mink and fox to the occasional sable, as well as a few more unusual coats, such as skunk. Most of their garments are culled from leading furriers and department stores who usually have accepted trade-ins on new garments; the rest come from well-heeled customers, many of whom buy fur garments as often as the rest of us purchase new shoes. Says Michael Kosof, whose grandparents started the original Ritz Thrift Shop, "Many of the better-quality secondhand furs in the country find their way to us, directly or indirectly—if we turn it down, it goes elsewhere." In 1984, the store rang up sales of $5 million.

If you were to enter the Ritz or a similar shop, you would be ushered to a private sales area, where a knowledgeable clerk would bring out a variety of fur coats, according to your specifications as to type of fur, price, length, and style. One of the first things you would notice on the coat is the tag, which is required by the Federal Fur Products Labeling Act of 1952. This tag must clearly state that the fur is secondhand, or used, and the type of fur—whether it be sable or squirrel—must be indicated. The tag should also say whether the coat is made of full or partial skins, if it is pieced, and if it has been dyed or is naturally colored. One thing that will not be indicated on the tag on a used fur garment is the country of origin; in the majority of cases, the shop selling the garment has no way of knowing this.

What should you expect to pay for a used fur? The price varies, depending on the quality, condition, and age of the coat. At the Ritz, the average coat is $1,800 and from two to three years old. Says Keith Tauber, manager of the store for over fifteen years, "Generally, we try to sell furs for about one third or less of the original retail price." This means that a fur that originally sold for $15,000 will be about $5,000 at the Ritz, although greater savings are not uncommon. Mr. Tauber cites a designer coat of baum marten, sold for $7,000 which when new "probably sold for more than $35,000."

## WHAT TO KEEP IN MIND

Buying used furs requires a bit of caution, as what you see isn't necessarily what you get—at least on the surface. While an older fur may look presentable on the outside, closer examination could reveal broken guard hairs and dried-out leather. Most reputable secondhand dealers, however, will not knowingly sell you a coat that is in poor condition. Says Keith Tauber, who is married to one of Kosof's nieces, "We look for coats that are guaranteeable, that meet more than minimum standards of quality. As we get most of our customers by word of mouth, a satisfied customer is our best advertisement."

What should you look for—and avoid—when buying an older fur? Here are a few pointers:

■ Check for bald spots, rips, and tears. This is particularly important in areas that receive a great deal of stress, such as the shoulders, elbows, pockets, underarms, and collar. Although most secondhand fur shops—including the Ritz—do repair damage of this type as a matter of course, extremely worn areas can only be fixed by actually replacing the skins; this may or may not be warranted, depending on the type and value of the fur. A sable, mink, or fisher, for example, might warrant repair, while a rabbit, opossum, or muskrat might not.

If you discover that the fur has already been repaired, the coat is probably not a good investment.

■ Check under the lining for brittle undersides. The leather should always feel soft and supple and bend easily in the hand without making a crackling sound.

■ Look at the guard hairs. They should not be broken off or bent; this is especially important in long-haired furs such as fox. Sheared furs should feel soft and even.

■ Take a critical look at the fur in good light. If the fur has a reddish or yellowish tint, it means it has oxidized.

■ As with a new fur, make sure the furrier stands by the garment. At the Ritz, this means replacing a fastener or fixing a minor tear free of charge, as well as offering complimentary summer storage.

■ Before making a final purchase, do some comparison shopping. You should have a good idea of how the fur you want compares with not only other pre-owned furs, but new garments as well.

---

**Fur Facts and Fancies:** *A coat of* kojah—*a hybrid of mink and sable—was bought in 1970 by Richard Burton for Elizabeth Taylor for $125,000.*

---

Mr. Kosof also recommends that the potential buyer think of fur in the same manner she does a head of human hair. Does it look soft and lustrous, with no split or broken ends? Is it something that she would want to touch?

It is also recommended that you shop with a friend whose judgment you trust. Comments Mr. Kosof: "In many cases, a friend has a more objective view of what suits the customer than she does herself. It's often a good idea to shop for furs for awhile, then go out and discuss your options over a cup of coffee, and then, come back to make a final decision." Apparently, this advice has been well-heeded: Mr. Tauber cites statistics stating that one of every 2.9 women who come to the store eventually leaves with a purchase.

## OTHER OPTIONS

Suppose, for one reason or another, you are not too keen about purchasing a fur garment from a secondhand shop. There are several other choices you have.

### One-to-One Transactions

Buying a coat from a private individual can be a good—or bad—experience, depending on the circumstances. Since most people know precious little about furs, it is very difficult to discern whether a coat that is being sold for $5,000 is actually worth that much, or a fraction of the price. Add to this the uncertainty of dealing with strangers and you have a less than ideal situation.

It's advisable to buy a coat from someone that you know, or at the very least, a person who you are acquainted with. If the fur in question is a costly one, you might want to get the opinion of an expert to determine exactly how much the fur is worth. Although many may balk at this, buying a fur garment is an investment—would you purchase a $4,000 used car without first giving it a test drive?

### Selling Your Fur

Now let's look at used furs from a different perspective—that of the seller. How would you go about finding a buyer for your fur?

Perhaps the safest route is to sell your garment to a secondhand dealer or store. There is a huge market for such furs, not only in Canada and the United States but in Europe and South America as well. Once again, the reputation of the individual or firm you are dealing with is very important.

How much can you expect to get for your fur garment? As a rule of thumb, you will most likely be offered a price anywhere from 15 to 30 percent of the original retail value. Although this figure may seem very low, remember that whether you have a $100,000 sable coat or a $500 rabbit jacket, the moment you walk out of the furrier's with it, it begins to depreciate: by the second year alone, the garment's value has decreased by about 50 percent. Fur garments depreciate rapidly during the first two to three years; after that, they tend to level off.

You must also keep in mind the fact that the secondhand dealer or shop has to make a profit on the transaction, too. As used-fur dealers generally try to sell a fur for about one third of the retail price, they are not in the position to offer you a large amount for the garment. Let's see why this is so.

Say you have a good quality mink coat which is several years old and was bought for $9,000. The secondhand dealer wants to sell the coat for $3,000 in his shop, but also wants to make a profit of about twice the price he paid for the garment—standard in retailing. Therefore, he must purchase the coat for considerably less than $3,000, and offers you $1,500—a little more than 17 percent of the original value of the garment. This allows him to make a profit of $1,500 on the coat.

If you are hesitant about selling your garment to a secondhand dealer, there are several other options you might want to explore, the first of which is to find a customer among your friends and acquaintances. You can also advertise, but as we've already seen, this presents certain problems, including dealing with strangers.

You also might want to give the garment to charity. Although this avenue does not present an immediate cash return, you will be eligible for a tax deduction that can be fairly sizable, depending on the value of the coat.

Fur coats are also sold at auction, but this route is open only to those with garments of exceptional quality, including antiques.

## VINTAGE FURS

What's the difference between a vintage or antique coat and a plain old used fur?

According to Harriet Love, a nationally known expert on antique clothing and the author of *Harriet Love's Guide to Vintage Chic:* "The term 'vintage' can mean a variety of things, but generally, I use it to describe a garment that is in good condition, and shows exceptional styling and workmanship."

---

> **Fur Facts and Fancies:** *In Great Britain, the famous dome-shaped hats worn by the unsmiling Brigade of Guards are still made of black bearskin. The Guards apparently "still regard their headgear as having been taken from the French as a victor's right after Waterloo, in which the 18th Grenadiers took part."*

She adds, "Good-quality antique furs are harder and harder to come by these days. Many women who own such furs and might have once considered selling them are coming to realize how valuable they are, and are holding on to them. There are, however, a few bargains to be had—mostly in smaller pieces." She recommends that the vintage fur buyer look for boas of sable, mink, and other fine furs, which look terrific with a tailored suit or a winter coat.

Vintage furs can be found in a variety of places, from auctions to antique clothing shops to flea markets and garage sales. The latter two sources, however, are risky, as purchases usually cannot be returned and are strictly cash and carry. With any garment that is not purchased from a shop that deals strictly with fur, remember that you will probably have to pay extra for storage and repair; these services are usually offered free of charge at most secondhand fur stores.

When buying vintage furs, Harriet Love recommends that you keep in mind the *CPW* (cost per wearing) of the garment, which simply means that you should weigh the cost of the coat or jacket against its condition and the number of wearings you expect to get out of it. For example, a ten-year-old fox jacket in good condition, on sale for $350, may be worth a good two years of wear; it is probably a good investment. On the other hand, a ten-year-old mink that costs $1,500 and needs $1,000 worth of repairs to make it wearable is probably not a good deal.

Here are some other things to keep in mind when purchasing vintage furs:

■ Mink is probably the best all-around buy when it comes to older furs, as it is durable, attractive, and long-wearing.

■ Fox is also a good buy, but is a little harder to find. It is also important to check for rips and tears—these are harder to see on a long-haired garment.

■ Other good, long-wearing furs include nutria, sable (if you can find it), Persian lamb, and Alaska fur seal.

As a general rule of thumb, Ms. Love advises against buying furs from the twenties and thirties, as "they are just *too* old." Her assistant, Kevin Kiely, adds that he once saw a huge bearskin coat from the twenties for sale. It looked presentable from a distance, but upon closer examination, the sleeve fell off! Some coats from the forties and fifties, however, can be good buys.

Here are some furs to *avoid* when looking for vintage garments:

■ Muskrat. Very popular in the thirties and forties, "the poor woman's mink" was often dyed to resemble the wild version of this fur, which can fool some inexperienced buyers. Muskrat tends to dry out and will fall apart if it has not been stored properly.

■ Rabbit. In plentiful supply, these also tend to fall apart quickly. Some coats from the forties and fifties were stenciled to resemble leopard, ocelot, tiger, etc. Many who think they have an authentic big cat coat actually have a lowly lapin.

■ Monkey and mole. Monkey was very popular in the thirties and forties for short "chubby" coats and jackets; mole was often used to trim the cuffs and collars of cloth coats, and later on was used in full-length garments. Both furs are porous and fragile even when new.


## GARMENTS FROM ENDANGERED SPECIES

In 1973 the Endangered Species Act was passed, which was designed to protect certain species of wildlife from extinction. Species covered include everything from exotic plants to fish and birds. Of particular concern, however, was the dwindling population of spotted big cats such as ocelot, leopard, and cheetah, which had been nearly annihilated by the demand for their beautiful pelts.

The Endangered Species Act forbids the export, import, or "sale or offer for sale in interstate or foreign commerce" of all products made from the hides of these animals—*unless* a special permit has been obtained from the U.S. Fish and Wildlife Service, and these are almost always given for reasons of "scientific study," *not* commercial activities. In addition, if you try to bring a coat from an endangered species into the country, it will be confiscated, and you might also be fined.*

As big cat coats were very popular from the thirties to the early sixties, there are still a substantial number of them available. This means that if you feel you must have a coat from an endangered species, you will probably be able to purchase one "under the table," although this is definitely not recommended. No reputable secondhand fur dealer will sell you one, and although it is unlikely that a U.S. customs agent will chase you down the street in an attempt to confiscate your garment, popular opinion against furs of this type is so strong that after one wearing, you will probably have received so many unfriendly glances and negative comments that you will never want to see the coat again.

In conclusion, previously owned furs—whether it be a "fun fur" from the 1970s or a boa from the 1950s—are a practical and inexpensive way to add to your fur wardrobe.

## ▊CLOSEUP
# THE COSTUME INSTITUTE: A WALK THROUGH FASHION HISTORY

For the student of fashion history, perhaps no facility offers better opportunities for research than The Costume Institute of the Metropolitan Museum of Art in New York City.

Originally implemented in 1937, the Costume Institute became a part of the Metropolitan Museum of Art in 1946. In the early seventies, it came under the directorship of fashion doyenne Diana Vreeland. Vreeland, the former editor of *Vogue*, is credited with transforming the Institute from a rather stuffy and little-known part of the museum into a major attraction whose special exhibits, all centered around a specific era in costume history—e.g., "The Eighteenth Century Woman," "Man and the Horse" (underwritten by Polo/Ralph Lauren), and more recently, "The Courtly Costumes of India"—have been enthusiastically received by both the press and the public.

*For more information about what can and cannot be brought into the U.S. from abroad, including wildlife products, write for the free booklet, *Customs Hints for Returning U.S. Residents—Know Before You Go*. It's available from the U.S. Customs Service, P.O. Box 7118, Washington, D.C., 20044.

The Institute is also a research facility for students of costume design. It accomplishes this through a unique system of "live storage," where 50,000 costumes spanning five continents and three centuries are as "easily accessible as a book in a library."

Special care is given to the costumes, many of which are irreplaceable. The pieces are hung in specially designed modular units made of "chemically inert" materials. Each compartment is covered by Venetian blinds, which allow air to circulate but protects the costumes from light, which is very harmful to older clothing. Accessories and other small pieces are stored in special acid-free tissue paper. Humidity and temperature levels are carefully controlled, and the air is 95 percent dust-free.

Anyone with a serious interest in fashion history can arrange to study the costumes and accessories that are of particular interest to them free of charge, from the design student who is researching different types of seam finishes to the romantic novelist who wants to add a note of authenticity to her description of Regency costumes. However, as general tours of the Costume Institute's facilities are not given, it is important that the individual have a good idea of what he or she wants to see.

One of the criteria for inclusion in the collection is that the garment be "a work of art," which automatically rules out most of the clothing that 98 percent of us wear. This also means that the everyday garb of ordinary folk is barely represented (an acquisition of the year 2075, for example, might include a Galanos gown, but not a pair of Calvin Klein jeans)!

## Furs of Yesteryear

Although the Institute has no fur collection *per se*, it does include many fur accessories and fur-trimmed pieces, as well as some full-length garments. One of the pieces, a coat of wild Russian mink from 1913, shows surprisingly contemporary styling. Moving forward a little in time, one of the famous men's raccoon coats of the 1920s—with its original wool lining and Abraham and Strauss label still intact—reveals how bulky these garments were. Another piece from the twenties, a black silk evening coat trimmed with monkey, illustrates the fickleness of fashion, as this fur is very rarely used today.

Mink began to come into its own in the 1940s, and an example from this period is a coat of let-out white mink with a scalloped hem. The garment is trimmed with an oversized collar and cuffs in white fox.

The collection also includes a wide variety of fur accessories, some of which are more than one hundred years old. These include an ermine cape and a stole of chinchilla, both from the turn of the century. A hood dating back to 1895 is made of dark mink and trimmed with a big velvet ribbon and artificial flowers. Lined with white rabbit, this charming piece made a cozy addition to a sledding costume of the Belle Epoque.

In addition to the many items of "Western Urban Dress" described above, the Institute also has a vast collection of "Regional Traditional" garments, many of which incorporate fur. Perhaps one of the most beautiful pieces in this era is a kimono of royal blue silk which is more than 150 years old. The robe is embroidered in a palette of jewel-tone colors with traditional dragon and peony motifs, and is lined from cuffs to hem with silky white fur.

A visit to The Costume Institute is more than a walk through history—it is an excursion for the imagination that enables one to eavesdrop on the powerful but silent language of clothes. Every garment has a tale to tell, from the scruffiest pair of sneakers to the most opulent ball gown, but the words are locked forever in the silent folds of the clothing, and the inventive observer can only wonder at their secrets.

# THE ACCESSORY STORY

## NINE

One of the most marvelous things about fur garments is their adaptability. With the right choice of accessories, your fur can go from a football stadium to a Broadway premier with equal finesse—something your old wraparound wool melton duffel coat just can't do.

There are an infinite number of ways to accessorize your fur, ranging from opulent fur on fur effects to casual knockabout looks. In this chapter you'll discover some ways to accessorize your fur for a custom look.

## THE LITTLE FURS

A little fur can mean anything from a fur hat to a toasty muff. This category also includes stoles, vests, capes, capelets, ponchos, and parkas, which can cost a few hundred or a few thousand dollars. Little furs can range from simple rabbit-skin capes to elaborate haute couture designs incorporating such materials as suede, leather, and even precious stones. Why the upsurge in their popularity?

According to a recent article in *Fur World*: "The chief reason is the resurgence of glamour, élan, and the generally positive way women are viewing themselves in society." Designers such as Lenore Marshall are busy creating luxe accessories, some of which cost nearly as much as full-length fur coats.

Fur accessories have been around for many, many years. Remember the muffs and tippets that were the mainstay of women's and men's fashions for centuries? When thinking of fur accessories, many picture enormous, fluffy hats á la Anna Karenina and long stoles worn by wealthy matrons with blue-tinted hair.

Not only can they add extra panache to a fur garment, they can give a tired cloth coat a whole new lease on life. Here are some of the possibilities:

*Shawls and Other Pieces.* Fur capes, shawls, and similar little furs are very adaptable—they can be worn over full furs, with cloth coats, and in warmer climates, can even be worn by themselves. They can be

Accessories can add dash and drama
to your wardrobe.

paired with evening clothing for grand entrances, and also blend with
casual attire. Shawls may be made entirely of fur and trimmed with
tails, or can be made of cloth and trimmed with fur.

*Fur Hats.* This category runs the gamut from perky mink berets to
sophisticated sable turbans, dramatic cuff hats of fox, and head cover-
ings combining luxe fabric with fur. A fur hat can add an elegant finishing touch to any ensemble, as well as making a definite fashion
statement. There's another very good reason for wearing a fur hat: over
half the body's heat escapes from the neck and head area, so they are
practical as well as warm.

When choosing a fur hat, you should keep in mind your proportions.
A small woman, for example, might be overwhelmed by a huge, bushy
hat, while a neat beret or cloche might do nicely.

You should also keep in mind the style of your fur garment. Your
accessories should fit in with the general style of your fur. For example,
a fluffy cuff hat and matching barrel muff would probably not work
with a waist-skimming bomber jacket, while a pair of fur earmuffs

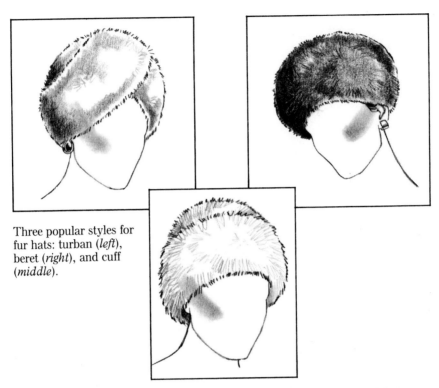

Three popular styles for
fur hats: turban (*left*),
beret (*right*), and cuff
(*middle*).

might look somewhat odd with a dramatic (and expensive) sable greatcoat. Earmuffs, however, are an option when a more casual, fun look is
desired, and can range from about $10 or so for rabbit to $200 for
sable.

*Fur Scarves*: One dramatic way of keeping warm that looks terrific
with furs and with a variety of other garments as well is a fur scarf.
When thinking of fur scarves, you may remember those rather creepy,
long things with their heads and claws still attached, sometimes with
beady little glass balls inserted where the eyes once were. Mercifully,
these "choker scarves," very popular before World War II, are largely
out of fashion, and the only time you're likely to encounter one is in
your grandmother's attic or at a vintage clothing store.

Popular types of fur scarves include the boa and the fling. The boa is
made from one or two skins, and is approximately six inches by forty
inches when finished, although the length varies. It has a roughly rec-
tangular form with a slight curve, which enables it to fit around the
neck and the shoulders. A snap is mounted underside at both ends,

making it possible to wear it in a variety of ways. Boas are often made out of fluffy furs like fox or sable.

The fling, which has gained popularity in recent years, is a long, thin, tapered scarf, which may or may not have a tail-trim edge. It may be made out of fox, mink, lynx, or a number of other furs. Most flings are from seventy-two to eighty inches long, although some may be made as long as nine or ten feet.

Both types of scarves are often dyed in a host of unusual colors, including fuchsia, peacock blue, and kelly green. Flings and boas can not only be worn with other furs, but in a variety of other ways:

## SIX WAYS TO WEAR A FUR SCARF

- Over a cloth coat or jacket
- With a slinky evening gown or cocktail dress
- Draped over a tailored wool suit
- With a sweater coat
- With a trouser suit
- Over knit separates

*Muffs.* Muffs make occasional comebacks on the fashion scene, but even though they're extremely warm, they are more or less intended as showpieces. They are just not suited to the vagaries of modern life—can you imagine wearing one on the subway? They can be made of sable, mink, or a variety of other furs.

For those who want their accessories to do double duty, David Leinhoff has designed a new accessory combining a knitted hat and a seven foot fur boa that can be snapped apart and worn separately, as well as in a number of other ways. Called the Chap-Boa, it is available in fox, finnraccoon, and other long-hairs.

*Gloves.* Gloves can be lined or trimmed with fur, and can be decorated with metal studs or even precious stones. One of the nicest (and warmest) types of gloves to look for is lined with fine or soft leather and cuffed with fur such as fox, mink, or rabbit.

*Some Unusual Accessories*: For those with an open mind—and pocketbook—there are fur handbags, fur pens, and even fur eyeglass cases! Some designers are even showing totally coordinated ensembles incorporating accessories made wholly or partially with fur.

One such designer is Spain's Elena Benarroch, who has shown designs that include matching mittens and leg-warmers! New York's Kip Kirkendall takes this concept one step further with her boots of Swa-

Accessories in the grand manner.

kara, which match her clothing designs. For the woman with a real sense of adventure, Ms. Kirkendall envisions a pair of mink-trimmed roller skates, embellished with snakeskin and her signature cowrie shells.

Whatever your preference, when it comes to fur accessories, you should use the same criteria for selecting your small fur pieces as you would your coat or jacket. The underfur should be full and soft, the guard hairs silky, the coloring even, and the leather soft and supple.

## NONFUR ACCESSORIES

If fur hats, gloves, and scarves don't interest you or if you want to explore additional ways to create your own special look, whether you have a rabbit stroller or a fisher greatcoat, nonfur accessories are ideal. Some of the ways to wear them include the following:

A oversize silk square goes well with a fur coat, either as a shawl or a scarf.

*Scarves.* A scarf is a versatile addition to any wardrobe, and most are priced so affordably that you can own them by the drawerful. The clever seamstress can even make her own with less than a yard of fabric. As well as being warm and dramatic, they also help protect your coat from becoming soiled by cosmetics or oils that might rub off from your skin.

Scarves come in silk, cotton, wool, linen, and lace—what could be more sexy or feminine than lace combined with fur? (As for synthetic fibers, although fine-quality polyester and rayon are acceptable, stay away from acetate—scarves of this fabric usually have a look and feel that say bargain basement.) Long muffler scarves are always fashionable, and come in everything from silky polyester (very affordable) to pure cashmere (very expensive). The most versatile length is fifteen by seventy-two inches.

What about color? Scarves in solid colors to contrast with your fur are a possibility—how about a fringed vermillion scarf in silk charmeuse with a ranch mink coat, or a jet-black cashmere muffler teamed with an ermine jacket?

For fur garments that already possess unique patterns of their own,

184

especially lynx, fitch, and many of the mutation foxes, some fashion experts recommend that you stay away from scarves and other accessories with bold designs, such as polka dots and large abstract prints. The only way to find out what works well for you is to experiment. Paisleys and small foulard prints usually go beautifully with fur. (Hint: you can find a wide variety of scarves in these subdued prints in the men's accessory department of better stores.)

Square scarves are another alternative that can be worn in a variety of ways. Oversized squares, which are thirty-six by thirty-six inches or more, can be worn ascot-style, or even as shawls to be draped jauntily over a shoulder.

*Hats and Gloves*. You can top off your own special look with a beret, fedora, or head-hugging cloche in wool felt, velvet, or some other fabric. Knit hats are warm and reasonably priced, but should usually be reserved for those occasions when you want a more casual look. Generally speaking, leather gloves look best with fur coats. They are available in a wide variety of colors and price ranges, and many are so affordable that you can have a rainbow of them.

## THE TAIL END OF FASHION

Those who are handy with a needle and thread might want to add some pizzazz to their wardrobe with fur. Fur tails—ranging from inexpensive raccoon to costly sable—can easily be added to the shoulders of a sweater, the hem of a cloth coat, a slouchy, oversized velvet beret, or even a shoulder bag. Use your imagination!

If fur tails are not available in your area, they can be ordered by mail from Fur Trims by Sam Chaklai, 207 W. 29th Street, New York, New York, (212) 947-0171. Tails can also be ordered from Furrtique, P.O. Box 3393, Farmington, MI 48018-8393.

## PUTTING IT ALL TOGETHER

When it comes to accessorizing your fur coat, there are very few don'ts. Wear what you feel looks best with your fur and, more importantly, what makes you feel comfortable. Here are a few pointers to keep in mind:

■ Do choose appropriate accessories to fit in with the style of your fur: sporty styles look best with more casual accessories, while more formal coats usually are more attractive with dressier hats, gloves, scarves, etc.

■ Choose accessories that are right for the occasion—you wouldn't want to wear a big barrel muff, for example, to a football game.
■ Do keep proportion in mind. This is especially true of the larger woman as well as petites, who may be overwhelmed by some styles.
■ Don't be afraid to experiment. Your fur is versatile enough to allow you almost unlimited fashion options. Don't be afraid to explore a number of them!

## FUR FOR THE HOME

As Queen Semiramis and her 8,000 tiger skins proved way back in 21 B.C., using animal pelts to decorate one's living environment is a fine idea. It is also said that the Queen of Sheba, along with gold and precious stones, brought hundreds of leopard and lion skins as gifts to King Solomon on her legendary visit to the Hebrew king.

Until recently, only the very wealthy could afford to use fur to decorate the home. Today, however, fur pillows, rugs, throws, and other items are so affordably priced that everyone from commoner to king can take advantage of the glamour, warmth, and beauty that this natural decor provides.

Fur can be used in a number of ways in the home. There are fur throws, bedspreads, and even wall hangings. One famous New York furrier has an entire wall of his office covered with lynx.

Some designers, including Kip Kirkendall, predict a complete fur environment for the home of the future. Ms. Kirkendall (whose New York office/studio is decorated with reindeer-skin rugs) says, "I envision a woman being surrounded by the luxury of fur from the moment she gets up in the morning until she goes to bed at night." To this end, she is planning an array of exclusive accessories for the home, including chairs, bedspreads, tables, and vanities.

## CLOSEUP
# FUR AROUND THE WORLD

More so than any other business, the fur trade is international. Once confined to a handful of nations—primarily the U.S., Canada, and the Soviet Union—the fur industry has expanded its scope to include a number of nontraditional countries, such as Hong Kong and Korea. Let's take a look at the way furs are made and sold around the world.

## The Orient

The Orient is increasingly becoming a source for lower and moderately priced furs. Two leading exporters of these garments are Hong Kong and South Korea. In the first half of 1984 alone, these two countries accounted for $50.8 million and $31.9 million, respectively, worth of imports to the United States and these figures are rising every year. Although Asian countries manufacture thousands of coats made from rabbit, opossum, and other poor furs, many of the imported garments are mink, which can sell for as little as a quarter of the price of their American counterparts, although their quality is usually not so high.

Hong Kong is increasing in importance as a center of fur manufacture. Each year, an international fur fair is held there that attracts buyers form all over the world.

Although business is booming in South Korea (total sales to the U.S. in 1984 came to $110.5 million, compared to $23.3 million in 1979), manufacturers there are concerned about the nation's reliance on exports. This is because the government does not permit domestic sales of such luxuries as diamonds, foreign cars, and furs because they feel that the sale of such goods would heighten tension between the rich and poor in this frugal nation.

The People's Republic of China also has a growing fur industry, although it is still a predominantly agricultural nation. Besides manufacturing garments, the nation produces some 2.5 million mink pelts. Wild furs include weasel, lamb, goat, civet cat, and Asian leopard (obviously not sold in North America). Many pet lovers would also be shocked to find out that the fur of the gai wolf, a type of dog resembling a Chow Chow, is a popular fur in this nation. The major centers of fur manufacture are Shanghai and the area around Canton.

A modest number of furs are also produced in Japan. However, this island nation is perhaps more important as a consumer market. Japanese women seem to love fur even more than their North American counterparts do and, like Western women, they prefer mink over any other type.

# Europe

## Southern Europe

The Italians are known throughout the world for their high-fashion styles, and seem to have a knack for creating dramatic, one-of-a-kind pieces. Italian women are very fashion-conscious, and pay attention to designer labels.

Surprisingly, style-conscious Italian furriers are also more willing to work with furs such as rabbit and muskrat, and are known for letting out the latter fur so that it resembles fine ranch mink. Some Italian furs are imported to the United States, including those manufactured by Rome's Fendi sisters. Another well known manufacturer of high-fashion furs is Milan's Tabak, which is represented in the United States by New York's Alixandre.

Spain, a country known more for its leather goods, also has a small but thriving fur industry. Fur garments are becoming increasingly popular with affluent Spanish women.

With its sun-kissed Mediterranean climate, few would associate Greece with the manufacture of fur garments, but this country is one of the top five exporters of furs to the United States, and is one of the world's largest producers of pieced mink garments. The center of the Greek fur industry is Kastoria, which has been involved in the trade since the Middle Ages, when it supplied the ermine that lined the robes of Byzantine nobles. A recent article in *The New York Times* states that "a visitor cannot fail to notice the preoccupation with fur. The buzz of sewing machines comes from every house. Outside the workshops, large wooden boards, pelts stapled to them, are left to dry in the sun. On a makeshift table at the lakeside, fur workers wet narrow strips, then hang them on trellises or spread them out on the sidewalk. In Kastoria one can literally walk on mink." Kastorians have also exported their expertise to other parts of the world; an estimated twenty-five thousand live and work in New York, another ten thousand in Frankfurt.

## Western and Northern Europe

Leipzig was once the center of the European fur industry, and at one time, West Germans consumed twice as many fur products as Americans, even though this nation has only one fourth the population of the United States. However, the German fur industry is not what it once

---

was, due in part to the relentless efforts of the antifur movement, which is much stronger in Europe than it is in the U.S., particularly in Switzerland, the Netherlands, and Britain.

However, the German fur industry now shows signs of revitalization, and at least one German furrier—Rosenberg and Lenhart, one of the country's oldest and most respected firms—has recently opened an office in New York. Says Helmut Rothe, the firm's young vice president, "Germans, and European women in general, are much more advanced when it comes to fur as fashion than American women are. They tend to go for unusual effects and colorations." The world's largest and oldest fur fair is held in Frankfurt every year.

## Scandinavia

Denmark, Sweden, Norway, and Finland also produce fur garments, although they are better known for their fur farms. In fact, the Scandinavian countries, represented by SAGA, are responsible for 85 percent of the world's ranched fox pelts and approximately 45 percent of the mink.

## Canada and Other Countries

Canada is also an important fur-producing country, and the United States and Canada are each other's largest customers. Like American furs, Canadian garments are known for their high quality.

Wild furs, such as raccoon, beaver, fisher, and lynx, seem to be the Canadians' forte. Monies earned from the trapping of these animals add greatly to the income of the country's many native peoples, who inhabit broad, largely unpopulated expanses of Canada where there is little other economic activity.

Israel produces a large number of furs, most of which are exported. Fur garments are also produced in the Dominican Republic, where labor costs are very low.

Of all the fur-producing countries, however, none can rival the United States for the quality of the pelts produced and fine workmanship. When your fur says "Made in the U.S.A.," you can be assured that you're buying the best in the world.

# FUR FOR MEN

## MEN IN FURS

What do Liberace and Joe Namath have in common besides being constantly in the public eye? They are men who have discovered the beauty, luxury, and warmth of fur. At one concert, Liberace wore a $150,000 cape of white fox on stage.

Furs for men are not new. In the Middle Ages, men considered the wearing of fur not only a right, but a privilege. In some countries women were prohibited from wearing expensive furs such as ermine, sable, and marten, and were limited to rabbit, cat, squirrel, and other poor furs.

This situation changed with the advent of the twentieth century. Says Edythe Cudlipp, "After centuries of wearing fur, fur suddenly became effeminate. With the exception of the raccoon coats that were a must for male escorts of the flappers in the roaring Twenties, the only fur worn by men was inside their coats as linings, out of sight and out of mind, and as occasional fur collars."

Ms. Cudlipp's words seem to be borne out by the fact that until recently, the only men to be found in fur were athletes, entertainers, and some members of the gay community. Indeed, it seemed that any man who wore fur—unless he was a six-foot-three-inch linebacker—was sure to have his masculinity questioned.

---

Modern furs for men are still a fairly new item, having been on the fashion scene only since the mid-seventies. Although they account for about only 10 percent of the thousands of furs sold in the United States, this percentage is increasing. Men's furs have "come out of the closet," so to speak, and are finding greater acceptance by everyone from celebrities to stockbrokers.

Men today are no more limited to dull, run-of-the-mill styles than women are. There is the right fur for every man who desires one, from the conservative businessman who wants a classically styled coat to the young contemporary customer with an eye for high fashion. Internationally known menswear designers such as Perry Ellis and Jeffrey Banks have even added furs to their collections.

What's behind the increasing number of men in fur? Warmth is one important factor, of course. Like women, men have learned that even the coziest cloth coat can't compare to even a modest fur on blustery winter days.

Smart men also realize that fur garments are more practical. Besides being much more durable than cloth coats, furs have a longer fashion life. Think about it: a cloth coat bought in 1985 will look dated just five years later, and unless it is of extremely fine quality, would probably not be worth the expense of remodeling. A good-quality fur coat, especially of a durable fur such as mink, lends itself well to restyling.

Price is also a factor. Although you will probably initially spend more for a fur garment, the cost will be justified in the long run. Wool has become more and more expensive, while the price of fur has remained relatively stable.

Perhaps most significant, however, is the change in attitude by both males and females who have learned that "masculine" doesn't necessarily mean "macho." Says Lawrence Schulman of Alixandre, one of New York's best-known luxury furriers: "In the past ten years or so, there's been a total revolution in terms of the way men feel about themselves. They've become more conscious of their appearance, and have become more willing to spend money on grooming and quality clothing, including furs. They realize when they are confident about their appearance, that self-assurance carries over to everything they do."

A strong sense of self-confidence may be the whole key to wearing fur, especially for men, for it appears that there is still some stigma attached to the idea of a male in what has traditionally been thought of as a "feminine" garment. One young man tells of his experience when he wore a fur coat for the first time: "When I walked down the street in my fur, I felt that everyone was staring and making assumptions about me on the basis of what I was wearing... it was an uncomfortable feeling." Other men report the exact opposite, and say that they are the center of attention for very different reasons—they maintain that a fur garment not only makes them feel special, it makes them *look* special.

However, the man who is a bit "fur-shy" is by no means limited to a traditional fur-out garment. There are wool trench- and raincoats with liners of fur that button out, as well as reversibles. For those active in cold weather sports, there are zip-up jackets suitable for every winter diversion from skiing to skating, as well as fur vests and casual bomber jackets. Today, a man is no more limited to a "dumb" fur coat than a woman.

## FUR FOR MEN—WHAT TYPE?

Men's coats and jackets are available in every type of fur from badger to sable, but some types are more popular than others. Coyote, for example, is often used in men's garments, while lynx, especially the rare Russian variety, is usually thought of as being a feminine fur. Swakara and broadtail are two other types of fur that are not used too often in men's garments.

Here are some of the types of furs that are used for men's coats:

*Coyote.* This is one of the few long-haired furs with a wide appeal to men. It is often styled into garments for active sportswear, as well as more traditional coats and jackets. However, like all long-hairs, it sheds, and does not last as long as many other types of fur.

*Fisher.* Elegant, expensive fisher, with its intriguing shades of brown, is becoming increasingly popular with those who are looking for an unusual fur that is very durable. Like mink, it is often made into traditionally styled garments.

*Fox.* Most varieties of fox have too feminine a connotation to appeal to most men. However, red fox occasionally finds its way into men's furs, as does the gray variety. Both can be styled into dramatic, masculine-looking garments.

*Mink.* This is another fur that is usually thought of as being feminine. However, mink, particularly the darker shades, is increasingly seen in classically styled coats and jackets for men.

*Muskrat.* Although traditionally thought of as a poor fur, muskrat can be styled to look rich and elegant. This is a very versatile fur; natural muskrat can be styled into casual garments, or can be processed to resemble ranch mink. It is also plucked and sheared.

*Nutria.* Long-haired nutria is often used for active sportswear. This rich brown fur, with its long, sleek guard hairs, makes a durable and warm garment. Sheared nutria is also a possibility. Like the other sheared furs, it is soft and drapeable and can be shaped into conservatively tailored garments.

*Opossum.* Opossum, especially the New Zealand variety, is often paired with cloth in short, sporty jackets. Soft and fluffy, it is warm as well.

*Otter.* This soft, brown "furrier's fur" is seen more often in men's garments than women's. It is soft and extremely durable, and is frequently used in active sportswear.

*Raccoon.* Those who associate raccoon with the garments of the twenties are in for a surprise, as today's modern raccoon coats bear little resemblance to their forebears; they are lighter and more supple. This silver-toned fur has a masculine look that is appealing to many men.

*Shearling.* Rugged shearling has been a traditional favorite for men's garments. In addition to being warm and durable, it is usually inexpensive.

*Spitz Beaver.* Like nutria, unplucked beaver has a rugged appearance that men find attractive. It is warm and very durable. Sheared beaver, like other sheared furs, is often used to line fine raincoats, and is used in reversible garments as well.

*Wolverine.* Wolverine is ideal for active sportswear because it does not hold moisture or freeze against the face, making it good for subzero temperatures.

This is not to say that there are no other options open for the man who is considering buying a fur coat. Marten and sable are two possibilities. One athlete had a coat made of marmot.

## MEN IN FUR—STYLES

The man who is considering a fur has a wide range to choose from: tailored and classic to sporty and casual. In fact, many men who might

---

**Fur Facts and Fancies:** *Canadian furs account for 12 percent of the American retail market.*

---

be reluctant to buy a fur to wear back and forth to the office—as more and more women are doing—are very willing to purchase furs for their off hours.

Andrew Marc Schwartz, an up-and-coming New York–based fur designer, seems aware of this fact. Although still in his twenties, his Andrew Marc collection, consisting of casual garments in fur, suede, and leather combinations for both men and women, has gained wide acceptance, and is sold nationally in stores such as Bloomingdale's and Neiman-Marcus.

The Andrew Marc collection consists mainly of shorter pieces in smooth-finished and embossed leathers and suedes. They are lined with furs such as New Zealand opossum, sheared beaver, raccoon, and kalgan lamb. Many of the jackets retail for under $1,000. However, although prices are modest, he insists that only the best quality leather and suedes are used. "The idea is," he says, "to make fur accessible to everyone who wants it. Everyone wants to wear fur. We provide them with the opportunity and the right price."

Says Schwartz of his unique design philosophy, "I basically look at designing from a ready-to-wear approach, where fur is not the primary focus of the garment. In my designs, I am taking the basic leather jacket one step further by adding fur. The customer can have a garment that is lined with fur for the same price of a good leather jacket, a jacket that is functional, rich-looking, and warm."

Then, of course, there are furs for active sportswear. Although the idea of a hooded fur poncho may seem strange to some, what could be warmer or more attractive? One furrier even goes skiing in an otter jacket. There are also fur vests that can be worn with heavy sweaters or even layered with other outerwear.

For the man who prefers his fur to be "undercover," there is a wide variety of fur-lined and reversible coats. Garments can be lined with sheared muskrat, nutria, beaver, or even mink, as well as New Zealand opossum. The shell may be of a classic Harris tweed, a rugged leather, or luxurious Ultrasuede.

Reversible coats and jackets come in much the same fabric, but are even more versatile, offering two looks for the price of one. And for the coast-to-coast commuter, what could be more practical—or luxurious—than a rugged Burberry-style raincoat with a zip-out liner of Lunaraine mink?

Then there are the "fur-out" coats. For the classicist, a double-breasted mink coat with brass buttons would be *de rigueur*, while the loose-fitting, belted bathrobe style garment would be the last word in nonchalant elegance for the man-about-town. A longer jacket—somewhere in length between a full-length coat and a very short bomber-style piece—might be an option for the man who wants a somewhat *sportif* look that is not too casual.

There are as many different choices for men as there are for women when it comes to fur, and if you just can't seem to find a fur you like, you can always have one custom-made.

## BUYING A FUR

When it comes to purchasing your fur, you'll want to keep in mind many of the guidelines listed in chapters five and six. Some of these considerations include:

■ *Your Lifestyle.* Where will you be wearing your coat? Will it be a part of your business or professional life? Or will you wear it mainly on your off hours? At first, you might want to invest in a full-length, all-around fur, and perhaps later on supplement your wardrobe with an inexpensive fur jacket that can be worn to sporting events and other leisure activities.

■ *Climate.* This is another important factor. Those who live in areas with cold winters will probably want to buy a fur with long guard hairs, such as unplucked beaver and muskrat, instead of a flat fur, which is not as warm. Sheared furs also tend to mat, which could be a problem in areas of the country which get a great deal of rain or snow.

■ *Price.* Men's furs are about the same price as women's. However, even if you are very price-conscious, you should never buy a coat just because it seems like a good bargain. With furs, value is the most important thing.

Once again, where you buy your fur is important. Many establishments are increasing their stock of men's furs. Whether you buy from a department store or an exclusive specialty shop, you'll want to make sure that the firm is reliable.

Then there is the matter of fit. You should try on as many garments as possible to get the feel of the various types of furs. Spitz beaver and natural raccoon, for example, might feel too heavy to some, while others may find their bulk appealing. Some men might not like the look of mink, while others may find that it suits them perfectly. Whatever your choice, remember that buying a fur is a very personal matter, and you should take your time in deciding what's right for *you*.

## J CLOSEUP JAMES P. MCQUAY—THE BLACK FURRIER

In the New York fur world, James P. McQuay is unique. Not only is he a first generation furrier in a field where many of the major firms have been in business for decades, but in a profession dominated by Jews of Eastern European origin and, increasingly, Greeks, he is New York's only black manufacturing furrier.

In business for more than two decades, Mr. McQuay has achieved a level of success that many would envy. His firm employs more than a dozen people, among them his son, James P. McQuay, Jr., and counts among his mostly black clientele not only entertainers and sports figures, but many business leaders and socialites. His furs have been featured in such nationally known magazines as *Ebony*, *Black Enterprise*, and *Essence*, as well as numerous fashion shows, and he was recently given the honor of creating the $50,000 golden sable coat offered as a prize in a contest sponsored by a leading cigarette company. His furs have also appeared on such programs as *The Bill Cosby Show*. Indeed, Mr. McQuay is the personification of the American dream, the quintessential self-made man.

The path to success has not been an easy one. Although McQuay, who looks decades younger than his sixty years, went to work for a furrier at age fourteen in Yonkers, New York, and except for a three-year stint in the army, had always worked within the industry, he found that the doors to advancement were largely closed. His original goal had been to obtain a position in New York's wholesale fur district, but in a classic Catch-22 situation, he was told by prospective employers that he would need a union book to obtain a position, while the union repeatedly informed him that in order to get a union book, he must first have a job.

Finally, despite his skills and qualifications, he was offered a position as a floor boy, where his duties consisted mainly of picking up after other people. After two years on this dead-end street, Mr. McQuay realized that he would never obtain the goals he had set for himself if he did not set out on his own. With savings of less than five hundred dollars, he went into business for himself, opening up his first store in Harlem.

During his first seven years in business, Mr. McQuay discovered discrimination of another kind, on the part of blacks who were "not used to buying from one another, and had difficulty in seeing other blacks as professionals." He found that he had to "begin a re-education process to combat these negative feelings that many blacks held." This problem has been overcome, and Mr. McQuay finds that many do seek him out from all parts of the nation, not only because he is the only black furrier, but because his twenty-five years of experience enable him to create a fine product.

Does he feel his self-described designation as "The Black Furrier" puts limitations on his business? Mr. McQuay answers with an emphatic "No!" He states, "I feel that black people should have a certain pride in their race and in this respect I don't feel I should make a change. If a black kid in, say, Peoria, Illinois, reads about me and what led me to start my own business with $460 in savings, then I hope that he'll say to himself, 'Hey, I can do it too!' no matter what field of endeavor he chooses."

James P. McQuay works with "anything that is fur," including such staples as the ever-popular mink (ranch mink, he states, outsells other varieties by about eight to one), fox, raccoon, beaver, and the more expensive furs such as sable and fisher. He does a substantial business in furs for men, who he finds prefer coyote, raccoon, and mink, in that order. Among younger customers, he finds that long-haired furs such as fox are growing in popularity. Styles run the gamut from conservative to avant-garde, and one of his exclusive creations consists of a garment with a body made of short-haired furs paired with sleeves made from long-haired furs.

Although pictures of celebrities line his walls, most of his customers are "just plain folks"—albeit affluent ones. Despite the high incidence of black poverty, few realize that blacks constitute the nation's largest consumer market, spending $180 billion in goods and services per year—the equivalent of the GNP of Canada or Australia. Prosperous blacks are even more likely than their white counterparts to spend a large amount of their disposable income on luxury items such as furs, expensive cars, and jewelry, and McQuay counts among his customers many men and women who are buying their second or third furs. He states, "I'm seeing a whole new generation of fur customers from middle-class backgrounds who have had some experience with fur, as their mothers, aunts, or some other relative had owned one."

More common, however, is the first-time fur buyer. Like others in the industry, Mr. McQuay reports that many young professional women in their twenties are purchasing furs for themselves as opposed to having a husband or male admirer buy it for them. He comments, "this type of customer realizes she is on her own, and in many instances prefers to be in a position to have this type of buying power. It gives her a certain amount of freedom and, definitely, pride."

Mr. McQuay is optimistic about the future, as he feels that the enormous interest in fur on the part of the affluent working woman can only lead to increased business. His tentative plans for the future include expansion into such cities as Chicago and Washington, D.C.

Undoubtedly, one of the reasons for Mr. McQuay's success is his positive attitude, even in the face of enormous obstacles. He states, "If a person fails or is unsuccessful after his first attempt, he should get up and try again. I can't tell you how many times things did not turn out the way I wanted them to, but that was never enough to make me say that I am not going to try it again. To get ahead in life, one has to take risks, and be prepared to do whatever has to be done in order to achieve success."

# FUR AND THE ENVIRONMENT

## ELEVEN

Although the fur industry is currently enjoying an unprecedented growth in sales, there are those who oppose the wearing of fur garments. The arguments on the "anti" side are many: that fur coats are an unnecessary luxury item, that synthetic furs are a viable alternative, and that the fur industry, particularly in regard to the trapping of wild animals, causes needless suffering and cruelty just to assuage our vanity.

On the "pro" side, the arguments are equally convincing. Critics of the anti-fur groups charge that the fur industry creates hundreds of thousands of jobs, that furs are a renewable resource, and that trapping is a valuable wildlife management tool. In this chapter, we'll briefly examine each of these arguments.

## PRESERVATION VS. CONSERVATION

In speaking of natural resources, the terms "preservation" and "conservation" are used interchangeably; however, they are *not* one and the same. Preservation is the *non-use* of a natural resource, while conservation can be defined as the *wise use of a renewable natural resource*.

According to George F. Hubert, Jr., a Furbearer Biologist with the Illinois Department of Conservation, "Like trees, furbearers are a renewable resource; they produce an annual surplus that can be safely harvested by man for his benefit. Wild animals cannot be stockpiled, that is, the annual surplus of individuals that comes from the animal's natural propensity to over-produce cannot accumulate for long . . . In summary, conservation implies management of animals, their habitat, and the people who use them."

## THE FUR INDUSTRY UNDER FIRE

In the 1960s, in the general spirit of rebellion that pervaded the air, many people turned their attention to issues that addressed our relationship with the environment. Although the primary focus was on air and water pollution, the fur industry also came under attack, particularly in regard to its sometimes careless use of certain dwindling species. According to the World Wildlife Fund, a highly respected conservation organization, "Heavy trade in the large cats between the late 19th century and the 1960s threatened the survival of many cat species."

Protests against the fur industry were quite effective, causing sales to plummet from $335 million in 1967 to $279 million in 1970, and prompting some to charge that environmentalists were causing *furriers* to become an endangered species!

### The Endangered Species Act

One important piece of legislation that was passed during this period was the Endangered Species Act of 1973. This law requires that all plants and animals "which are of esthetic, ecological, educational, historical, recreational, and scientific value to the Nation and its people" and which are considered threatened or "endangered" be safeguarded until the population is up to an acceptable level. The U.S. Fish and Wildlife Service (a division of the Department of the Interior), which is in charge of the program, describes an "endangered species" as one that is "in danger of extinction throughout all or a significant portion of its range," whereas a "threatened" species is one that is likely to become endangered throughout all or some of its range.

The Endangered Species Act has proven to be highly effective, and has been credited with saving such creatures as the Florida alligator and the brown pelican from extinction.

## The CITES Convention

Another important piece of legislation, which perhaps has had even a greater effect on the status of endangered species because of its global scope, is the Convention on International Trade in Endangered Species (CITES), which was implemented in 1975. The main purpose of this treaty is to protect wildlife against over-exploitation by trade and to prevent international trade from contributing to the extinction of the species. To date, eighty-nine countries have signed this agreement.

To accomplish its aim, the Convention has implemented a worldwide system designed to control the traffic in wildlife and wildlife products by requiring that government permits are required for such trade. Security paper and stamps are often used for these permits to prevent such abuses as forgery.

An organization called TRAFFIC—The Trade Records Analysis of Flora and Fauna in Commerce, which is under the auspices of the World Wildlife Fund—helps determine whether or not a species is endangered by trade.

The main problem with the CITES treaty is lack of cooperation. Adherence to the treaty is purely voluntary, and to date, several members of the world community, including Spain, Hong Kong, and Singapore, have not signed it. In these places, it is quite possible to purchase products made from endangered or threatened wildlife, although bringing them into North America is another matter.

Another international program which monitors the trade in wildlife is the IUCN, or the International Union for the Conservation of Nature. Based in Switzerland, this organization publishes the *Red Data Book*, in which the endangered species of each nation are catalogued.

The fur industry has also taken steps to ensure the survival of the world's wildlife through such organizations as the International Fur Trade Federation. Through its delegates, the IFTF keeps members fully informed of any developments in the field of conservation and maintains close connection with organizations particularly concerned with conservation.

In addition, individual states and provinces have enacted legislation protecting endangered species. In New York State, where the bulk of fur processing takes places, the use or sale of skins, hides or other parts of endangered species by the industry is strictly forbidden by the Mason Act.

This brings us to an important point: *no reputable furrier in the*

*United States, Canada, and most European nations will manufacture or sell a garment made from the pelts of a protected species.* Even if a manufacturer wanted to make and sell, for example, a leopard or cheetah skin coat, importation of pelts from endangered species into North America is strictly illegal, and penalties for violation of laws such as the Endangered Species Act are substantial.

## THE TRAPPING CONTROVERSY: BENEFICIAL OR BARBARIC?

The issue that is of most concern to animal rights organizations is trapping. According to one group: "Innocent animals are dying by the thousands in steel-jaw traps—to provide furs." It does seem that such suffering cannot be justified for the sake of mere vanity. This brings us to an important point—why is trapping necessary?

For wildlife, raw nature was and still can be a place of violent, lingering, and gruesome death from predator wounding, starvation, plagues such as mange, distemper, rabies, ringworm, guinea worm, and tularemia. Very few wild animals die from old age.

If the surplus population of animals is not removed, disaster may result. Few realize, for example, that fully 75 percent of the fall muskrat population may consist of surplus animals. According to Duane Pursley, a Wildlife Biologist for the West Virginia Department of Natural Resources, "If the muskrat population is too large in a local area, an 'eat-out' often occurs. An eat-out describes a situation in a pond or marsh where muskrats have completely eaten the existing aquatic vegetation, including the root systems which bond the organic soils together. This converts the pond or marsh to a mucky area and destroys waterfowl, fish, and other wetland wildlife's habitat." Despite the fact that 5,482,147 muskrat were harvested in the 1983–1984 season in the United States alone, muskrat, as are most of the other wild animals used by the fur industry, are in abundant supply. If left uncontrolled, wild animals can pose a threat to man, sometimes with disastrous results.

Before we take a closer look at the trapping issue, let's examine the device most often used to catch wild animals—the steel leghold trap. Since its invention in the early 1800s, the use of this device has been under attack, and it has been labeled "a cruel instrument of torture."

With proper use, this trap is very effective, as it can be used for both short- and long-legged animals. It can be set on land or anchored in water, where it causes a speedy death by pulling the animal under.

This sort of trap also gives the trapper the option of releasing, usually without permanent damage, a "non-target" animal.

However, in all fairness, it must be said that the leghold trap, while perhaps not a "cruel instrument of torture," has been recognized by conservationists, wildlife management specialists, and many in the fur industry as being far from perfect. While the "ideal" trap may not exist, improvements are constantly being sought.

One device that seems to hold some promise is the so-called "soft-catch" trap. This device uses rubberlike pads with concave faces that rotate in against the leg to confine the animal without injuring it. In preliminary tests, it was found that this device was successful in producing significantly less trap-related damage to the animal than did conventional leghold traps, but more study is needed.

Both public and privately funded efforts are underway to improve upon existing traps. For instance, the Fur Institute of Canada recently invested more than $1.5 million in such a project.

## Trapping Facts and Fallacies

**Statement:** The leghold trap is a device which has jagged teeth that clamp down on an animal's paw, causing intense pain.
**Reply:** The steel-toothed trap is illegal in most states. In New York State, only traps up to six inches in length are permitted. As for steel-toothed devices, they are not even made any more.
**Statement:** Traps are seldom checked, so that animals caught in them languish in agony for hours, sometimes even days.
**Reply:** In most states, the law requires that trappers check their sets periodically. However, anti-harvesting forces argue that these laws are rarely, if ever, enforced.

Angie Berchielli, a trapper and Wildlife Consultant to the New York State Trappers' Association, comments, "If I have twenty traplines set—which is a considerable investment in time and money—it doesn't make sense for me to keep the animals in the trap any longer than I have to. Secondly, other trappers may come along and steal what I've caught—therefore, it's to the trapper's best advantage to check his or her lines every day."
**Statement:** The steel leghold trap often catches many "non-target" animals, including household pets such as dogs and cats, and endangered species. Such animals are killed and discarded as "trash."
**Reply:** Comments George F. Hubert, "Trappers in Illinois capture furbearers with a great deal of expertise. Based on trapper surveys

conducted during the past few years, non-target catches comprise about 2.5 to 3.0 percent of the animals captured in the state. This means that one non-target animal is taken for every thirty-two to thirty-nine furbearers trapped. Many non-target catches are released. An estimated 91 percent of all the dogs accidentally trapped are released unharmed."

Trapping of domestic pets such as dogs or cats, however, is a considerable problem, because of the growing numbers of individuals who own pets and allow them to run loose. To help reduce this problem, trappers should always gain the landowner's permission before he or she sets a trap, and should carefully note where they are located.

**Statement:** Although it has been claimed that trapping is a valuable wildlife management tool, it has been shown that as a means of disease control, it is worthless.

**Reply:** Trapping has *not* proven effective in controlling the spread of certain diseases, such as rabies and distemper. However, studies have shown that trapping is a proven means of controlling other ailments.

Trapping is effective in reducing the incidence of density-dependent ailments—diseases that become dangerous when animals reach a critical level of population. Comments Charles M. Pils, Furbearer Biologist for the state of Wisconsin, "The most important fact to remember is that trapping reduces the potential threat to humans and domestic animals posed by wildlife diseases. Furthermore, trapping as a wildlife management technique allows private and public natural resources agencies to monitor the prevalence and distribution of several wildlife diseases such as canine parvovirus, Lyme disease, and mange." A number of well-known organizations, including The National Wildlife Federation and Atlanta's Center for Disease Control have also come out in support of trapping as a means of disease control.

**Statement:** If all trapping was banned, it would not constitute an economic hardship for most trappers, as only *one* percent of America's two million trappers, are "professional" (i.e., persons for whom the sale of pelts comprises a major portion of their yearly earnings).

**Reply:** The majority of trappers live in rural areas, many of them economically depressed, where job opportunities are scarce. Many trappers are students, retired individuals, or members of other low-income groups, and trapping does contribute substantially to their incomes.

In Canada, Greenland, and Alaska, trapping of furbearers by native peoples, including the Inuit, Metis, and Indian, provides not only cash

---

for pelts but meat for food, as well as skins for clothing. Although the actual percentage of wild furs trapped by native peoples is relatively small, trapping is a vital part of the rich and ancient culture of these people.

Alarmed by increasing agitation by animal rights organizations, the native peoples of these regions have formed a group called Indigenous Survival International. The purpose of this organization is to defend the interests of native peoples against these forces, some of which not only oppose trapping, but hunting and fishing as well. Comments Dave Monture, a Mohawk Indian and spokesperson for the group, "The issue for native peoples is one of survival."

It would be unwise to paint too rosy a picture of the trapping issue. Abuses do occur. However, in the long run, a trap is only as effective as the trapper who sets it. This is why trapper education is so important. In many states and provinces, potential trappers must take mandatory courses before being issued a license. Such programs appear to be effective: in a recent study, it was found that of twenty major groups surveyed, trappers were the second most knowledgeable in the field of wildlife management and conservation.

## FUROR OVER FUR FARMING

If you still have reservations about wearing a fur from a wild animal, you should remember that the majority of furs used in garments come from ranched animals, who are raised for their pelts in much the same manner that other creatures, such as poultry and cattle, are raised for use by man.

Although it is difficult to pinpoint an exact figure, it is estimated that in the United States and on an international scale, 75 to 90 percent of the pelts used for fur garments come from ranched animals, including 95 to 98 percent of all mink, most varieties of fox, rabbit, chinchilla, lamb, black fitch, nutria, some opossum, and some types of sable and raccoon. The Russians are even said to be experimenting with ranching lynx and beaver.

In many cases, fur animals are used for other purposes. Rabbits are used for meat as well as fur, and mink provide oils that are useful as emollients for both cosmetics and leather (many of you have probably used mink oil to waterproof leather boots). Mink manure is used to fertilize crops.

Although ranched animals, including mink, are raised under carefully controlled conditions, the fur farming industry has come under attack. Animal rights activists charge that the "people who raise fur-bearing animals are primarily concerned with profit. The needs and feelings of the animals are rarely considered."

Is this a true depiction of fur farming? According to Harold DeHart, a third generation fur farmer and president of the Wisconsin-based Fur Farm Animal Welfare Coalition, it is not. "Many of these organizations present a distorted and unrealistic picture of fur farming."

The Coalition seeks to "promote the general welfare and health of Fur Farm animals; to educate the public as to the proper and humane practices employed by fur farmers for the protection and health of Fur Farm animals, and to educate the public as to the value of ranch-raised fur garments." The Coalition employs the services of a number of independent advisors, including veterinarians and many others with doctorates in such diverse fields as chemistry, physiology, biochemistry, and animal nutrition.

Pelts from American ranch-raised fox and mink are generally regarded as being of the finest quality and mink farmers maintain that their creatures are the "world's best cared for farm animals." Naturally, a farmer is concerned with profit; this is the only way he can provide for his family and reinvest in his farm, but the feeling and respect the agriculturist has for the land and his livestock goes much deeper than this.

Mr. DeHart comments, "The quality of American mink is a direct result of good care and good nutrition. Mink are at the end of the food chain, and what they need for a healthy, well-balanced diet cannot be used for human consumption. Their diet consists of carefully balanced meat and meat by-products, poultry by-products, eggs, fish, special grains and other dietary essentials."

In addition, "mink are an aquatic animal, consequently, they need extra water during warm months. Water is, therefore, amply provided by the farmers. For their own protection and safety, mink are kept in comfortable, well-ventilated housing."

## FUR FARMING FIRSTHAND

A visit to the Jim Preston Fur Farm seems to bear out the claims made by the Fur Farm Animal Welfare Coalition. Located outside Pittsburgh, Pennsylvania, this family-run farm raises 21,000 mink in a variety of colors including black, mahogany, and white.

The mink are kept in outdoor sheds which provide adequate coverage from the elements. They are fed two to three times a day with a mixture that includes an assortment of multi-vitamins. The animals are also innoculated against such diseases as botulism and distemper. The animals are "pelted out," or harvested, in late November. Approximately two-third's of the herd is culled; the remaining animals are kept as breeding stock.

The Jim Preston Mink Farm is typical of the well-run facilities that raise fur-bearing animals. Any individual who desires a mink coat can wear it with pride, knowing that mink are indeed "the world's best cared for farm animal."

## FUR—OR FAKE FUR?

One argument that anti-fur forces use is that fake furs are a more acceptable alternative to the real thing: they are "more ecologically sound, cost the consumer far less money, and cause no suffering to animals."

Most fake furs are made of acrylic, modacrylic, (many fake furs are made of 80 percent acrylic and 20 percent modacrylic fibers, the former which is highly flammable) or some other fiber that uses natural oil or gas in the manufacturing process. The production of both these fibers involves the use of highly toxic chemicals.

The substitution of synthetic substances such as modacrylic cloth for fur and plastic for leather products might save animals, but the increase in use of these materials can pollute air, streams, rivers, and oceans to the point where far more is destroyed than gained. With proper management, it is possible to harvest fur-bearers indefinitely. Such animals such as raccoon, beaver, and muskrat have been used by the fur industry for centuries, and all three species are in plentiful supply. However, natural gas resources are limited; it has been estimated that by the year 2000, they may be all but depleted. Our oil resources are also finite, and perhaps will last for another seventy-five years.

Are fake furs really less expensive for the consumer? They usually do cost less initially, but many people are unaware that a light adhesive solution is usually used to seal the fabric together at the darts and seams. This solution tends to disintegrate with dry cleaning, so that no more than five or six dry cleanings is advisable. Fake furs, therefore, have a much shorter lifespan than real furs. And when a fake fur is discarded, it will be a burden to the environment for years to come, as petroleum products are not biodegradable.

# THE ANIMAL RIGHTS CONTROVERSY

Some of the most emotional arguments against the fur trade are of a philosophical bent. Many opponents of the fur industry carry the idea of preservation one step further and subscribe to the "animal rights" viewpoint, which claims that animals, like people, have certain inalienable rights, including the right to live free of pain, stress, and fear. Animal rightists believe that the idea of using furbearers as a renewable natural resource is just another example of "speciesism"—an evil akin to racism and sexism.

While it is not within the scope of this book to debate the animal rights issue, it would appear that it would be very difficult, if not impossible, to exist without placing some form of stress on our environment. Said the great humanitarian and physician Albert Schweitzer, "Man is under the law of necessity which forces him to kill or injure, with or without his knowledge."

Every day we use products that are made in whole or part from animals. We wear leather shoes and carry handbags and briefcases made from animal hides; we wash ourselves with soap made from animal fat and use cosmetics that contain collagen (an animal protein). We nourish our bodies with meat, poultry, and fish, as well as other animal products, including eggs and Jell-O (this popular dessert contains gelatin, made from boiling the bones and hides of animals, usually beef cattle).

Many feel that we do have the right to intelligently exploit our animal population, as long as it is done humanely. In regard to the fur industry, this means that three guidelines should be followed:

■ The use of animals whose population has reached critically low levels should be prohibited until a favorable balance is restored.

■ The trapping of wild animals should be carried out in tandem with scientific wildlife management principles, to assure that an optimum level of population is maintained, and in the most humane matter possible.

■ Animals should be dispatched in the manner that causes them the least amount of pain, stress, and suffering.

On both a national and global level, the fur industry is moving toward implementing these guidelines. However, there are still some areas of concern facing the industry in regard to conservation, particularly concerning the trapping issue. Problems such as these are not easily addressed, but must be resolved if we are to keep from destroying our environment.

# OF SEALS AND MEN

In the late sixties and early seventies, millions were shocked by the seemingly meaningless slaughter of baby harp seals. The annual harp seal hunt became a media event of sorts, as millions watched "the good guys"—members of such organizations as Greenpeace and The Fund for Animals—protect the appealing, white-coated little creatures, often with their own bodies, from "the bad guys"—the club-wielding sealers.

Public outcry against the hunt was so widespread that the annual harvest of pelts declined from 170,000 in 1976 to about 19,000 in 1985. The European Economic Community also placed a two-year ban on the importation of the seal pelts which was renewed in 1985. For all practical purposes, the market for sealskin coats of any type, at least in North America and Western Europe, is nonexistent.

The harp seal ranges throughout the Arctic and sub-Arctic regions of the world; with a population of more than three million, it is the world's third most abundant seal. The harp seal has a long lifespan and can live up to thirty years or more. They have few natural predators, except for sharks, killer whales, and polar bears.

Harp seals consume enormous amounts of fish, putting them in competition with the commercial fishing industry. According to the Canadian Wildlife Federation: "Harp seal are estimated to consume 1.5 metric tons of food per animal annually. At current population levels, the harp population now consumes more food annually than the total Canadian fish catch. Uncontrolled expansion of the seal population can be expected to seriously curtail the supply of fish available to all countries now fishing the region and will have serious economic implications for Canada's east coast fishing industry."

## THE HUNTERS AND THE HUNTED

The harp seal hunt has a history that goes back 400 years. Each part of the animal is utilized—the flesh is eaten (some of it is even canned and sold commercially) and the pelts are used for clothing and shelter. Oil from the seals also provides heating and cooking fuel.

Most of the income of the residents of the sub-Arctic area comes from fishing; however, in the winter, huge ice floes make this activity impossible. In the bleak environment of the Arctic, sealing is an important commercial activity. At one time, the industry brought in about one million dollars to the region annually.

The "Save the Seals" campaign has already proven disastrous for many native communities. In the town of Resolute, Northwest Territories, collective income generated by the seal hunt dropped from $54,000 to $1,000 in one year. According to Indigenous Survival Internationale, depression, alcoholism, and suicide are some of the indirect effects of the anti-seal campaign, which has succeeded in depriving many not only of their livelihoods, but of a sense of dignity and purpose as well. This serious situation has led one highly respected environmental rights organization, Greenpeace, to publicly apologize to the people of Greenland for the role it played in the anti-seal campaign.

Other seal hunters consist of "landsmen," who are mainly inshore fishermen from isolated bays and inlets of northern Newfoundland. The landsmen take harp seals of all ages; only 20 percent of the total catch consists of baby animals in the "whitecoat" stage. The landsmen have also suffered economically because of the anti-seal campaign.

The Canadian seal hunt is overseen by the Canadian Department of Fisheries and Oceans, which is responsible for issuing licenses to the sealers, and also has the power to revoke them. The taking of seal pups must conform to the provisions of the Canadian Seal Protection Regulations. Although it did not appear so to the uninformed observer, clubbing was found to be the most effective method of disposal, causing the least amount of stress to the animal.

In their campaigns, anti-sealing organizations have stressed that the harp seal is an endangered species. Although at one time harp seals were overharvested, there is *no scientific evidence* to corroborate this claim. The harp seal is not even a threatened species. In fact, at the 1983 biennial meeting of the parties to the CITES treaty, a proposal to include harp and hooded seals in an Annex to the Convention was not approved, meaning that the Convention did not feel that continued unregulated trade in the products of the animals endangered the survival of the species. In addition, to insure that the harp seal population is at an optimum level, seal specialists from several nations meet every year to study the status of the harp seal and to advise the Canadian government on the scientific management of the population.

If, indeed, the seal hunt was conducted in accordance with sound wildlife management principals and the killing was accomplished humanely, why was there such opposition to it?

According to one environmental group, the seals represented "the fragility of nature in the hands of humans; the killing symbolizes the destruction of all that is beautiful." Many also opposed the use of seal products, such as meat, fur, and oil, although few would extend such criticism to the commercial meat industry.

The Department of Fisheries and Oceans tells a different version of the story. To them, it appears likely that sympathy for the harp seal was due in large part to the animal's undeniable emotional appeal. The Department wryly points out that "it is ironic ... however, that a lamb, a calf, or a piglet is just as endearing as a seal pup, yet their killing is accepted without question by most members of society ... decisions about the management and protection of any species cannot be based upon what the animal looks like, but must be guided by sound scientific advice. Otherwise truly endangered, but less photogenic species (such as the Nile crocodile) risk having their plight ignored because people have difficulty forming sentimental attachments to them."

Janice Scott Henke, a conservationist and licensed New York State Wildlife Rehabilitator, comments that, "It has been argued that everyone has a right to his or her opinion about such matters, yet an uninformed opinion that results in harm to a species and to thousands of humans as well is not defensible. The issue of cruelty to harp seals has been one nurtured by a combination of ignorance and clever fundraising. The resulting public-generated legislation in Europe and the United States is destined to have an effect on the biology of the species for years to come."

# GLOSSARY OF FUR TERMS

**The American Fur Industry.** A trade organization consisting of manufacturers, retailers, and others involved in the fur industry. In addition to promoting "the fashion image of fur apparel to the consumer," the AFI is actively involved in conservation on both the national and international level.

**American Legend—The Mink Source®.** A trade organization representing the former members of EMBA, the Mutation Mink Breeders Association, and GLMA, the Great Lakes Mink Association.

**Blackglama®.** A trade name describing a very dark brown shade of mink that appears almost black.

**Bleaching.** A chemical process in which furs are lightened or made white. Bleaching generally weakens the leather of a fur.

**Blending.** See Tip-dyeing.

**Breath of Spring®.** A term used in describing mink which refers to a shade lighter than the designated color (an EMBA trademark).

**Bukhara.** Trade name for Persian Lamb (caracul) from the U.S.S.R.

**CITES.** The Convention on International Trade in Endangered Species, a treaty signed in 1973 by members of eighty-seven nations, which regulates trade in endangered or threatened species. In the United States, the CITES convention is operated under the auspices of the World Wildlife Fund.

**Commercial grade.** A fur of less than prime quality.

**Cording.** See *Grooving*.

**Cost-utility ratio.** A term used when determining the advisability of having a fur remodeled.

**Dressing.** See *Tanning*.

**Drumming.** A process in which furs are cleaned and fluffed by putting them in a drum with chemically treated sawdust. The abrasive action of the sawdust as the fur revolves in the drum cleans and fluffs the furs.

**Dyeing.** A process in which the color of a fur is changed.

**Endangered species.** Plants, animals, and insects whose existence is threatened because of overharvesting, destruction of habitat, etc. Endangered species are not used by American or Canadian furriers.

**Endangered Species Act.** A law passed by Congress which forbids the sale or possession of animals and other wildlife whose existence is threatened.

**Feathering.** Clipping fur in shingled layers to produce an effect similar to eyelash fringe. Feathering is also another term for *tip-dyeing*, as this process was often done with a feather.

**Flat fur.** A type of fur with leather and only one kind of fur or hair, such as hair seal or Persian lamb.

**Fleshing.** Scraping the leather side of a raw pelt to remove excess fats and other material.

**Fur Farm Animal Welfare Coalition.** An organization composed of American mink farmers, whose purpose is to ensure the proper treatment of ranched mink. The organization also conducts educational programs to inform the public about fur farming.

**Grooving.** Shearing fur in "stripes" of alternating widths and depths. The result is similar to corduroy; the stripes can be wide or narrow. Also called cording.

**Grotzen.** A Yiddish word referring to the guard hair along the center back of a pelt. It is longer and coarser than the rest of the fur and sometimes resembles a short mane.

**Guard hair.** The long lustrous outer hair of a fir that protects the animal from inclement weather. Guard hairs are lacking in flat furs such as antelope.

**International Fur Trade Federation (IFTF).** An organization composed of thirty fur-producing countries whose purpose is to ensure that the industry follows guidelines designed to preserve the existence of fur-bearing species.

**International Union for the Conservation of Nature (IUCN).** An organization based in Switzerland which is involved in preservation of natural resources. Publishes the *Red Data Book*, which lists the endangered species of every nation.

**Leathering.** A process in which strips of fur are alternated with strips of leather. It is used to lighten very heavy furs, such as wolverine and badger, and to create different styles.

**Letting out.** A method in which pelts are scored into very narrow, fine strips, and then resewn. The shape of the pelt is changed, but not the square area.

**Majestic®.** Trade name for Canadian mink.

**Mutation.** A fur that is a variation of the naturally occurring color of the fur. Rabbit, chinchilla, fox, and mink are bred in mutation colors.

**Natural.** Natural furs have been dressed, but are sold in their natural colors and textures.

**Natural ranch mink.** A term referring to mink which ranges in color from chocolate brown to off-black.

**Norka®.** Trade name for Russian mink.

**Oxidation.** A natural process in which fur changes color over time. Although all furs will eventually oxidize, modern tanning techniques make the change in color look natural.

**Partial skins.** Portions of pelts, including flanks or sides and bellies, that are used in fur garments. The fur is usually softest in these areas, and the desirability of the fur depends largely on the markings, color, and texture.

**Pieced fur.** Furs made from very small trimmings from full pelts—may be as small as a half an inch in length. The cuttings are usually sewn into large sheets, called plates. Such furs as fox, mink, or Persian lamb can be pieced. Pieced furs are less expensive than other types, but also wear the most poorly, and for this reason should always be reinforced on the leather side.

**Plates.** Sections of fur—often measuring eighteen by twenty-four inches—that have been sewn together like cloth. The fur pattern is placed on the plate, which is cut like fabric. Pieced furs are made from plates.

**Plucking.** A process in which the guard hairs of a fur are removed by tweezing or plucking. In some cases, only the uneven or coarse hairs are plucked. It is necessary to pluck the furs before *shearing* them.

**Processing.** Any method of changing the appearance or texture of a given fur including dyeing, grooving, and bleaching.

**Puch.** Yiddish term referring to the softness and density of the underfur.

**Ranched fur.** Fur from animals which are raised on farms, including mink, chinchilla, sheep, fox, and nutria. Approximately 85 to 90 percent of the furs used in the United States are from ranched animals.

**Ribbing.** A process in which very narrow strips of leather are alternated with strips of fur. Often used for less expensive coats and jackets.

**SAGA®.** Trademark for the finest quality ranch-raised Scandinavian mink and fox pelts.

**Shearing.** A process in which the fur is shaved or cut down to an even, plushlike texture, similar to silk velvet. This is often done on furs from aquatic creatures, such as nutria, beaver, and sometimes mink. In order to be sheared, the fur first must be plucked.

**Skin-on-skin.** A method of making fur garments in which the skins are not let out, but trimmed, and then fit to a pattern. Skin-on-skin coats are less expensive to make and do not require as much skill as let-out garments. This process is often used with larger skins, as well as with less expensive pelts. However, sable and mink garments are made skin-on-skin in Europe.

**Sobol®.** Trade name for Soviet-produced sable, considered the finest in the world.

**Soft-catch trap.** A type of leg-hold trap that uses rubber pads to confine an animal, causing much less injury and distress than the steel leghold trap.

**Specialty fur.** A fur combining unusual techniques and materials to create a one-of-a-kind garment.

**Tanning.** A process in which the raw pelts are skinned, fleshed, soaked, and washed in special solutions to prepare them for use in garments.

**Tip-dyeing.** Coloring only the tips of the guard hairs for uniform shading. Obviously, only long-haired furs can be tip-dyed.

**Underfiber.** The underfur of a fur with guard hairs. The underfiber, or underfur, should be dense, soft, and compact. This is what keeps you—and the animal—warm.

**Vintage fur.** A previously owned garment that combines a high degree of workmanship with quality materials to create a valuable antique fur.

# BIBLIOGRAPHY

Arnim, Faye. *Fur Craft.* New York: Key Publishing Co., 1968.
  An interesting little book that shows the reader how to construct a variety of items, including fur-trimmed slippers, gloves, and even a dog's fur coat.

Calasibetta, Dr. Charlotte. *Fairchild's Dictionary of Fashion.* New York: Fairchild Publications, 1983.
  An encyclopedia of fashion, from antiquity to the present.

Ewing, Elizabeth. *Fur in Dress.* London: Batsford Books, 1982.
  A fascinating look at fur fashions of yesteryear, told from a British perspective.

Henke, Janice Scott. *Seal Wars! An American Viewpoint.* St. John's, Newfoundland: Breakwater Books, 1985.
  A provocative analysis of the harp seal controversy by a licensed New York State wildlife rehabilitator and conservationist. (Order from: Breakwater Books, Ltd., 277 Duckwater Street, St. John's, Newfoundland, A1C 1G9.)

Herscovici, Alan. *Second Nature: The Animal-Rights Controversy.* Toronto, 1983: CBC Enterprises/Les Enterprises Radio-Canada, une division de la Societie Radio-Canada, C. P. 500, Succursale "A"/Toronto (Ontario) Canada, M5W 1E6.
  An in-depth discussion of the animal rights movement by a Montreal journalist and novelist. The book is a transcript from the CBC *Ideas* program called "Men and Animals: Building a New Relationship with Nature." (Tapes of the program may be ordered from: Audio Products, CBC Enterprises/Les Enterprises Radio-Canada/P. O. Box 4039, Station A/Toronto, Canada M5W 2P6.)

Krohn, Margaret B., and Phyllis W. Schwebke. *How to Sew Leather,*

*Suede, Fur.* New York: Collier Books, a division of Macmillan Publishing Co., 1970.
For the serious fur seamstress, this book contains instructions for a variety of interesting projects.

Van Gelder, Richard G. *Animals and Man: Past, Present, Future.* Ringsted, Denmark: J. Theilade & Co.
A discussion of man and his relationship to the environment by the curator of mammals at the American Museum of Natural History in New York.

# INDEX

Accessories, 178–86
  fur, 178–83, 185, 186
  fur tails, 185
  for the home, 186
  nonfur, 183–85
  pointers, 185–86
  *see also specific accessories, e.g.* Hats;
    Muffs; Scarves
Age of customers for fur, xi–xii
Age of fur, decision to remodel and, 154
Alaska, 204–5
Alixandre, 40, 188, 191
Alley cat, 3
Allure of fur, xi–xiv
American Fur Industry, 94, 141, 144
American Indians, 19, 22, 23, 204–5
American Legend—The Mink Source,
  34, 85
Ancient world, 1–2, 17, 18
Animal rights controversy, 208–9
Antelope:
  maintaining, 156
  profile of, 52–53
Anthony, John, 144
Antique furs, 172–74
Asian complexions, 107
Astor, John Jacob, 24
Astrakhan, *see* Persian lamb
Auctions of skins, 34–35, 119
Auctions of used furs, 172, 173
Availability of fur, xiii
Average figure, furs for, 98–99

Badger:
  maintaining, 156
  profile of, 53
Banks, Jeffrey, 40, 191
Baronduki, 16
  maintaining, 157
  profile of, 54
Bassarisk:
  maintaining, 157
  profile of, 53–54
Bearskin, 173
Beaver, 25, 30, 207
  hats, 5, 6, 12, 17, 22
  maintaining, 157
  for men, 193
  New World fur trade in, 6, 22, 23
  profile of, 54–55
  supernatural powers of, 17
  for working woman, 137
Bedspreads, fur, 186
Belted coats, 100, 104
Bemberg rayon, 43
Ben Kahn, Inc., 45–47
Benarroch, Elena, 182
BEPS (Body Energy Performance Standard) rating, xii
Berchielli, Angie, 203
Bernard Teitebaum, Inc., 135
*Berserkers*, 19
Bible, 1
*Bill Cosby Show, The*, 196
Bisang, André, 144

Bisang, Lisa, 144
*Black Enterprise*, 196
Black furrier, profile of a, 196–98
Blackglama, 34, 84–85
Black skin tones, 107–8
Blass, Bill, 40, 144
Bleaching of furs, 37, 38, 121, 144, 152
Blending of furs, 36, 38
Blondes, 106–7
Bloomingdale's, 194
  Northern Lights salons, 111
Blumer, Marilyn, 128–30
Blye, Sandy, 94–95, 110
Boa, 8, 181–82
Boutiques, shopping for furs in, 116
Breeders' associations, 34
Britain, 5, 173, 189
  fur trade, 22, 24
Brownettes, 107
Brown skin tones, 107–8
Brunettes, 107
Brushing furs, 148
Buffalo, 19
Bundles, 34
*Business of Fur, The*, xi
Bustle, 10, 11
Buying the right fur, *see* Selecting and
  buying the right fur

Cabbage Patch Kids, furs for, xiii
Calf:
  maintaining, 157
  profile of, 55–56
Canada, 6, 26, 86, 189, 204–5, 210–11
  fur market in, xii
  fur trade in, 22
Canadian Department of Fisheries and
  Oceans, 210, 211
Canadian Seal Protection Regulations,
  210
Canadian Wildlife Federation, 209
Canine parvovirus, 204
Capes, 179–80
  in fashion history, 8, 9, 11, 14
  figure types and, 103, 105
Caracul, *see* Persian lamb
Caring for your fur, *see* Maintaining your
  fur
Carol and Irwin Ware Fur Collection,
  111
Cat, spotted:
  maintaining, 156
  profile of, 56
  *see also* Endangered species
Catherine the Great, 8
Catholic clergy, 3
Cat lynx, *see* Lynx
Census Bureau, U.S., 134
Center for Disease Control, 204
Chanel, Coco, 92
Chap-Boa, 182
Charity, giving a used fur to, 172
Cheetah, 174
Chicago, Illinois, xii, 22
China, People's Republic of, 187

Chinchilla, 144, 205
  maintaining, 157
  profile of, 56–57
Chinese, 2, 18
Christensen, Birger, 39
CITES Convention, 201–2, 210
Cleaning, 151
Clergy, 3
Climate and selection of fur, 88–90, 195
Cloaks, fur-lined, in fashion history, 8, 9,
  10
Close-out sales, 118
Closing of furs, 42
Coats, fur:
  buying, *see* Selecting and buying the
    right fur
  in fashion history, 12, 13, 14, 15, 16
  maintaining, *see* Maintaining your fur
  for men, *see* Men, furs for
  for working women, *see* Working
    woman, fur and the
Coleco, xiii
Collar treatment, figure type and, 102
Coloring processes, 36–39, 121, 126–
  27
Color of fur:
  your coloring and, 106–8
  figure type and, 102
  for working woman, 136
Combing furs, 148
Compromising, 123
Coney, *see* Rabbit
Conservation, 199–200
  *see also* Environment, fur and the
Convention on International Trade in
  Endangered Species (CITES), 201–
  2, 210
Cooper, J. G., 18
Corset, 13, 15
Costume Institute, The, 175–77
Coyote:
  maintaining, 158
  for men, 192
  profile of, 57–58
  for working woman, 137
Crinoline, 9
Crusades, 4
Cudlipp, Edythe, xiii, 123, 156, 190
Custom-made coats, 106
*Customs Hints for Returning U.S. Residents—Know Before You Go*,
  175n.
Cutters, 40
Dasa Furs, 40
Definitions, 32–33
Degradé process, 37
DeHart, Harold, 206
Denmark, 189
Department stores, 110, 111, 195
  independent fur salons in, 111, 114
Designers, 12–13, 87, 143
  of accessories, 179, 182–83, 186
  of men's furs, 191, 194
  role of, 39–40
  of specialty furs, 128–33

Details, excessive, 136
Dior, Christian, 15–16
Diseases, wildlife, 204
Dominican Republic, 189
Double-breasted coats, 100, 102
Doublet, 4
Dressing gowns, fur-lined, 8
Dressing of skins, 35–36
Drumming of skins, 36
Durability of a fur, xii, 51
  see also individual types of fur
Dutch fur trade, 22, 24
Duty on furs purchased overseas, 119
Dyeing of furs, 36, 37, 121

Earmuffs, 180–81
Ebony, 196
Edward III, King of England, 3
Egyptians, ancient, 2, 18
Eighteenth century, 8–9
Elizabeth Arden, 47, 48
Elizabeth I, Queen of England, 5, 17
Elle, 143
Ellis, Perry, 40, 191
EMBA (Mutation Mink Breeders' Association), 34, 85
Endangered species, 201, 210
  purchased overseas, 119, 174–75,
    202
  purchasing previously owned furs
    from, 174–75
  see also Environment, fur and the
Endangered Species Act, 174–75, 200,
    202
Environment, fur and the, 199–211
  animal rights controversy, 208–9
  attacks on the fur industry, 200–209
  endangered species, see Endangered
    species
  environmental status of a fur, 51
  fake furs, 207
  fur farms, 205–7
  hunting of seals, 209–11
  preservation vs. conservation, 199–
    200
  trapping controversy, 202–5, 209
Ermine:
  in fashion history, 3, 4, 9, 15
  maintaining, 158
  profile of, 58
  Russian, 30, 144
  as symbol of virtue, 17–18
Essence, 196
European Economic Community, 209
      Evans, Inc., 26, 44, 137
Ewing, Elizabeth, 10–12

"Fake" furs, 16, 207
Farthingale, 4–5
Fashion as factor in selecting a fur, 90–
    95
  jackets, 94–95
  length of garment, 92–94
  long- vs. short-hair furs, 90–92
  sports furs, 95
  style, 92
  type of fur, 90
Fashion Institute of Technology, 28
Feathering of furs, 38

Federal Fur Products Labeling Act of
    1952, 120, 169
Federal Trade Commission, 127
Female skins, 122
Fendi of Rome, 143, 188
Figure type and fur selection, 97–105
  the average figure, 98–99
  the full-figured woman, 101–3
  other special figure types, 103–5
  the petite woman, 99–101
  the tall figure, 98
Finland, 189
Fish and Wildlife Service, U.S., 174, 200
Fisher, 25, 144–45
  maintaining, 158
  for men, 192
  profile of, 58–59
  for working woman, 138
Fit as factor in selecting fur, 96–97, 125,
    195–96
  for working woman, 136
Fitch, 16, 205
  maintaining, 158
  profile of, 59
  white Russian, 29–30, 59
  for working woman, 139
Flea fur (countenance), 5–6
Fleshing, 35
Fling, 181, 182
Forrest, Michael, 40
Fort Manhattan, 22
Fox, 30, 205, 206
  in fashion history, 3, 10, 15
  maintaining, 158–60
  for men, 192
  profile of, 59–63
  supernatural powers of the, 18
  vintage, 173
  for working woman, 138
France, 173
  fur trade, 22, 24
Frankfurt, West Germany, 188, 189
French bottom, 43, 125
Full-figured woman, furs for the, 101–3
Function as factor in selecting a fur, 88–
    90, 195
Fund for Animals, The, 209
"Fun furs," 16
Fur department stores, 114–16
Fur Farm Animal Welfare Coalition, 206
Fur farms, 33, 205–7
Fur Galleria, xiii
Fur in Dress (Ewing), 10–12
Fur industry, 21–28, 118–19
  environmentalists' attacks on, 200–
    209
Fur Institute of Canada, 203
Fur-lined cloth coats, 155, 192, 194
Fur Products Labeling Act of 1952, 36
Furrier's knife, 40
Furrtique, 185
Fur salons, shopping at, 113–14
  in department stores, 111, 114
Furs: An Appreciation of Luxury, A
    Guide to Value (Cudlipp), xiii
Furs by Antonovich, 112
Fur shows, 44
Fur tails, 185
Fur Trims by Sam Chaklai, 185

Fur Vault, The, 111, 114–16, 135, 137,
    141
Fur World, 141, 179

Glamour of furs, xiii
Glazing, 43
GLMA (Great Lakes Mink Association),
    34
Glossary, 212–15
Gloves, 182, 185
Glutton, see Weasel
Goat, mountain:
  maintaining, 158
  profile of, 63
Goodman, David, 155
Gorbachev, Mikhail S., 30
Gorbachev, Raisa Elena, 30–31
Graf, Ernest, 45–47, 135
Graf family, 45, 46
Gray-haired women, 108
Greatcoat length, 94, 102
Greeks, ancient, 2
Greeks in the fur industry, 27, 188
Greenland, 204–5
Greenpeace, 209, 210
Griegé degrade, 121
Grooving of furs, 38
Grotzen, 32–33, 41
Guard hairs, 32–33, 126, 170
Gus Goodman, Inc., 155

Hair color and fur color selection, 106–8
Hanging your fur, 147, 148
Harp seal hunting, 209–11
Harriet Love's Guide to Vintage Chic
    (Love), 172
Hats:
  fur, 181
    beaver, see Beaver, hats
    in fashion history, 5, 6, 12
  nonfur, 185
HBA Fur, 40
Heat source, keeping fur away from, 148
Heavy lower body, furs for women with,
    103–4
Henke, Janice Scott, 211
Henry VI, King of France, 22
Henry VIII, King of England, 4
Herrera, Carolina, 143
History of fur in fashion, 1–20
  the ancient world, 1–2
  the eighteenth century, 8–9
  the Middle Ages, 2–4
  the nineteenth century, 9–11
  the Renaissance, 4–6
  the seventeenth century, 6–7
  supernatural powers associated with
    fur, 17–20
  the twentieth century and beyond,
    12–17
Hollywood's influence on fur fashion, 15
Home accessories made of fur, 186, 187
Hong Kong, 187, 201
Hubert, George F., Jr., 200, 203–4
Hudson's Bay Company, 22–23, 24, 25,
    28
Hyena, 17

Illinois Department of Conservation,
    200

*Illustrated Encyclopedia of Traditional Symbols, An*, 18
I. Magnin, xii, 111, 137
Imported furs, 27, 42
Indigenous Survival International, 205, 210
Informed buyer, being an, xiii–xiv
Iniuts, 204–5
Insect damage, 149
Insurance, 149–50, 151–52
Intaglio designs, 38
Intarsia design, 38, 39
International Fur Trade Federation, 201
Israel, 189
Italy, 188
IUCN (International Union for the Conservation of Nature), 201

Jackets, 94–95, 101, 103, 123, 136
Japan, 18, 187
Jewelry, 148, 150
Jews in the fur industry, 25, 27
Jim Preston Fur Farm, 206–7
J. Mendel Fur Salon, 36, 47–49
Josephine, Empress, 9
J. Walter Thompson, 19

Kahn, Ben, 45
Karan, Donna, 39
Kidskin:
    maintaining, 160
    profile of, 63–64
Kiely, Kevin, 174
Kirkendall, Kip, 130–32, 182–83, 186
Klein, Anne, 40
Kolinksy, 30
    maintaining, 160
    profile of, 64
Kosof, Michael, 169, 170, 171

Label, reading the, 120–22, 169
Labor unions, 25, 27–28
Lamb, 205
    maintaining, 152–53, 160–61
    profile of, 64–68
    for working woman, 138
Landau, Adrienne, 145
Lauren, Ralph, 38
Lawer, Jill, 28
Layouts:
    decision to remodel and, 154–55
    let-out, 41–42
    pieced, 43–44
    skin-on-skin, 43
Leather, 32
Leghold trap, steel, 202–3
Leinhoff, David, 182
Length of the fur garment, 92–94
    figure type and, 102–3, 104
    remodeling, 155
Leopard, 174
    in fashion history, 16
    supernatural powers of, 18, 19
Leopard Societies, 19
Let-out furs, 41–42, 102, 126
Liberace, 190
Lifestyle considerations, fur selection and, 88–90, 195

Light source, keeping fur away from, 148
Linings, 42–43, 125, 170
    fur, 155, 192, 194
Lishman, Paula, 132–33
Long-haired furs, 90–92
Love, Harriet, 172–73, 174
Lunaraine, 34
Luxe furs, 141–45
Lyme disease, 204
Lynx, 19, 30, 44, 122, 144, 192
    maintaining, 161
    profile of, 68–69
    supernatural powers of the, 18
    for working woman, 139

McFadden, Mary, 40
Mackie, Bob, 40, 144
McQuay, James P., 196–98
McQuay, James P., Jr., 196
Mail-order firms, shopping for furs from, 117–18
Maintaining your fur, 146–65
    chart by fur type, 156–65
    cleaning, 151
    dos and don'ts of everyday care, 146–48
    dos and don'ts when wearing your fur, 150
    insect damage, 149
    oxidation, 148–49
    remodeling, 153–56, 165–66
    repairs, 153
    safety precautions, 149–50
    special care, furs requiring, 152–53
    storage, 151–52
    weather damage, 149
Majectic (Canadian) mink, 86
Male skins, 122
Mange, 204
Mantles, fur-lined, in fashion history, 10
Manufacturer/retailers, shopping for furs at, 116–17
Marco Polo, 2
Market Time, 44
Marmot:
    maintaining, 161
    for men, 193
    profile of, 69
Marshall, Lenore, 179
Marten, 3, 22, 25, 30
    maintaining, 161–62
    for men, 193
    profile of, 69–70
    for working woman, 138
Martin Paswall Furs, Inc., 144
Mason Act, 201
Master furriers, 45–49
Medes, 2
Men, furs for, 190–96, 197
    masculinity and, 190–92
    styles of, 193–95
    tips for buying, 195–96
    types of, 192–93
Mendel, Gilles, 47–49
Metis, 204–5
Metropolitan Museum of Art, The Costume Institute at, 175–77
Middle Ages, 2–4

Miniver, 3, 4
Mink, 19, 30, 83–86, 137, 145
    colors of, 85
    in fashion history, 15, 16
    maintaining, 162, 166
    for men, 192
    mystique of, 84–85
    profile of, 70–72
    raised on fur farms, 205, 206–7
    vintage, 173
    for working woman, 137, 138
Mink International, 19
Mohl Furs, 40
Mole:
    maintaining, 162
    profile of, 72
    vintage, 174
Molly Moses, 47
Mongol tribes, 2
Monkey, 15, 16
    vintage, 174
Monture, Dave, 205
Mosaic designs, 38
Moth repellents, 149
Mountain goat:
    maintaining, 158
    profile of, 63
Muffs, fur, 182, 187
    in fashion history, 5, 6, 7, 8, 9, 10, 11, 13
Muskrat, 15, 30, 202, 207
    maintaining, 162, 166
    for men, 192–93
    profile of, 72–73
    vintage, 174
    for working woman, 138–39

Namath, Joe, 190
Name of fur on the label, 120, 169
Napoleon I, 9
National Bureau of Standards, 99
National Wildlife Federation, 204
Natural history of a fur, 51
    see also individual types of fur
Neiman-Marcus, 143, 194
Netherlands, 189
Newfoundland, 210
New Jersey, 28
New York City fur industry, 25, 26–27, 28, 45, 188
New York State, 201, 203
New York State Trappers' Association, 203
*New York Times, The*, 188
Nineteenth century, 9–12
Nine-tenths length, 94
Norka (Russian) mink, 86
North America (New World):
    fashion in the, 8
    fur trade in the, 6, 21–24
Northern Lights salon at Bloomingdale's, 111
North West Company, 24, 25
Norway, 189
Novelty furs, *see* Specialty furs
Novick, Barry, 137
Nutria, 205
    maintaining, 163
    for men, 193

profile of, 74
vintage, 174
for working woman, 139

Ocelot, 15, 174
Opossum, 15, 205
  maintaining, 163
  for men, 193
  profile of, 74–75
  for working woman, 137, 139
Orient, fur industry in the, 187
Origin of fur on the label, country of, 121, 169
Otter, 18, 25
  maintaining, 163
  for men, 193
  profile of, 75–76
Overseas purchases of furs, 118–19
Oxidation, 148–49, 170

Pacific Fur Company, 24
Pahmi (Asian ferret badger):
  maintaining, 163
  profile of, 76
Palace of Furs, Leningrad, 30
*Pannier*, 8
Paquin, Madame, 12, 13
Paris Exposition of 1900, 12
Paswall, Evelyn, 144
Patterned furs, 126
Payment plans, 112
Pear-shaped figure, furs for woman with, 103–4
*Pelzkappe*, 6
Penn, William, 22
Perfume, 147
Perris, Bernard, 49
Persian lamb, 12, 15, 144
  maintaining, 161
  vintage, 174
  for working woman, 139
Persians, 2
Petite woman, furs for the, 99–101
Pieced furs, 43–44, 126
Pillows, fur, 187
Pils, Charles M., 204
Plastic bags, 147
Plates, 43–44
Plucking process, 33
Pocketbooks, 150
Poiret, Paul, 13
Ponchos, 105
Pony, 15
  maintaining, 163
  profile of, 76–77
Preliminaries, fur, 32–33
Preservation, 199–200
  *see also* Environment, fur and the
Previously owned furs, 122, 167–77
  The Costume Institute, 175–77
  garments from endangered species, 174–75
  one-to-one transactions, 171
  pointers for selecting, 169–71
  Ritz Thrift Shop, 168–69
  selling your fur, 171–72
  vintage furs, 172–74
Price of furs, 191, 195
  range of, xii–xiii, 51–52

Pricing of furs, 44–45, 122–23, 127
  mark up, 44, 172
  used furs, 169, 172
Printing, 37, 38
Processing information on fur label, 121–22, 169
Processing of fur, fundamentals of, 33–36
Profiles of the most important furs, 50–83
  how to use, 50–52
  the profiles, 52–83
Purses, 150
Pursley, Duane, 202
Pushkino sable farm, 30

Quality fur, 136
  factors that determine a, 124–25

Rabbit (coney), 44, 205
  in fashion history, 3
  maintaining, 163, 166
  profile of, 77
  vintage, 174
  for working woman, 139
Raccoon, 19, 207
  maintaining, 164
  for men, 193
  profile of, 77–78
  for working woman, 139
Ranches, *see* Fur farms
Reagan, Nancy, 16
*Red Data Book*, 201
Redheads, 107
Remodeling, 153–56, 165–66
Renaissance, 4–6
Repairs, 153, 170, 173
Reversible garments, 90, 140 ,155, 192, 194
Revillon, 143
Revillon, Victor, 12–13, 150
Ritz Thrift Shop, 168–69, 170
Romans, ancient, 2, 17
Rosenberg and Lenhart, 189
Rothe, Helmut, 189
Roy, Hippolyte, 9
Russia, 5, 21
  for industry in, 29–31, 85, 86
Russian broadtail, 29, 126, 144, 192
  in fashion history, 15
  maintaining, 160

Sable, 143–44
  in fashion history, 3, 10, 15
  maintaining, 164, 166
  for men, 193
  profile of, 78–80
  Russian, 29, 30, 31, 78, 80, 122–23, 143
  vintage, 174
  for working woman, 139
Sable, Jean Baptiste Point du, 22
Safety precautions, 149–50
SAGA, 34, 86, 189
Scandinavia, 19, 85, 86, 189
Scarves:
  fur, 16, 181–82
  nonfur, 147, 184–85
Schulman, Lawrence, 191

Schwartz, Andrew Marc, 194
Schwartz, Fred ("Fred the Furrier"), 26, 116, 135, 137, 141
Seal, 17
  in fashion history, 12, 15
  hunting of, 209–11
  maintaining, 164
  profile of, 80–81
  vintage, 174
Secondhand furs, *see* Previously owned furs
Selecting and buying the right fur, 87–128
  assessing your selection, 124–27
  custom-made coats, 106
  fashion as factor in, 90–95
    jackets, 94–95
    length of garment, 92–94
    long- vs. short-haired, 90–92
    sports furs, 95
    style, 92
    type of fur, 90
  figure-type and, 97–105
    the average figure, 98–99
    the full-figured woman, 101–103
    other special figure types, 103–105
    the petite woman, 99–101
    the tall figure, 98
  fit, as factor in, 96–97, 125, 136, 195–96
  function as factor in, 88–90, 195
  making a compromise, 123
  for men, 195–96
  a pleasurable experience, 128
  price, 122–23, 191, 195
  reading the label, 120–22, 169
    name of fur, 120, 169
    origin of fur, 121, 169
    processing of fur, 121–22, 169
  size, your, 120
  skin and hair color and, 107–8
  taking your time in, 124
  when to buy, 127
  where to buy your fur, 108–19
    department stores, 110, 111, 114, 195
    finding a furrier, 108–10
    the fur department store, 114–16
    fur salons, 113–14
    mail-order firms, 117–18
    manufacturer/retailers, 116–17
    other options, 118–19
    shopping options, 110–19
    specialty stores/boutiques, 116, 195
  *see also* Previously owned furs
Selection of pelts for a garment, 40, 41
Selling your fur, 171–72
Semi-let-out furs, 42
Semiramis, Queen, 2, 186
Seven-eights length, 92
Seventeenth century, 6–7
Shawls, 179–80
Shearing, 33, 126
Shearling for men, 193
Sheba, Queen of, 186
Shedding, 90
Sheepskin in fashion history, 3, 15
Shopping options, 110–19

Shortening a garment, 155
Short-haired furs, 90–92
Short-waisted figure, furs for, 105
Silk linings, 43
Silver-haired women, 108
Singapore, 201
Size, determining your, 120
Skin brokers, 35
Skin dealers, 35
Skin-on-skin furs, 43, 126
Skin tone and fur color selection, 106–8
Skunk:
    maintaining, 165
    profile of, 81
Sleeve style and figure type, 100, 102
Smoking, 148
Smolarski, Arlette, 165–66
Snake, *see* Boa
Soft-catch trap, 203
Solomon, King, 186
Sorbara, Jerry, 143
South Korea, 187
Soviet Union, *see* Russia
Spain, 201
Specialty furs, 128–33
    care for, 152–53
Specialty stores, shopping for furs in, 116, 195
Spiegel *Ambiance* catalogue, 117
Sports furs, 95
Spotted cat, *see* Cat, spotted
Squaring, 41
Squirrel, 30
    in fashion history, 3, 10
    maintaining, 165
    profile of, 81–82
Stenciling, 37, 38
Stillman, Eve, 87
Stoles in fashion history, 10
Storing your fur, 151–52, 170, 173
Streaking of furs, 37
Stroller length, 92
Sumptuary laws, 3, 4

"Sunburst" back, 102
Supernatural powers associated with furs, 17–20
Suslik:
    maintaining, 165
    profile of, 82
Swakara, 126, 144, 182–83, 192
Sweden, 189
Switzerland, 189, 201

Tabak, 188
Tall figure, furs for, 98
Tanning, *see* Dressing of skins
Tanuki:
    maintaining, 165
    profile of, 82
    for working woman, 139
Tauber, Keith, 169, 170
Teitelbaum, Carol, 135
Teutonic tribes, 2
Tennyson, Alfred Lord, 3
Three-quarter length, 92
Tiger:
    in fashion history, 16
    supernatural powers of the, 18
Time of year to buy your fur, 127
Tipdyeing, 36, 38
Tippet, 5
Trade-ins, 123
TRAFFIC (The Trade Records Analysis of Flora and Fauna in Commerce), 201
Trahey, Jane, 84
Trapping, 202, 205, 208, 209
Travel, 88, 90, 150
Twentieth-century fashion, 12–16
Twenty-first century, outlook for the, 17

Underfur, 32, 33
United Food and Commercial Workers Union, 25
United States, quality of furs produced in the, 189

Used furs, *see* Previously owned furs

Vintage furs, 172–74
V/O Sojuzpushnina, 29, 31
Voltaire, 8
Vreeland, Diana, 175

Waist, figure with no or short, furs for, 105
Wall hangings, fur, 186
Ware, Carol, xii, 137
Ware, Irwin, xii
Warmth of fur, xii, 51, 191
    *see also individual types of fur*
Weasel, 30
    maintaining, 165
    profile of, 82–83
Weather damage, 149
West Germany, 188–89
West Virginia Department of Natural Resources, 202
*What Becomes a Legend Most?—The Blackgama Story*, 85
When to buy your furs, 127
White-haired women, 108
Wizcheria, 9
Wolverine, 30
    maintaining, 165
    for men, 193
    profile of, 83
Working woman, fur and the, 134–41
    advice for buying a "working fur," 135–36
    dressing for success, 135
    list of appropriate furs, 137–39
    other options, 140
    when it isn't appropriate, 140–41
Workmanship, 125
World Wildlife Fund, 200, 201

Zippers, 150
Zulu warriors, 19

## About the Author

A native of Buffalo, New York, Melissa A. Simmons now makes her home in Pennsylvania, where she is working on a novel.

# CREDITS

pp. 7, 10, 11, 13, 14, 23, and 24: Bettmann Archive; p. 46: Courtesy of Ben Kahn Furs; p. 48: Courtesy of J. Mendel; p. 55: Courtesy of Amsel and Amsel; p. 57 Courtesy of Grosvenor Canada, photo by Victor Skrebneski; p. 61:(above) Courtesy of SAGA Furs of Scandinavia, (left) Silva-Cone for the American Fur Industry; p. 65: Courtesy of Grosvenor Canada; p. 67 Courtesy of Gus Goodman, Inc.; pp. 71 and 73: Courtesy of Amsel and Amsel; pp. 79 and 89: Courtesy of Martin Paswall, Inc.; pp. 96, 109, and 111: Silva-Cone for the American Fur Industry; p. 112: Grosvenor Canada; p. 113: Courtesy of Ben Kahn Furs; p. 115: Courtesy of Amsel and Amsel; p. 119: Courtesy of Ben Kahn Furs; p. 129: Courtesy of Marilyn Blumer Designs; p. 131: Courtesy of Kip Kirkendall, photo by Rosemary Howard; p. 132: Courtesy of Paula Lishman, Ltd.; p. 142: Courtesy of Revillon; p. 145: Courtesy of Adrienne Landau, photo by Adrienne Weinfeld-Berg; p. 168: Bettmann Archive; p. 179: Bob Jefferd for the American Fur Industry.

Special thanks to Charles Carpelis for coordinating the fur glossary. Thanks to the following for supplying fur swatches: Christie Bros. (coyote, Canadian lynx); Al Kauffman (beaver, chinchilla); Antonios Lolis (red fox, nutria, American opossum); Sharfstein and Feigin, Inc.(Canadian sable, Russian sable); Sekas Bros. (ranch mink, white mink, Blue Iris mink, Umpa Glo mink); Bernard Teitelbaum, Inc. (otter, lakota seal, tanuki); Toscos Furs (badger, natural muskrat, skunk); Johnathan Tracy (sheared beaver, long-haired nutria, dyed nutria, New Zealand opossum, raccoon); Valerie Furs (fisher, fitch, baum marten, stone marten); World Fox (crystal fox, sterling dyed fox, blue fox).